THE END
OF YOUR LIFE
BOOK CLUB

THE END
OF YOUR LIFE
BOOK CLUB

Will Schwalbe

ALFRED A. KNOPF NEW YORK TORONTO

2012

THIS IS A BORZOI BOOK
PUBLISHED BY ALFRED A. KNOPF AND
ALFRED A. KNOPF CANADA

www.aaknopf.com
www.randomhouse.ca

Knopf, Borzoi Books, and the colophon are registered trademarks of
Random House, Inc. Knopf Canada and colophon are trademarks.

Owing to limitations of space, all acknowledgments for permissions to reprint previously published material may be found at the end of the volume.

Library of Congress Cataloging-in-Publication Data
Schwalbe, Will.
The end of your life book club / by Will Schwalbe. — 1st ed.
p. cm.
ISBN 978-0-307-59403-7
1. Cancer—patients—United States—Biography. 2. Cancer—Patients—
United States—Family relationships. I. Title.
RC265.5.S39 2012
616.99'40092—dc23
[B]   2012018989

Library and Archives Canada Cataloguing in Publication
Schwalbe, Will
The end of your life book club / Will Schwalbe.
Also issued in electronic format.
ISBN 978-0-307-39966-3
1. Schwalbe, Mary Anne. 2. Schwalbe, Will—Family. 3. Schwalbe,
Mary Anne—Books and reading. 4. Schwalbe, Will—Books and
reading. 5. Educators—United States—Biography. 6. Cancer—
Patients—United States—Biography. I. Title.
LA2317.S38S38 2012   370.92   C2012-902055-9

Jacket design by Carol Devine Carson

Manufactured in the United States of America
First Edition

My sister, my brother, and I all had extraordinary times and conversations with our mother throughout her life and during her last years. Dad spent more time with her than anyone— over decades of marriage and at the end—and his care for her, and their love for each other, inspired all of us.

What follows is my story. If it's mostly about Mom and me, and less about my father and siblings, that's only because I believe that their stories are theirs to tell, if and when they choose.

This book is dedicated with love and gratitude to Nina, Doug, and Dad— and David.

CONTENTS

Author's Note   ix

Crossing to Safety   3
Appointment in Samarra   8
Seventy Verses on Emptiness   28
Marjorie Morningstar   49
The Hobbit   61
Daily Strength for Daily Needs   84
People of the Book   102
"I Am Sorrow"   114
The Uncommon Reader   121
The Lizard Cage   131
Brat Farrar   136
Continental Drift   144
The Painted Veil   161
Murder in the Cathedral   170
Wherever You Go, There You Are   181
Kokoro   195

The Price of Salt   202

The Reluctant Fundamentalist   213

The Year of Magical Thinking   219

Olive Kitteridge   227

Girls Like Us   240

Suite Française   249

The Bite of the Mango   258

The Elegance of the Hedgehog   270

The Girl with the Dragon Tattoo   276

Brooklyn   283

My Father's Tears   292

Too Much Happiness   306

Epilogue   323

Acknowledgments   327

Appendix   331

AUTHOR'S NOTE

I didn't know I was going to write this book while we were living through most of the events in it. So I've had to rely on my memory, along with notes I scribbled randomly; papers, lists, speeches, and letters that Mom gave me; emails between us; the blog we kept; and help from family and friends. I'm certain that I've occasionally muddled chronology and facts and confused some conversations. But I've tried to be true to the spirit rather than the letter of our discussions and to give an honest depiction of what we went through together. Mom would say: "Do your best, and that's all you can do." I hope I have.

THE END
OF YOUR LIFE
BOOK CLUB

Crossing to Safety

We were nuts about the mocha in the waiting room at Memorial Sloan-Kettering's outpatient care center. The coffee isn't so good, and the hot chocolate is worse. But if, as Mom and I discovered, you push the "mocha" button, you see how two not-very-good things can come together to make something quite delicious. The graham crackers aren't bad either.

The outpatient care center is housed on the very pleasant fourth floor of a handsome black steel and glass office building in Manhattan on the corner of 53rd Street and Third Avenue. Its visitors are fortunate that it's so pleasant, because they spend many hours there. This is where people with cancer wait to see their doctors and to be hooked up to a drip for doses of the life-prolonging poison that is one of the wonders of the modern medical world. By the late autumn of 2007, my mother and I began meeting there regularly.

Our book club got its formal start with the mocha and one of the most casual questions two people can ask each other:

"What are you reading?" It's something of a quaint question these days. More often in lulls of conversation people ask, "What movies have you seen?" or "Where are you going on vacation?" You can no longer assume, the way you could when I was growing up, that anyone is reading anything. But it's a question my mother and I asked each other for as long as I can remember. So one November day, while passing the time between when they took Mom's blood and when she saw the doctor (which preceded the chemo), I threw out that question. Mom answered that she was reading an extraordinary book, *Crossing to Safety* by Wallace Stegner.

Crossing to Safety, which was first published in 1987, is one of those books I'd always so intended to read that I spent years pretending not only that I'd actually read it but also that I knew more about its author than that he'd been born in the early years of the twentieth century and wrote mostly about the American West. I worked in book publishing for twenty-one years and, in various conversation lulls, got into the habit of asking people, especially booksellers, the name of their favorite book and why they loved it so much. One of the most frequently named books was and is always *Crossing to Safety*.

Raving about books I hadn't read yet was part of my job. But there's a difference between casually fibbing to a bookseller and lying to your seventy-three-year-old mother when you are accompanying her for treatments to slow the growth of a cancer that had already spread from her pancreas to her liver by the time it was diagnosed.

I confessed that I had not, in fact, read this book.

"I'll give you my copy when I'm finished," said my mother, who was always much thriftier than I am.

"That's okay, I have a copy," I told her, which was, in fact, true. There are certain books that I mean to read and keep stacked by my bedside. I even take them on trips. Some of my books should be awarded their own frequent-flier miles, they've traveled so much. I take these volumes on flight after flight with the best of intentions and then wind up reading anything and everything else (*SkyMall! Golf Digest!*). I'd brought *Crossing to Safety* on so many trips and returned it to my bedside unread so many times that it could have earned at least one first-class ticket to Tokyo on Japan Airlines.

But this time it would be different. That weekend I started it, and then, at about page twenty or so, the magical thing occurred that happens only with the very best books: I became absorbed and obsessed and entered the "Can't you see I'm reading?" mode. For those of you who haven't read *Crossing to Safety* (or are still pretending to have read it), it's a story about the lifelong friendship of two couples: Sid and Charity, and Larry and Sally. At the start of the novel, Charity is dying of cancer. So once I read it, it was natural that I would want to talk about it with Mom. The novel gave us a way to discuss some of the things she was facing and some of the things I was facing.

"Do you think he'll be all right?" I would ask her, referring to Sid, who is very much alone at the end.

"Of course it'll be tough on him, but I think he'll be fine. I'm quite sure of it. Maybe not right away. But he'll be fine," she would answer, also referring to Sid but perhaps to my father as well.

Books had always been a way for my mother and me to introduce and explore topics that concerned us but made us uneasy, and they had also always given us something to talk about when we were stressed or anxious. In the months since her diagnosis, we'd started talking more and more about books. But it was with *Crossing to Safety* that we both began to realize that our discussions were more than casual—that we had created, without knowing it, a very unusual book club, one with only two members. As in many book clubs, our conversations bounced around between the characters' lives and our own. Sometimes we discussed a book in depth; other times we found ourselves in a conversation that had little to do with the book or the author who had sparked it.

I wanted to learn more about my mother's life and the choices she'd made, so I often steered the conversation there. She had an agenda of her own, as she almost always did. It took me some time, and some help, to figure it out.

Over the course of Mom's illness, before and after *Crossing to Safety,* Mom and I read dozens of books of all different kinds. We didn't read only "great books," we read casually and promiscuously and whimsically. (As I said, my mother was thrifty; if you gave her a book, she would read it.) We didn't always read the same books at the same time; nor did we meet over meals, nor on specific days, nor a set number of times per month. But we were forced to keep coming back to that waiting room as Mom's health got worse and worse. And we talked about books just as often as we talked about anything.

My mother was a fast reader. Oh, and one other thing I should mention. She always read the end of a book first because she couldn't wait to find out how things would turn out. I realized, when I started writing this book, that, in a way, she'd already read the end of it—when you have pancreatic cancer that's diagnosed after it's spread, there isn't likely to be a surprise ending. You can be fairly certain of what fate has in store.

You could say that the book club became our life, but it would be more accurate to say that our life became a book club. Maybe it had always been one—and it took Mom's illness to make us realize that. We didn't talk much about the club. We talked about the books, and we talked about our lives.

We all have a lot more to read than we can read and a lot more to do than we can do. Still, one of the things I learned from Mom is this: Reading isn't the opposite of doing; it's the opposite of dying. I will never be able to read my mother's favorite books without thinking of her—and when I pass them on and recommend them, I'll know that some of what made her goes with them; that some of my mother will live on in those readers, readers who may be inspired to love the way she loved and do their own version of what she did in the world.

But I've gotten ahead of myself. Let me go back to the beginning, or rather the beginning of the end, to before Mom's diagnosis, when she started to get sick and we didn't know why.

Appointment in Samarra

Mom and I loved opening lines of novels. "The small boys came early to the hanging" was one of our favorites, from Ken Follett's *The Pillars of the Earth*. How could you not go on reading? And the first sentence of John Irving's *A Prayer for Owen Meany*: "I am doomed to remember a boy with a wrecked voice—not because of his voice, or because he was the smallest person I ever knew, or even because he was the instrument of my mother's death, but because he is the reason I believe in God; I am a Christian because of Owen Meany." And E. M. Forster's first line in *Howard's End*: "One may as well begin with Helen's letters to her sister." It's the "may as well" that draws you in—casual, chatty even, yet it gives the reader a strong sense that there's a lot of story to come.

Some novelists start with opening lines that foretell the major action of the book; some begin with hints; others with words that simply set a scene or describe a character, showing the reader a world before a deluge—with no hint as to what is to come. What never needs to be written is: "Little did she know her life was about to change forever." Many authors adopt something like this when they want to create suspense. The truth is that people never realize their lives are about to change in unforeseen ways—that's just the nature of unforeseen ways.

We were no different.

The year 2007 had begun with Mom and Dad spending some weeks in Vero Beach, Florida, a place Mom discovered late in life and loved. I remember now with some guilt repeating to her a line I'd heard a comedian say about Florida: "It's where old people go to die and then don't."

All of us were scheduled to visit at one point or another, and everyone in the family was, at the time, happily busy. My brother, Doug, had just produced a new film version of *Lassie, Come Home*. My sister, Nina, was working for the TB Alliance, fighting the spread of tuberculosis around the world. I was getting David Halberstam's book on the Korean War ready for publication and was also promoting a book about email that I'd written with a friend. Dad was busy with his business representing concert artists: conductors, singers, and musicians. We obsessed about the anxieties and minor tiffs and tiny ailments (toothaches, headaches, insomnia) that all people have. And then there were birthdays to remember and events to be planned and travel arrangements to be made and schedules to be shared. With my family, there was a ceaseless flow of requests, made of one another on behalf of our friends and causes: Could we come to a fund-raiser? Could we make an introduction? Could we recall the name of the woman at the concert who was wearing the red dress? We also bombarded one another with recommendations, often phrased as commandments: You must see . . . You must read . . . You must watch . . . The bulk of these came from Mom.

If our family was an airline, Mom was the hub and we were the spokes. You rarely went anywhere nonstop; you went via Mom, who directed the traffic flow and determined the priorities: which family member was cleared for takeoff or landing. Even my father was not immune to Mom's scheduling, though he was given more leeway than the rest of us.

The frustration among us offspring had to do with how carefully everything needed to be planned. Just as one late plane can throw off the whole operation of an airport, resulting in backed-up flights and people sleeping in corridors, so, Mom felt, any change could throw our lives into chaos. My brother, sister, and I were, as a result, mildly terrified of making even the smallest alterations to plans once they had been discussed with Mom.

When I called Mom in Florida that February to let her know I'd decided to take an afternoon flight from New York instead of a morning one as we'd previously discussed, she first just said, "Oh," but I could hear a massive hint of exasperation in her voice. Then she added: "I was thinking that if you got in that morning, we could go see the couple next door for lunch; they leave that evening, so if you're on the later flight, then you won't be able to see them at all. I suppose we could ask them over for coffee in the afternoon, but that would mean that we couldn't go to Hertz to add you to the registration on the car, and then I would need to drive to Orlando to pick up your sister. But it's okay. I'm sure we can figure out how to make it all work."

Mom didn't confine herself to coordinating our lives. She

was also helping to coordinate, almost always at their request, the lives of hundreds of others: at her church, at the Women's Commission for Refugee Women and Children (she'd been the founding director), at the International Rescue Committee (she'd been board-staff liaison and founded the IRC's UK branch), and at all the other myriad organizations where she'd worked or served on boards. She'd been director of admissions at Harvard when I was growing up—and then a college counselor at one New York school and head of the high school at another—and she remained in contact with hundreds of former students and colleagues. There were also the refugees she'd met in her travels all over the world, and with whom she kept in touch. And there were all her other friends, too—who ranged from childhood intimates to people who'd happened to sit next to her on a plane or crosstown bus. My mother was always introducing, scheduling, weighing in, guiding, advising, consoling. Sometimes she said it exhausted her—but it was pretty obvious that mostly she loved it.

One of the organizations Mom was busiest with was a foundation to help establish libraries in Afghanistan. She fell in love with that country and its people the first time she went there, in 1995, going across the Khyber Pass from Pakistan to report on the conditions of refugees. She went back to Afghanistan nine times, always for the Women's Commission or the International Rescue Committee (which is the Women's Commission's parent organization), to learn ever more about the changing plight of refugees there; then she would come back to the United States and advocate for policies that would help them, especially policies attuned to the lives and needs of women and children. Her trips on behalf of refugees took her not just to Kabul, and not just all over Afghanistan—including to Khost, where she spent the night in a run-down guesthouse, the only woman among twenty-three mujahideen warriors—but all over the world, including to most of the countries in Southeast Asia and West Africa.

This year, while in Florida, she was in constant contact with a man named John Dixon, an old Afghan hand who knew as much about the country as almost anyone and was helping achieve the vision of a person who knew even more than he did: a seventy-nine-year-old woman named Nancy Hatch Dupree, who for decades had divided her time between Kabul and Peshawar. Mom and John, both of whom had met with Nancy many times in Pakistan and Afghanistan, were working together to form a U.S. foundation to help Nancy raise money for a national cultural center and library—something Afghanistan didn't have—to be built at Kabul University, and for mobile libraries for villages all over the country, bringing books in Dari and Pashto to people who'd rarely or never seen a book in their own language if they'd seen a book at all. Nancy and her husband, who'd died in 1988, had amassed a collection without rival of 38,000 volumes and documents on the crucial last thirty years of Afghan history. So she had the books; what was missing was money and support.

In the spring of 2007, Mom was given the opportunity to join an International Rescue Committee delegation to Pakistan and Afghanistan, and everything seemed to be coming together nicely: in Peshawar and Kabul, she'd be able to spend a lot more time with Nancy to firm up a plan for raising money for the libraries. While in many families it would be big news if one member was to up and visit one of the most dangerous places on earth—a place where Mom had previously been shot at (though she always said they were shooting at the tires, not at her), where she had met with the military leader Ahmed Shah Massoud (who was later assassinated by two suicide bombers), where the Taliban still controlled much of the country, and where more than two hundred members of the U.S. and Coalition forces would die before the year was out—for our family it was business as usual. I can't recall if I even remembered Mom was going there, she traveled so much.

SO WE DIDN'T expect anything would be different this time she went traveling; nor did we suspect anything would be different when she returned sick. She was no sicker than she usually was after a visit to a war-torn land. She came back from most of her work trips—Liberia, Sudan, East Timor, Gaza, Côte d'Ivoire, Laos, to name a few—with some kind of ailment: a cough, exhaustion, headaches, a fever. But she would simply soldier on with her busy life until her various ailments faded away.

There had certainly been occasions when Mom came back from a trip sick and stayed sick for a long while. There was a cough she acquired in Bosnia that lasted about two years, becoming so much a part of her that we noticed it only when it suddenly disappeared. And there were various skin ailments: spots, bumps, and rashes. But in all those cases, she didn't get sicker. She came home sick and stayed sick until she got well or until everyone, including her, forgot that she'd ever been better.

We always insisted that Mom see doctors—and she did: her GP, and various tropical disease experts, and occasionally other specialists. But except for a frightening bout with breast cancer that was detected early enough that surgery sufficed and no chemotherapy was required, and a gallbladder that needed to be removed, she'd never had anything else seriously wrong with her. The assumption was always that there was nothing the matter with Mom that couldn't be cured if only she would slow down.

Which she wouldn't.

We all also believed that if Mom would just once take a full course of antibiotics, she would rid herself forever of all her travel-related ailments. I don't know if it was thrift or stubbornness or distrust of medicines, but after consuming half the prescription, she would save the rest for later, which was maddening. Even reminding her that she might be creating a superbug didn't have much effect.

The summer of 2007, however, Mom stayed sick. Fairly quickly, every doctor and specialist confirmed what she had: hepatitis. She was turning yellow; the whites of her eyes were the color of organic egg yolks—not the pale yellow of supermarket eggs, but blood-tinged gold. She was losing weight and had no appetite. And it was fairly obvious where she'd contracted the hepatitis, since she'd just come back from Afghanistan. Something she ate, perhaps. Or some shower water getting in her mouth. But the doctors at first couldn't figure out what type of hepatitis it was. Not A, not B, not C—not even D. They thought that it might, perhaps, be the very rare hepatitis E. Still, even the fact that no one was completely sure what strain Mom had wasn't much of a worry. If we couldn't understand Afghanistan's complicated political and religious situation, did we really expect to have identified every weird virus and disease you could pick up there?

Her doctors were not incautious—early on, they did tests to rule out other things and felt pretty confident that they had ruled them out. They provided some recommendations: she would need to rest and also not drink any alcohol (for her not a big deal, although she did like a glass of wine with dinner, and champagne at celebrations). That was all.

The summer progressed, however, with Mom getting progressively sicker. She was tired. And she was aggravated to be tired, and to have hepatitis, and not to be feeling herself. She didn't complain, but to those closest to her, she occasionally noted it. Now that I think back, every mention she made of her hepatitis sounds ominous. She would occasionally say to my father or to one of us something like "I don't know why they can't figure out what's wrong with me." Or "I rest and rest and never feel rested." Nevertheless, she pushed herself to do just about everything she wanted to do.

Did she ever really rest? It was difficult to say. For her, a "lazy" day was one devoted to catching up on email or "attacking" her desk (always the word she used, as though it were a paper-spewing monster that needed to be fought lest it take over and destroy everything in its path). Only when she was reading was she truly still.

Watching Mom struggle to keep up with the demands of her life caused tension to build in the rest of the family. We couldn't get mad at her for not feeling well and for refusing to relax, so we got far more annoyed at one another than we usually did for all sorts of little crimes: being early, being late, forgetting a birthday, making a sarcastic comment, buying the wrong flavor of ice cream. We tried to keep Mom from overhearing these squabbles but didn't always succeed.

She was usually able to solve them, dismiss them, or referee them—which made the combatants feel guilty for having quarreled at all.

This summer was a busy one, and neither Mom nor I was able to read the way we liked to during summers—that is, most of the day, day after day, indoors and outside, at home or at the vacation houses of friends—so we tended toward short books. I read *On Chesil Beach* by Ian McEwan, which even a slow reader can start and finish in an afternoon. Mom had it on her list of books to read and asked me what I thought.

We'd both read several novels by Ian McEwan over the years. McEwan's earlier works feature a catalog of cruelties, including sadism and torture. Mom had spent so much time in war zones, she said, that she was drawn to books that dealt with dark themes, as they helped her understand the world as it is, not as we wish it would be. I'm drawn to books with dark themes mostly because I always feel better about my life in comparison. In his more recent novels, however, McEwan had become less extreme, if not exactly cheery. *On Chesil Beach* was his latest and had just been published.

In some ways, *On Chesil Beach* is an odd book to discuss with your seventy-three-year-old mother—given that it involves a just-married couple in 1962 about to have sex for the first time, and describes their disastrously clumsy and messy attempt in vivid detail. That, I didn't mention to her. Instead I talked about the book's fascinating and melancholy coda, which explains what will happen to each of the two main characters. *On Chesil Beach* had moved me so much that I didn't want to pick up a new book for a while.

"I wonder if things could have turned out differently," I added, after I told her about the couple's fate. The great thing about knowing that my mother always read the ends of books first was that I never had to worry about spoiling them.

"I don't know," Mom answered. "Maybe not. But maybe the characters think that things could have turned out differently. Maybe that's why you found it so sad."

We continued talking about the book for a little while, with me still neglecting to mention the pivotal sex scene—not because Mom was prudish but because I have the classic child's horror of having such subjects discussed in the presence of my parents. (I remember vividly the trauma of seeing Peter Shaffer's play *Equus* with Mom and Dad when I was thirteen. At the point when the boy and girl take off all their clothes and attempt to have sex, I'd wanted to become a pattern on the seat's upholstery.)

Eventually our discussion on that July day returned from my thoughts on the McEwan book to family logistics—who would be where when. Then, at some point, as in most conversations that summer, Mom said that she still couldn't get rid of the hepatitis, that she still wasn't herself, that she didn't have much of an appetite, and that she felt not great. But she was sure, sure, that she would soon feel better, regain her appetite, get stronger. It was only a matter of time. Meanwhile, there was just too much to do—for family, friends, and the libraries to be built in Afghanistan. All needed her attention, and she loved giving it. If only she felt a bit better.

THAT AUGUST THE whole family (my brother and his wife; my sister and her partner; me and mine; all five grandchildren) and several friends traveled to Maine to celebrate Dad's eightieth birthday. Mom had organized just about everything and was at almost every event: group breakfasts, a boat trip, and a visit to the Rockefeller Garden in Seal Harbor.

Dad was then, and still is, hardy. He has a full head of hair. Once portly, he's now slimmer than many of his friends. He may puff a little when climbing stairs, and he's by no means what people call a sportsman, but he likes to garden and go on long walks and be outside. He's not fussy—he prefers quirky old restaurants that have seen better days to fancy ones—but he does like a level of comfort. He also likes baroque music and action movies, roadside diners, and having time and leisure to read books on the British Raj. He's completely uninterested in schools and real estate, which were two of Mom's favorite topics, and while he's capable of chatting with great charm about topics that amuse him, he also loves to challenge others when he's decided they're spouting nonsense. He's happiest when it's a little chilly and a bit misty. And he also likes lobsters and a good clambake, as do we all. So Maine was the perfect place to celebrate his birthday.

But in the midst of all the shore dinners and boat rides and enjoying Maine sunsets with a drink firmly in hand, all the adults, especially Dad, noticed how much Mom was struggling, a fact she was determined no one should acknowledge until the weekend was over.

She looked increasingly drawn and weary. Her skin wasn't more yellow, but she was thinner and her face was more creased; her cheeks sagged, making her perpetual smile seem slightly pensive. Still, all the lines seemed to disappear when the grandchildren marched in front of her on one mission or another. During that trip, Mom turned to me one evening and said that it was hard to imagine herself or ourselves any luckier.

What had gone so terribly awry for the people in Mc-Ewan's *On Chesil Beach,* one character thought, was that they'd never had love and patience at the same time. We had both.

The last morning of our stay, which was in a sprawling, shingle-style, classic Maine hotel, I came down to find Mom on the porch with the four younger grandchildren around her. She was reading them a story. It was a crisp Maine summer morning. I pulled out my iPhone and hastily snapped a few pictures. I remember realizing that Nico, the oldest grand-child, wasn't in the picture. I mean, why would he be? At sixteen, he wouldn't have been listening to his grandmother reading a picture book.

I ran to his room and told him I needed him—so he un-plugged himself, put down his own book, and followed.

We walked together to the porch, and then Nico joined the crew so I could get a picture of Mom with all five of her grandchildren. I'm not sure why I felt compelled at that moment to do it. I never take photographs. Maybe I sensed that something was about to happen beyond the control of love, patience, or any of us, and this was my last chance to fix time.

THE FINAL WEEKEND of the summer, mid-September, my partner, David, and I spent with a friend who always rented a particular house on the beach in Quogue, about two hours from Manhattan, on Long Island.

Mom loved when I told her about visiting this friend, be-cause the house belonged to John O'Hara's daughter, Wylie, and to O'Hara himself before that. O'Hara was one of Mom's favorite authors. The house was a ramshackle Cape on a rap-idly crumbling bluff overlooking the beach and ocean, and it had the perfect porch for lying around and reading. Not surprisingly, the bookshelves were filled with John O'Hara books. On this visit, I'd decided to cheat on the book I'd brought and read O'Hara instead.

First, though, I'd figured I better find out a bit about O'Hara. I learned from books in the house that O'Hara was born in 1905 in Pottsville, Pennsylvania. His father was a distinguished Irish doctor, and the family was able to send him to Yale. But his father died when he was at college, and his mother couldn't afford to continue to pay his tuition, so that was the end of Yale for him. The experience of having to drop out gave O'Hara a lifelong obsession with money, class, and social exclusion. He first drew notice in 1928, during Mom's parents' era, writing stories on these themes for *The New Yorker,* and then, in 1934, at age twenty-nine, he wrote *Appointment in Samarra,* which made him famous. Mom said that O'Hara was, at first, someone she was told she should read and then soon became someone whose books she eagerly awaited.

When I got back to the city after my Quogue weekend, my father was in the hospital with septic bursitis in his elbow, having let it swell to the size of a small grapefruit before Mom made him seek emergency-room treatment. I called Mom to get the update. He hated being in the hospital, but he was doing well.

"So I finally read *Appointment in Samarra,*" I told her. "I'd always thought that book had something to do with Iraq."

Appointment in Samarra is not set in Samarra or anywhere else in the Middle East but in the fictional town of Gibbsville, Pennsylvania, in the 1930s. The novel tells the story of a young married car dealer named Julian English, who thinks he has all the right breeding and connections and who impulsively throws a drink in the face of a wealthier and more powerful man whom he loathes for no good reason. Three days later, and after two additional impulsive acts—including making a pass at the girlfriend of a gangster—Julian has lost literally everything.

"I can't believe you hadn't read it. And it does apply to Iraq, even if that's not at all what it's about. It's a book about setting things in motion and then being too proud and stubborn to apologize and to change course. It's about thinking that being raised a certain way gives you the right to behave badly. It seems Bush was fated to get us into a war there no matter what." Mom was not a fan of our then-president, and she was horrified that he'd used al Qaeda and 9/11 as a pretext for invading Baghdad. Dad sometimes played devil's advocate to Mom's most liberal views, but on this subject he felt similarly, and they'd both taken recently to sharing books dissecting American foreign policy.

As we talked more about *Appointment in Samarra,* we soon found ourselves discussing the book's epigraph, which is, in fact, a speech from a play by W. Somerset Maugham, a writer on whose stories we would both later jointly binge.

Maugham's parable is a retelling of a classic Iraqi tale. The speaker is Death:

> There was a merchant in Baghdad who sent his servant to market to buy provisions and in a little while the servant came back, white and trembling, and said, Master, just now when I was in the marketplace I was jostled by a woman in the crowd and when I turned I saw it was Death that jostled me. She looked at me and made a threatening gesture; now, lend me your horse, and I will ride away from this city

and avoid my fate. I will go to Samarra and there Death will not find me. The merchant lent him his horse, and the servant mounted it, and he dug his spurs in its flanks and as fast as the horse could gallop he went. Then the merchant went down to the market-place and he saw me standing in the crowd and he came to me and said, Why did you make a threatening gesture to my servant when you saw him this morning? That was not a threatening gesture, I said, it was only a start of surprise. I was astonished to see him in Baghdad, for I had an appointment with him to-night in Samarra.

Later, we would have more time and cause to talk about fate and the role it did or didn't play in the events of our lives—particularly in the events that lay ahead. But during that phone call in September, my mother and I soon moved on to other topics. When it sounded like the conversation was drawing to a close, Mom had one more thing she wanted to mention.

"I just wanted to let you know that your sister is insisting I see another doctor and go in for more tests." The new doctor was going to do another scan and try to determine why she couldn't get rid of the hepatitis.

"That sounds like a good idea, Mom."

Then we were back to me. "And are you going to get some rest?" she asked.

"There's so much to do before I leave," I hedged. "I don't know how I'm going to get it all done." At the time, I was editor in chief of a book publishing house, and was headed, as I was every year, to Germany for the Frankfurt Book Fair, which is held the first week in October.

"You can only do what you can, and what doesn't get done, just doesn't get done." Mom was forever giving me advice that she would never herself take.

"Mom, I promise to take it easier if you do—we'll make a deal. But it sounds like no matter what, it's going to be a very challenging couple of days for you, especially when you're still not feeling well."

Every day, Mom was at the hospital for a few hours with Dad. Friends she adored were in town from London, so she was spending time with them. She was also planning to drive hours out of town with them to visit another friend, who had a brain tumor and had just been told he had anywhere from three months to two years to live. Then, at the end of the week, she had her appointment with the new doctor.

I realize now that all of us had reached a mad, feverish pitch of activity in the days leading up to Mom's diagnosis. Dinners, drinks, visits, benefits, meetings, scheduling, picking up, dropping off, buying tickets, yoga, going to work, cardio at the gym. We were terrified to stop, stop anything, and admit that something was wrong. Activity, frenzied activity, seemed to be the thing we all felt we needed. Only Dad slowed down, and that wasn't until he was trapped in a hospital getting intravenous antibiotics. Everything would be all right, everything would be possible, anything could be salvaged or averted, as long as we all kept running around.

While I was at the Frankfurt Book Fair a week later, just before heading off to co-host a table full of publishing pals for dinner, my mother called to tell me that she almost certainly had cancer. The hepatitis wasn't viral; it was related to a tumor in her bile duct. It would be good news if the cancer was only there, but it was far more likely that it had started in the pancreas and spread to the bile duct, which would not be good news at all. There were also spots on her liver. But I was not to worry, she said, and I was certainly not to cut my trip short and come home.

I can't remember much of what I said, or what she replied. But she soon changed the subject—she wanted to talk to me about my job. I'd recently told her that I'd become weary of my work, for all the same boring reasons privileged people get sick of their white-collar jobs: too many meetings, too much email, and too much paperwork. Mom told me to quit. "Just give two weeks' notice, walk out the door, and figure out later what to do. If you're lucky enough to be able to quit, then you should. Most people aren't that fortunate." This wasn't a new perspective that came from the cancer—it was vintage Mom. As much as she was devoted to intricate planning in daily life, she understood the importance of occasionally following an impulse when it came to big decisions. (But she also recognized that not everyone was dealt the same cards. It's much easier to follow your bliss when you have enough money to pay the rent.)

After we hung up, I didn't know if I would be able to make it through the dinner. The restaurant was about a mile from my hotel. I walked to clear my head, but my head didn't clear. I confided the news about Mom's cancer to my co-host, a good friend, but to no one else. I had a feeling of dizziness, almost giddiness. Who was this person drinking beers and eating schnitzel and laughing? I didn't allow myself to think about Mom—what she was feeling; whether she was scared, sad, angry. I remember her telling me on that call that she was a fighter and that she was going to fight the cancer. And I remember telling her I knew that. I don't think I told her

I loved her then. I think I thought it would sound too dramatic—as though I were saying goodbye.

When I got back to my hotel after dinner, I looked around the room and then out the window. The river Main was barely visible under the city streetlights; it was a rainy night, so the roadway glistened in such a way that the lines between the river, the sidewalk, and the street were obscured. The hotel housekeeping staff had folded my big, fluffy white duvet into a neat rectangle. Beside my bed was a stack of books and some hotel magazines. But this was one of the nights when the printed word failed me. I was too drunk, too confused, too disoriented—by the hour of night, and also by the knowledge that my family's life was changing now, forever—to read. So I did the hotel room thing. I turned on the TV and channel-surfed: from the glossy hotel channel to the bill channel (had my minibar item from the night before really cost that much?) to Eurosport and various German channels, before settling on CNN and the familiar faces and voices of Christiane Amanpour and Larry King.

When Mom and I later talked about that night, she was surprised at one part of my story: that I had watched TV instead of reading. Throughout her life, whenever Mom was sad or confused or disoriented, she could never concentrate on television, she said, but always sought refuge in a book. Books focused her mind, calmed her, took her outside of herself; television jangled her nerves.

There's a W. H. Auden poem called "Musée des Beaux Arts," written in December 1938, just after Kristallnacht. In it is a description of a painting by Brueghel, in which the old master depicts Icarus falling from the sky while everyone else, involved in other things or simply not wanting to know, "turns away / quite leisurely from the disaster" and goes about daily tasks. I thought about that poem a lot over the next few days of the fair as I chatted about books, kept my appointments, and ate frankfurters off cardboard-thin crackers. The poem begins, "About suffering they were never wrong, / The Old Masters: how well they understood / Its human position; how it takes place / While someone else is eating or opening a window or just walking dully along." While at the fair, I felt the "someone else" was me. Mom was suffering; I was going on with my life.

I did manage to talk with my brother and sister, their spouses, and Dad (now out of the hospital and fully recovered), and David. All of us were saying hopeful things to each other: there was cause for alarm but no reason to panic. And yet the calls were exponential—every conversation was relayed to everyone else, leading to ever more calls, calls upon calls, calls about calls. We all spent time on the Web and read the same grim things about this particularly vicious cancer. But there were more tests to be done. It was still early. There was a lot to learn. No one should jump to any conclusions.

"Are you sure I shouldn't come home right away, Mom?" I asked each time when I spoke to her from the trip.

"Don't be silly," she said. "Enjoy yourself." In one conversation, she finally relayed exactly how she got the news—and talked about the first oncologist she'd visited, to whom she and my sister had taken an instant dislike when he'd asked Mom if she worked outside the home. Mom said to me, "Do you think a doctor would ever ask a man that?" She told me that Nina had been amazing—organizing, arranging, asking all the right questions. My sister had spent years working in.

Soviet Russia and had learned there how to push when neces-sary.

"The lesson of all of this . . ." Mom began, and then paused. I waited. I couldn't imagine what the lesson was. "The lesson is this," she continued. "Relief organizations need to tell peo-ple who have gone on trips to places like Afghanistan not to assume that any sickness they get while there or after is related to the trip. It may just be a coincidence. We need to make sure people understand that."

This was the silver lining? A new protocol for humanitar-ian aid workers returning from overseas trips to exotic locales?

"Also, I have a favor to ask," Mom added. "Bring me back a wonderful book from the book fair. And your father could use a new book too."

I grabbed too many books to carry home and then tried to figure out which I would put in my luggage and which I would mail, but all I could think about was whether things could have been different if we'd made Mom see more doc-tors earlier, or whether, perhaps, she'd had an appointment in Samarra and nothing could have changed that.

Seventy Verses on Emptiness

H i, Mom, I'm home. How are you feeling?"
"Better."

It was Saturday night, and I'd just returned from Frankfurt. The next topic on the phone call was my flight—any delays, books I'd read on the plane. As always, it was only with some effort that I turned the conversation back to Mom. Much of her activity had been centered on her grandchildren. She also wanted to talk about my sister's reluctance to go through with an impending move to Geneva. Before Mom was diagnosed, Nina had applied for and accepted a job there working for the GAVI Alliance, helping to set global vaccination and immunization policy. Now, days away from moving there with her partner, Sally, and their two children, Nina had second thoughts and was contemplating turning down the job and keeping her family in New York so that they could spend whatever time Mom had left with Mom.

"Your sister doesn't want to go. I told her she has to."

Mom was getting more and more jaundiced, but it wasn't

slowing her down at all. She'd gone, at the recommendation
of a friend, to see the Dalai Lama at, incongruously, Radio
City Music Hall, that glittering monument to entertainment
excess. There was a booklet she'd been given there that she
wanted to loan me—it contained *The Diamond Cutter Sutra* and
Seventy Verses on Emptiness. I asked her what she thought of the
event, and she said that while she'd been very moved to see
and hear the Dalai Lama, she'd found, honestly, much of his
talk confusing. It had still given her a lot to think about, she
said—especially when she read in printed form the verses that
were the subject of his speech.

I also found things to ponder in the booklet, but there was
much that I didn't, and still don't, understand. These aren't
works that reveal themselves casually—they require study. *The
Diamond Cutter Sutra*, which is largely about impermanence,
was composed by the Buddha around 500 B.C. A woodblock
copy dated A.D. 868 was found in 1907 in western China and
is the oldest printed book in the world. *Seventy Verses on Emptiness* was written around A.D. 200. Its author, Nagarjuna,
was born into the Brahmin upper caste in southern India
and converted to Buddhism. Neither I nor Mom—even after
the lecture—had the necessary context for interpreting these
works, which led Mom to remark that the older she got, the
more she learned how little she knew. And yet there was one
passage from *Seventy Verses on Emptiness*, translated into English
by Gareth Sparham, that Mom had underlined: "Permanent is
not; impermanent is not; a self is not; not a self [is not]; clean is
not; not clean is not; happy is not; suffering is not."

This passage made a deep impression on me, and I found
myself turning to it again and again. Although I wasn't sure
exactly what it meant, it calmed me.

Mom told me that she and my sister had met, the Friday before I returned from Germany, a new oncologist, Dr. Eileen O'Reilly. A phrase the doctor used had reassured Mom—"treatable but not curable." Just the word *treatable* was making a difference. It might mean she had more than the six months that seemed to be the norm. So long as her cancer was treatable, there was reason to hope.

"Wait till you meet Dr. O'Reilly," Mom said. "She's tiny and so young and she couldn't be smarter. She's very efficient but also very kind. You'll love her." It was important to Mom that we all love her oncologist.

On the plane back from Frankfurt, I'd started *The Savage Detectives,* a big, ambitious novel by the Chilean poet and novelist Roberto Bolaño. The novel was written on Spain's Costa Brava in a frantic burst of creativity as Bolaño turned from poetry to prose to try to make money to support his son. It was originally published in 1998 but had just been launched in America in an English translation in 2007, four years after Bolaño's death at age fifty from liver disease. I'd brought it back with me from the fair for Mom but wanted to finish it first. Mom had just read *Man Gone Down* by Michael Thomas, a young writer originally from Boston who was now living and teaching in New York. *Man Gone Down* is another big, ambitious novel—about race, the American Dream, fatherhood, money, and love. Even though Mom had yet to read the Bolaño and I hadn't started *Man Gone Down,* we compared notes and decided that the two were quite similar: vast, bold, obsessive, and brilliant books about disappointment, writing, and running (metaphorically in the Bolaño; literally and metaphorically in the Thomas, as the main character is a jogger).

When I was finished with the Bolaño, we swapped. Mom

was fascinated with *The Savage Detectives,* even if its digressions occasionally maddened her. I think what she liked most was that it's a book obsessed with writers by a writer who was clearly in love with writing. Mom also liked that the literary allusions were foreign to her; neither she nor I had read or often even heard of most of the writers Bolaño referenced or lampooned. The experience appealed to her curiosity—the way you can be fascinated by a story that you overhear, on a train or in a coffee shop, about people you don't know, when the storyteller is highly animated, full of passion and wit.

Unlike the Bolaño, the Thomas has locations and references that were mostly familiar to us. It had just been published months before, and Mom was excited for me to read it. Told in one great rush of prose, *Man Gone Down* moves back and forth between the character's life as a young black kid in Boston, amid the violence that took place around the forced desegregation of schools, and New York, where he's now married to a white woman, is the father of three children, and has only a few days to keep their lives from falling apart.

"You'll race through it," Mom had said. "It's the most amazing portrait of the city and the country." I did, and it is.

The Bolaño and Thomas are now forever linked in my mind—not just because they are both books about chronic disappointment but because they were the first books Mom and I read together after we learned Mom's diagnosis, and they provided a different kind of hope than that which Dr. O'Reilly had given us. These two books showed us that we didn't need to retreat or cocoon. They reminded us that no matter where Mom and I were on our individual journeys, we could still share books, and while reading those books, we wouldn't be the sick person and the well person; we would simply be a mother and a son entering new worlds together. What's more, books provided much-needed ballast—something we both craved, amid the chaos and upheaval of Mom's illness.

This occurred to me only later. At the time, I remember feeling that I was a little too busy for it all, that reading these books with Mom was so time-consuming that it was keeping me both from being useful to her and from reading other books I'd been wanting to read. But there would be such disappointment in Mom's voice if I hadn't yet started a book she knew I'd love that I continued to read whatever she gave me or suggested, and to recommend books to her that I thought she'd like. So it's fair to say that Mom started the book club unwittingly and I joined it grudgingly.

IN MY DESIRE to do something, anything, to help, I'd fixed on two thoughts. The first was the idea that Mom should have a blog. She had so many friends, from her many different lives, I suspected it would exhaust her to spend time updating everyone all the time. When I suggested the blog, she and Dad instantly saw the need for it. But Mom didn't love the idea of writing it. She didn't consider herself a writer. And more than that, I think she thought it was self-aggrandizing, unseemly.

"Why don't you write the blog?" she suggested to me. I said I would.

My second idea was to have Mom talk to a friend of ours named Rodger, who had been the primary caregiver—my whole family is quick to adopt the language of whatever country we are in, and now that we were in the country of the sick, we were picking up phrases left and right—for a mutual friend who had lived nearly five years with pancreatic cancer.

I thought it would give her hope. Rodger was one of the most generous and brave people I knew: an almost-seven-foot-tall extreme athlete and former nuclear sub officer who had been a leader in the fight against AIDS. He had also written a book about caring for the ill.

As soon as Rodger told me that he and Mom had talked, I called her to find out how it went.

"So, was it helpful to talk to Rodger?"

There was a long pause. I wasn't sure Mom had heard me. Then she began:

"I didn't love my conversation with Rodger. It was a bit discouraging. He says I'm going to be so sick from the chemo that I won't be able to do anything for myself, that I'll need round-the-clock care, and that I'll be in terrible pain."

There are some genies that, once let out of their bottle, can't be put back in. It had seemed like such a good idea. I'd been certain that Rodger would know the right things to say, that he would be hopeful. It was the first time since the diagnosis that I heard my mother's voice crack. She kept telling herself and all of us how lucky she was—to have insurance; to have had such a wonderful long life; to have grandchildren she adored and meaningful work; to have excellent doctors and a loving family; to have a niece who worked in medicine who'd expedited charts and appointments. But as she repeated this mantra now, with that slight crack in her voice, I heard something new: fear. Just how wretched and painful was this going to be?

Why hadn't I seen this coming? Why hadn't I talked to Rodger first and vetted what he would say? Why did I always need to do something, like referring one person to another, just for the sake of doing something, when sometimes, perhaps, it was better to do nothing? I was so busy regretting my advice that I couldn't think of anything to say except to mumble that I was sure (how was I sure?) that things had changed a lot since the mutual friend had died, and that the treatments were gentler and more effective than they were even a few years ago.

You should talk to this person. You should read this guidebook. You should go to this restaurant. You should order this dish. My life has always been filled with suggesting, recommending. Sometimes my advice works out brilliantly, but sometimes not. And then I look back and wonder whether I really gave proper thought to my recommendations. Was that barbecue restaurant really the best in Austin—or just one where I'd spent a fun evening?

"Are you sorry you talked to Rodger?" I asked.

"No," Mom finally said, with slightly less than her usual assurance. "We'll just do our best and see."

THE NEXT MORNING my father told me that Mom had had a really bad night; she was terribly upset by her conversation with Rodger. Dad was too. Rodger had also told her that her hair would fall out in clumps; that her digestive system would fall apart entirely; that she would be so nauseated and sick, she wouldn't be able to get out of bed; and that she would need to take painkillers and so many other pills that she'd be like a zombie.

Dad sounded sad and worried but also irritated. And then I spoke to Mom.

"Did you get any rest?" she asked me, before I could say anything. "You sounded exhausted yesterday."

I told her I'd slept well. Which of course I hadn't—partly

from my habitual insomnia and partially from guilt over setting up the call.

Two of my nephews were being baptized that day, and we were all getting together for the occasion. Nina and Sally just hadn't gotten around to it before, but now that Mom was sick and they were supposed to be leaving for Switzerland, they'd arranged it fast. Milo was four and Cy two. "This is going to be a great day," Mom said. "Now all my grandchildren will have been baptized."

There were other things she needed to talk to me about too. Ever more people were starting to hear that she had cancer, and she wanted to make sure she got to everyone in the right order and with the right message: *not curable but treatable.* Mom wanted everyone to know that it was too early to hang crepe and that she was determined to fight the cancer. With prayers and a bit of luck, she would have a good long run, she told people. But she also wanted them to know that it wasn't something that could be zapped and dispensed with; that it was indeed pancreatic cancer, and they shouldn't expect a miracle, just pray for one. We all spent a fair amount of time explaining to people that no, alas, she wasn't a candidate for the Whipple, a grueling and brutal operation they do to remove the tumors and much of your pancreas if they think your cancer hasn't yet spread to other organs. Because with Mom it certainly had spread.

One of my cousins and his wife had written to say, in a way they knew would make her smile, that even though they were "heathens," they were praying for her. Mom loved this. She said to me—and to them—that she suspected heathen prayers were even more effective than Christian or Jewish or Muslim ones—perhaps because heathens prayed less.

We knew word had begun to get out widely when lots of food started to appear. A delicious roast chicken arrived. Some friends made soup or muffins and dropped them off. One of Mom's best friends since grade school arranged and paid for a cook to come once a week and serve dinner so Mom could host a small gathering of friends without exhausting herself, or just share a delicious home-cooked meal with Dad if she wasn't up for visitors.

Several people called me for advice. I understood their dilemma. What does one say to someone who has just been diagnosed with such a dire illness?

Every year pancreatic cancer kills more than 35,000 people in America—it's the fourth leading cause of cancer death. It gets only 2 percent of the National Cancer Institute's budget; maybe that's because it has so few survivors. Most people don't know they have pancreatic cancer until it has spread, because the symptoms usually come late, often as a result of the cancer affecting other organs, and they are common to many different illnesses. Weight loss, back pain, nausea, and loss of appetite can have hundreds of causes. The yellowing eyes and skin of jaundice is another symptom but is far more likely to be caused by viral hepatitis than anything else, so it's usually chalked up to that.

After Mom's diagnosis, I went to the Web to find a picture of the pancreas. It's a lumpy, cone-shaped gland tucked deep in the abdomen behind the stomach, resting in front of the spine and alongside the small intestine. The pancreas is the gland that makes hormones like insulin and also the enzymes that help us digest food. The bile duct links it to the liver and the gallbladder. Cancer cells easily spread from the pancreas to other parts of the body, hitching a ride on the blood that courses from the pancreas through the lymphatic system.

When it's not possible to remove the tumors by performing a Whipple operation—and it's not with about 85 percent of the people who are diagnosed—the only available treatment is various combinations of chemotherapy. This is usually palliative—it addresses the symptoms and helps slow the disease but can't stop the cancer from spreading.

At the time of Mom's diagnosis, and at the time of this writing, the type of pancreatic cancer Mom had is almost always fatal, unless it's caught in time for a Whipple. Fewer than five percent of all people diagnosed with all kinds of pancreatic cancer, including those who have the Whipple, will live five more years. For those, like Mom, who are diagnosed after the cancer has spread, the average life expectancy is three to six months, but that's just an average. Some people, we were told, are dead within a month; others will live for two years or even longer.

I gave people who didn't know what to say the best advice I could muster, which was that it was better to say anything rather than pretend that nothing was wrong. My hunch was that Mom would simply appreciate knowing that people were thinking of her. This turned out to be true enough. The messages she received brought her real pleasure, and she shared some with me. One of my oldest friends wrote a letter chronicling our families' decades of friendship and also inviting Mom to her annual holiday party—or a quiet supper. The sister of Mom's oldest godchild sent a lovely picture of "paper boats on a river of salt and sand to bear away some of your discomfort." Others wrote about the effect Mom had had on their lives. I cringed a bit at some of the pre-eulogizing—too much too soon, I thought, too much like being present at your own funeral. Yet those were among the messages she liked the most. And why not? Why not enjoy the pleasure of knowing that you touched others during your life while you still can?

She did, however, confess to a passing irritation with people who wrote or said, "I'm sure you'll be cured soon."

People also wanted to share with her their stories of friends and relatives who'd had pancreatic cancer. I grew weary of these tales, but my mother didn't seem to, always asking questions in case there was something useful she could learn, or perhaps just because she was much more comfortable in the role of the comforter than the comforted. Mom told one friend that she felt deeply selfish about her sense of relief that she would now be thinking only of herself and her family, and not about work or the scores of charities and schools and causes that had previously occupied her. The friend countered that that was hardly selfish, given the circumstances. But then in the next breath, Mom suggested a party for her beloved ninety-three-year-old office mate at the International Rescue Committee, and also volunteered to help plan a mission to Uganda that she couldn't go on but thought was extremely important.

Meanwhile my mother's bile duct was swollen shut, because of the pressure from the tumor in her pancreas. So Mom went into the hospital that week to have a stent put in, to ease the jaundice by helping her liver drain through her bile duct, but she simultaneously kept herself busy working her cell phone, organizing the party, the mission, and our lives.

Watching all this unfold, my sister was less and less sure about going ahead with the move to Geneva. The new job would give her the ability to influence policy and help save the lives of children around the world. But she really wanted to stay with Mom, go with her to chemo, and have Mom be able to spend as much time as possible with all her grandchildren. Sally, a nurse by training and now also in public health, was, as always, a calming and practical voice as my sister contemplated scrapping all the plans they had made together. If that was what Nina wanted to do, of course that was what they would do.

Mom would hear none of it.

"I'm going to fight this thing, and Nina can come back as much as she likes, and I'll spend lots of time in Geneva, but she and Sally and the kids must go." If Nina and her family stayed, against Mom's instructions, she would be signaling to Mom that there might only be months left instead of, perhaps, years. Mom relied on my sister for an enormous number of things—including hope. What would it say to Mom about her condition if days away from moving Nina canceled everything? And what about all the plans surrounding the impending move? If the slightest change of timing or itinerary generally drove Mom's anxiety level to DEFCON 1, then what would this do?

Still, Nina wanted to stay. Was it okay to stay simply because she wanted to do so, even if it upset Mom and increased Mom's feeling of doom? And what about the job? Was it selfish to go or selfish to stay—or did that word even apply? *A self is not; not a self [is not].*

"Are you sure you don't want me stay?" Nina asked Mom.

"Of course, I want you to stay. But I really want you to go," Mom answered.

"And if I were sick and you had the same choice I have, would you leave or stay?"

"Oh, sweetie, that's totally different. You have your whole life ahead of you."

"But you'd stay?" Nina asked.

Mom didn't answer.

And then Nina called me. "What on earth am I supposed to do with that?"

MOM HAD JUST given me *A Thousand Splendid Suns*, the new book by Khaled Hosseini, author of *The Kite Runner*. When Mom discovered *The Kite Runner*, soon after its publication in 2003, she was ecstatic—and made everyone she knew read it. The book and its author fascinated her. Hosseini was born in Kabul in 1965. He spent his early years in school in Afghanistan, but his father, a diplomat, was posted to Paris when he was eleven, so they moved there. After the Soviet invasion in 1979, his family was granted asylum in the United States. He would eventually become a doctor and would write *The Kite Runner* in the mornings before work. He had almost finished, and then came the September 11, 2001, attack on the World Trade Center, which made him think he should abandon it. But his wife insisted that he continue—she saw the book as his way of putting "a human face on the Afghan people." Mom felt he had done exactly that; this was the Afghanistan she knew and loved, because it was a book about everyone she'd met there. She no longer needed to try to explain her love of that misunderstood country—she just insisted everyone read *The Kite Runner*.

Mom and I didn't exactly agree about *The Kite Runner*. I liked it a great deal but thought it had too much plot. Did the evilest Taliban guy really need to be a Nazi too? There's also a key scene involving a slingshot that I had trouble believing. When we disagreed about a book she loved, Mom would just furrow her brow. It wasn't that she didn't think you had a right to your opinion—of course you did. It was just that she felt you were missing the main point—you were focused on one thing when you should have been focused on another. It was as if you were critiquing a restaurant based on the decor, while she was talking about the food.

When she first pressed *A Thousand Splendid Suns* into my hand—we were in New York, standing in her and Dad's dining room, sun streaming in through the French doors, making for a splendid sun effect right inside their apartment—she told me that she loved it even more than *The Kite Runner*, because this time Hosseini was focusing on women. It was the women of Afghanistan, my mother believed, who—once they'd been granted access to books and education—would be the salvation of that country. "And there are no Nazis in this one," she added emphatically, remembering my earlier criticism.

As soon as I finished the book, I went over to Mom and Dad's apartment to talk with her about it. Dad was still at his office; Mom at home waiting for a conference call. We found ourselves discussing the three kinds of fateful choices that exist in the two books: the ones characters make knowing that they can never be undone; the ones they make thinking they can but learn they can't; and the ones they make thinking they can't and only later come to understand, when it's too late, when "nothing can be undone," that they could have.

Mom had always taught all of us to examine decisions by reversibility—that is, to hedge our bets. When you couldn't decide between two things, she suggested you choose the one that allowed you to change course if necessary. Not the road less traveled but the road with the exit ramp. I think that's why we had all moved, at different times in our lives, to various foreign lands without giving much thought to it. If you stayed at home, you might not get the opportunity to go to that place again. But if you went, you could always come back.

At the same time Mom loaned me *A Thousand Splendid Suns*, she'd also given us all a much more prosaic work to read: *The Etiquette of Illness*, a book from 2004 by a social worker and psychotherapist named Susan Halpern, who is herself a cancer survivor. The subtitle is *What to Say When You Can't Find the Words.* But it's really about what to do when you feel scared that doing something, if it turns out to be the wrong thing, might be worse than doing nothing at all. For years, Mom and Dad had been fascinated with the subject of end-of-life care—including palliative medicine, which focuses not just on managing pain but also on helping patients and their families maintain the best possible quality of life throughout the course of an illness. In addition to having a standard will, always kept up-to-date, Mom had made living wills and filled out her "Do Not Resuscitate" paperwork long before she'd had any inkling that she was ill. It's not that she was obsessed with sickness and death or even particularly worried about either—she said she just didn't want to leave room for us to argue about her wishes if she wasn't able to express them.

A Thousand Splendid Suns and *Man Gone Down* were books Mom had said I must read. *The Etiquette of Illness*, however, was one she said she wanted me to read. I let it sit for days on my bedside table, untouched. I thought I didn't need such a book. Common sense would guide me.

One of the many things I love about bound books is their sheer physicality. Electronic books live out of sight and out of mind. But printed books have body, presence. Sure, some-times they'll elude you by hiding in improbable places: in a box full of old picture frames, say, or in the laundry basket, wrapped in a sweatshirt. But at other times they'll confront you, and you'll literally stumble over some tomes you hadn't thought about in weeks or years. I often seek electronic books, but they never come after me. They may make me feel, but I can't feel them. They are all soul with no flesh, no texture, and no weight. They can get in your head but can't whack you upside it.

As an insomniac, I find what I want to read at three A.M. is very different from what I crave during normal waking hours. So a few sleepless nights later, I found myself giving *The Etiquette of Illness* a quick glance, after my hand knocked against it and it fell onto the floor when I fumbled for my bedside lamp. Three hours later I looked up. David and I live in an apartment that's not huge but has a view south, to where the World Trade Center towers used to stand; east to the Brook-lyn Bridge; and west across the Hudson, which peeks out from between elegant Richard Meier glass buildings and various squat brick structures that fill the blocks between our place and the water. When I paused in my reading, I saw that it was no longer dark and that the patches of the Hudson River visible from our window were orange with the light from the east. I would finish the book a few hours later, just in time for work. The book had hooked me instantly with one exam-ple that made me realize that there is, indeed, an etiquette of illness; that there was no reason I should know it, but also no excuse for not being open to learning it.

Halpern wants the reader to think about the difference between asking "How are you feeling?" and "Do you want me to ask how you're feeling?" Even if it's your mother whom you're questioning, the first approach is more intrusive, insistent, demanding. The second is much gentler and allows the person simply to say no on those days when she's doing well and doesn't want to be the "sick person," or is doing badly but wants a distraction, or has simply answered the question too many times that day to want to answer it again, even to someone as close as a son.

I scribbled down on a scrap of paper a version of that question and two other things I didn't want to forget from this book and stuck the creased paper in my wallet. Here's what I wrote:

1 Ask: "Do you want to talk about how you're feeling?"
2. Don't ask if there's anything you can do. Suggest things, or if it's not intrusive, just do them.
3. You don't have to talk all the time. Sometimes just being there is enough.

The next morning, I called Mom the minute I awoke.
"Hi, Mom, do you want to talk about how you're feeling?"
And she did. She'd been feeling better—the stent they'd put in made a huge difference, and her jaundice had almost disappeared. Dad had gone with her for the procedure, and she was very proud of him, as he hadn't been squeamish in the least about any of it. (He always gets annoyed if people insist on describing operations or illnesses in detail, though I now realize that this is mostly because he just doesn't think it's a proper topic for conversation.) Mom's appetite was somewhat back. But she'd had her first chemo treatment and was get-

ting mouth sores—very irritating. On the other hand, Dr. O'Reilly gave her steroids, and that was helping improve her energy. She was just nervous about how she'd feel when the steroids wore off. She'd been thinking about my suggestion of a blog—but was even more convinced that it was unseemly for her to write about herself, and that I should write about her from my perspective. So we clunkily titled it *Will's Mary Anne Schwalbe News.*

Still, she thought, it would be easier for me if she composed the first post—but in my voice, as if I had written it and not her. She would dictate it to me, and I would type it up. So here is Mom, pretending to be me reporting on her:

Mom started her weekly treatment yesterday as an outpatient at Memorial Sloan-Kettering. She says the people are incredibly nice there and she was impressed with the whole setup.

A lot of people have asked Mom, Dad, Doug, Nina, and me about the best way to keep in touch—which is part of the reason for this blog! I'll post news when there is news to post, including dates on Mom's trips to London, Geneva, etc. . . . So you can check back on the blog as often as you like for any updates.

And, as I'm sure everyone has guessed, email to Mom and regular old snail mail are much better than phone calls. (My father has never been a great fan of the phone.) Of course, depending on her treatments and travels, she may not always be able to reply right away to emails or notes. So please don't worry if you don't hear back.

Thanks to everyone for your concern and kind thoughts and words. Mom is really grateful, as are we all.

Of course, she said, I should change or edit the post however I liked. But she did think it important to mention that she was planning to travel, so people wouldn't think she was on her deathbed quite yet. I didn't change the post at all. Mom apologized to me several times: "I'm sorry to put you to so much work when you have so much of your own to do." I tried to explain to her how little work it is to update a blog. She wanted me to promise her I would get some sleep.

Mom did have one other favor to ask me. Would I accompany her to her third chemo? I assured her that I wanted to go with her as often as I could. Over the course of her illness, my mother would ask all of us—my brother and sister and their partners, and David, as well as various friends—to accompany her to various appointments, of which there were many. I soon realized that this was a way for her to spend time with all of us—and to give us something significant to do for her. This strategy also allowed her to save Dad's time and energy for the more complex procedures or hospital stays that might be in her future. As the weeks passed, accompanying Mom to her chemo treatments would become part of my regular routine with her.

Mom was also eager to tell me about two resolutions she'd made. First, she was going to do more yoga. She loved it, and it relaxed her. And second, she was finally going to bring proper order to her desk, once and for all, while she still had the energy. Mom was particularly determined to remove all duplicates from her address book. I couldn't imagine why—but she seemed so excited about it I didn't question her. (*Do you want to talk about why you want to remove duplicates from your address book?*) "Clean is not; not clean is not." So said Nagarjuna, as quoted by the Dalai Lama. I guess there are many ways of looking at tidiness, and isn't it really all about removing that which doesn't need to be?

Mom also wanted more to read, now that she was finished with the Bolaño. I would drop off a copy of *The Coldest Winter,* David Halberstam's final book, his epic about the Korean War, when I returned the Hosseini. It was a book I'd just published. Halberstam had been a friend of Mom's from college days, when he'd dated a glamorous pal of hers, who was still one of Mom's best friends. He and his wife, Jean, had become friends of mine over the course of my publishing many of his books. Six months earlier, David had been killed instantly in a car accident when a graduate student in journalism who had volunteered to drive him to an interview made a sudden, reckless left turn into oncoming traffic. Days before his death, David had finished this enormous book, on which he'd worked for ten years.

Shortly after David was killed, I'd had to fly on business to Nashville, a city where Halberstam first made his name as a reporter on the civil rights movement. I was fine until right after I fastened my seat belt. For me, there's something about planes that isolates and intensifies sadness, the way a looking glass can magnify the sun until it grows unbearably hot and burns. On that particular flight, I waited for the familiar lift of takeoff, and then, for the first time since David's death, burst into tears.

In the summer, Mom and I had read slender books. Now we were reading one long book after another. Maybe that was a way of expressing hopefulness—you had to have a lot of time left if you were going to start reading Bolaño, or Thomas, or Halberstam. Even the Hosseini had heft. I remarked to Mom how all the books we were reading then shared not just length but a certain theme: fate and the effects of the choices people make.

"I think most good books share that theme," Mom said.

Mom was still worrying that Nina wouldn't move to Geneva. "Remind her: She can always go and come right back. But she has to go."

I didn't know what to say. So I looked at item three on my little *Etiquette of Illness* sheet and decided to say nothing. Then I called my sister.

"I'm going to go," Nina said. "I'll talk to her every day. We'll visit lots with the kids, and she says she'll come visit lots. And we can always move back if we need to. But Mom insists that I go, and she's going to be very unhappy if I don't." So Nina was going.

Happy is not; suffering is not. Somehow Nina's decision to go ahead with the move to Geneva made not just Mom feel better but all of us. Mom was sick, but life was going on. At least for the moment. When we had to make changes, we would.

Permanent is not. Impermanent is not.

Marjorie Morningstar

November brought my first visit with Mom to chemo. And it also brought the chance to talk to her about family in a way we'd never talked about family—or, really, any subject.

Mom sent over the instructions a few days before. I was to meet her at Memorial Sloan-Kettering's outpatient center on East 53rd Street. There was a bookstore across the street, if I got there early. And a deli of sorts on Lexington Avenue, if I wanted to bring a snack. Though she didn't think that would be necessary—there were both graham crackers and pretzels at the outpatient facility, she said. I was to take the elevator to the fourth floor and stake out seats if I arrived there before she did. She liked the chairs, not the long sofa that ran along the back of the room.

Hospitals are interruption factories. Someone is always bursting in to hook you up to something, unhook you, ask you how you're doing, check on you, remind you. On this first visit with Mom, as on all the others, we would eventually be summoned, after Mom had her blood taken, to the treatment rooms, which reminded me of a boarding school dorm with cubicles that don't quite reach to the ceiling. Every few weeks she saw the doctor first; other times she just went to have her blood taken and the treatment given. Once she was in a cubicle, a nurse would appear and ask questions, both medical ones and others related to Mom's comfort (Would she like a pillow for her arm? A blanket? Some more juice?), and then have Mom recite the hospital version of name, rank, and serial number (name, date of birth). Next came the torture of finding a vein, followed by the shout for a chemo check, which involved a second nurse coming in to confirm that it was the right patient (name, date of birth) and the right medicine.

But the interruptions didn't stop there. Especially at the start, there were social workers and people conducting studies and others needing consent forms for those studies.

Mom didn't like being interrupted. For several years I'd been in the habit of calling Mom most mornings at eight A.M. or so—not every morning, but most. She and Dad had call waiting, but it was a constant source of irritation to her. I'd be talking to her and what she called "the clicker" would go off, and she'd say, "Darn, there's someone on the other line," in a more than slightly aggrieved tone.

I don't like being interrupted either—but I interrupt other people. I often forget that other people's stories aren't simply introductions to my own more engaging, more dramatic, more relevant, and better-told tales, but rather ends in themselves, tales I can learn from or repeat or dissect or savor. Mom, on the other hand, rarely interrupted other people and wasn't given to topping other people's tales. She would listen and then ask questions—and not just the yes-or-no or numerical questions people ask to feign interest ("How many days were you in Phoenix?"). She used her questions to get people to talk more about how they felt or what they'd learned or who they'd met or what they thought would happen next.

Even though my first visit to the outpatient center was only Mom's third, she was already on nodding acquaintance with quite a few of the people there, staff and other patients. She had a favorite nurse, one who'd succeeded in finding a vein where two others had failed. And she didn't even seem to mind all the interruptions.

I was feeling extremely cranky about my job that morning. I tried not to dwell on it. It seemed an odd thing to complain about when surrounded by people battling cancer. So we sat silently.

"You really don't need to stay with me, Will. I'm fine. You have so much to do."

"But I'd like to," I said. "Unless you want some time alone?"

It was then, on that November day, that Mom told me she was reading Wallace Stegner's *Crossing to Safety*, the book I'd flown around the world, and then that I said I would finally read it myself.

"I guess if we keep reading books at more or less the same time, then it's sort of like being in a book club," I added. I'd once been in a traditional book club. Mom never had.

"But you don't have time for a book club!" Mom said.

"I have time to read. And we've always talked about books. So if we're reading the same books, and talking about them, why can't we call that a book club?"

"But don't people in book clubs cook things?" Mom asked.
I laughed. "We'll have the world's only foodless book club."

ONE OF THE first things people in book clubs tend to do is
tell one another about their childhoods. I mentioned this to
Mom—who smiled quizzically—and then I asked her to tell
me again about hers. I've never even thought of calling my
parents by their first names, so it's hard to write of Mary Anne
being born in 1934 and not of Mom being born that year, but,
of course, Mom wasn't born then—Mary Anne was.

Mary Anne and her younger brother, Skip, had a beautiful
and very unhappy mother, who was born in America but had
grown up in Paris. Their father was dapper and in the family
textile business, which he sold for a healthy sum while still
young. By all accounts, it was a very unpleasant marriage. It
ended after more than thirty years with a nasty divorce. This
chemo session was one of the few times I ever got Mom to talk
about her childhood, and the first and only time she ever told
me how bitterly unhappy her parents were with each other,
and how it made her determined not to complain about anything if she was ever lucky enough to have her own family.
Mary Anne went to public school and then to an excellent
girls' school, the Brearley School, on the Upper East Side of
New York, where she made friends she would keep for life,
and where she fell under the spell of Mildred Dunnock.

Millie, as she asked to be called, was a drama teacher
who inspired ferocious loyalty in her girls, and already a
well-known stage and movie actress. She went on to create the
role of Linda Loman, Willy's wife, in Arthur Miller's *Death of
a Salesman* ("Attention must be paid") on Broadway (which is

why Mary Anne was there at the opening, which she said was the most thrilling night of theater she would ever see) and was nominated for an Oscar playing the same role in the 1951 film. Mary Anne had always loved to go to the theater, but after studying and performing with Millie, she decided that she had to be an actress.

It was also at Brearley in the early 1950s that Mary Anne and her classmates were told something no generation of women prior to theirs had ever heard, and by the headmistress herself: that they could do anything and be anything—and have a husband and children to boot.

Most people and most other institutions said otherwise. Mary Anne went to Radcliffe, and when she attended services at Harvard's Memorial Church, she told me, she had to wear white gloves and sit in the balcony and wasn't allowed to join the men in the pews. When we lived in Cambridge, Mom always made a point of sitting in the pews downstairs and right at the front.

I knew most of that. As Mom and I sat in the treatment room, waiting for the next interruption, I asked her to tell me more.

"Well, what do you want to know?"

"Well, what were your favorite books?"

"When?"

"As a young girl."

"Nancy Drew. I read dozens of them. I loved the idea of a girl detective."

"And of all time?"

Without a moment of hesitation, she said, "*Gone With the Wind.*" I'd never known that. "I just loved it. I still do," Mom added.

"What else?"

"*Marjorie Morningstar* by Herman Wouk."

I didn't read *Marjorie Morningstar* until after Mom died, but I did know that it was about a good Jewish girl who wants to be an actress and who falls in love with a composer-director she meets at a summer theater. At the heart of the book is their carnal dance, which turns into a scandalous affair. Herman Wouk, who was born in New York in 1915, is also the author of other best sellers such as *The Caine Mutiny*, which won the Pulitzer Prize, and *The Winds of War*. In *Marjorie Morningstar* he created a huge, all-enveloping book that sucks you in like *Gone With the Wind*. It's even got a young, at-first-naïve female protagonist (though it's fair to say that Marjorie is a good deal more likable at the start than Scarlett), and you want her to find love and success and happiness. She begins life as Marjorie Morgenstern but renames herself Marjorie Morningstar because it's a better stage name (and also less Jewish).

I can see how my mother's generation fell in love with this book, which is set in the late 1930s, the time of their mothers, and which depicts not just America but the whole world on the eve of great change. It was a huge best seller. Wouk moves Marjorie first from her life in privileged Jewish New York to the more decadent environs of the theater camp but then to Paris and Switzerland, where she finds a new love, a man who is working to help Jews flee Europe—a man somewhat like a real historical figure, Varian Fry, who was one of the key figures in the early history of the International Rescue Committee, where Mom would eventually work.

Like Hosseini with his *The Kite Runner* and *A Thousand Splendid Suns*, Wouk is the kind of popular writer who is always teaching you something, but who knows how to tell a story and involve you in the lives of his characters. Both are also much better prose stylists than critics often acknowledge. You could say that they are thoroughly old-fashioned in their storytelling techniques—which might explain their tremendous popularity among people of different backgrounds and ages. People like stories. Yet the two of them also thoroughly engage contemporary themes. *Marjorie Morningstar* is a book about assimilation, anti-Semitism, and women's rights. While it ends with what many readers would regard as a bitterly disappointing outcome for Marjorie, I believe that's an essential part of Wouk's critique of the world in which Marjorie was raised. In the end, Marjorie can't overcome the expectations that have been set for her, and the book is more powerful for that than it would have been had she triumphed on the stage as she always thought she wanted.

I can also see how Mary Anne might have recognized herself in young Marjorie. In college summers, Mary Anne had gone off with a few friends to a summer stock theater called Highfield in Massachusetts. By all accounts a beautiful young woman, with lively brown eyes and a constant smile, she became instantly popular, and some of her deepest friendships started or were cemented there. Every now and then, during my childhood, Mom would make an enigmatic comment about her time at Highfield, with a smile that was both sly and rueful. Then when I was fifteen and going to a summer stock theater myself, to be an apprentice, Mom told me, as she drove me up to the house I would share with four strangers, that she hoped I would have as much fun at my theater as she had at hers; but then added, almost as an afterthought, a not entirely convincing caution about taking care not to lead people on. I've always been sure that there's a story that goes with that warning, but no matter how many times I asked her, Mom never said anything more specific about her theatrical summers.

College was different—Mom had lots of stories about Radcliffe. She talked most about how she'd fallen madly in love with a professor of hers, Bob Chapman, who was glamorous and charismatic beyond measure. (Marjorie's love interests couldn't even begin to compare). Bob had graduated from Princeton, taught at Berkeley, been a naval officer in Morocco and Paris in World War II, and had dated F. Scott and Zelda Fitzgerald's daughter, Scottie. He was a playwright, too, and with a friend adapted Herman Melville's *Billy Budd* for Broadway and for a 1962 film.

Mom's love was reciprocated, but platonically, as Bob was, in the parlance of the time, a "confirmed bachelor." Bob introduced her to his friends, and they became hers, too. Mom introduced Dad to Bob soon after she was engaged, and Dad wound up working with him for more than a decade, running Harvard's theater, and sharing a fondness for drinking martinis and collecting postcards. Bob became my sister's godfather and almost a sixth member of our family (the *almost* is because we would never dare argue or be mean to each other in front of him). He was the smartest and best-read person any of us had ever known, but he wore his learning so lightly and had such curiosity about other people that he had the ability to make everyone around him feel smart and well-read. He came over to our house for dinner every few nights—and we traveled with him as a family and individually through North Africa, Europe, and Asia. In 2001, at age eighty-one, Bob had a sudden and massive stroke, and Mom and I flew down to Florida to be with him when he was dying.

No one in the family has ever really gotten over Bob's death. We talk of him daily, recounting stories and imagining what his reactions would be to new books and recent events. He remains for my family the perfect model of how you can be gone but ever present in the lives of people who loved you, in the same way that your favorite books stay with you for your entire life, no matter how long it's been since you turned the last page. When I talked with Mom about Bob, I wondered if I would be able to talk about her the same way when she was no longer here.

As Mom and I sat together in the chemo room, waiting for the next interruption, I tried to turn the conversation from Bob and Wouk back to her experience at summer stock theater.

"It was a long time ago" was all she said, and all she was going to tell me. No one could be more stubborn than Mom when she didn't want to tell you something.

Maybe there was no great mystery to Highfield—maybe it was just a time and place Mom loved and wanted to treasure alone.

Mom loved *Marjorie Morningstar*. That much I knew. How much she was or was not Marjorie Morningstar herself remained her secret.

WE SAT SILENTLY for a while, listening to the sounds around us. The curtain to our little cubicle rustled as people walked by, dragging their IV towers with them on the way to the toilet. Mom's drip dripped. It could take anywhere from two to four hours for the bags to drain. I thought of water torture (wrongly called Chinese water torture), the medieval torment in which you are supposedly driven mad waiting for the next drop of water to plunk on your forehead. Here the drops were supposed to make you better. I mentioned this to Mom, who looked irritated. It was the same look she gave my father and brother when they got overly boisterous after a third martini, and to my sister whenever the two of them went shopping for shoes: always a disaster because of Mom's antipathy toward shopping and my sister's chronic difficulty making up her mind. I usually earned the look for odd and inappropriate comments.

So I quickly brought the conversation back to books—to David Halberstam's *The Coldest Winter* and the veterans he'd interviewed for it. "You know, Mom, almost none of them had ever talked to their families about the Korean War. I've heard from a lot of them, as well as from their children and grandchildren, who say their fathers and grandfathers are now talking about that war for the first time. I've also heard from people who were sent *The Coldest Winter* by a father or grandfather, men who still can't talk about the war."

"That's one of the things books do. They help us talk. But they also give us something we all can talk about when we don't want to talk about ourselves."

Mom went on to tell me, as we sat there, that she really believed your personal life was personal. Secrets, she felt, rarely explained or excused anything in real life, or were even all that interesting. People shared too much, she said, not too little. She thought you should be able to keep your private life private for any reason or for no reason. She even felt that way about politicians—so long as they weren't hypocrites—and worried that we'd never find enough good and interesting people to run for office if we pried into every corner of their past.

Mom also believed that there is such a thing as a good secret. Maybe something kind you did for someone but didn't
want that person to know, because you didn't want him
to be embarrassed or feel as though he owed you anything.
I thought back to a Harvard student of Mom's, an aspiring
playwright who won an award to travel in Europe—but the
award didn't exist. Mom had simply paid, anonymously, for
him to have enough money to go on what turned out to be a
life-changing trip. I write about this only because I was told
that years later this fellow figured it all out, when he went to
research who else had won this lucrative traveling fellowship
and discovered that the answer was no one.

As we were talking, a social worker came in with a ques-
tionnaire. Did Mary (I thought it was odd that they always
called her Mary even though her name was Mary Anne, and
odder that Mom refused to correct them) have time for some
questions? They were doing a study and wanted to see if she
might be a fit.

"Sure," said Mom. There was at least an hour of chemo
to go.

"Awesome." The person asking was a woman in her twen-
ties. She was smartly dressed in a skirt and a V-neck sweater,
with thick tights and Doc Martens—style shoes. Her face was
clear-skinned and earnest, a bit pinched but friendly. She ran
her hands frequently through her shoulder-length blond hair.

"Now," the young woman began, more or less reading from
a script. "This is a survey we are doing about the spiritual
health and support systems of people undergoing treatment
for cancer that has spread to other organs or throughout the
body, Stage Four cancers . . ."

I allowed my mind to drift as the young woman explained

that the participants would be divided into two groups. One group would get counseling, and one group would get none. They would assess everyone at the beginning and at the end, and they wanted to talk to several members of the family. Mom would need to bring the form home, read it, sign it, have my father sign it, and also have it signed by the other family members who were willing to participate. The woman then asked a series of questions: my mother's religion (Christian), how often she prayed (daily), whether she would describe herself as happy (yes—though she wasn't thrilled about the cancer). The woman laughed brightly but a bit nervously.

"Well," said Mom when she left, "that was something of a surprise. And I think your father is going to be surprised too."

"About the survey?"

"No. That I have Stage Four cancer. I had no idea."

The Hobbit

M om, what are you talking about? I think Stage Four just means your cancer has spread to other parts of your body, which is why they can't operate. You know that it's spread, right?"

"Of course, I know that." She sounded a bit annoyed, or maybe she was just tired. "I just didn't know it was Stage Four."

The Etiquette of Illness. I tried to think of what I should or shouldn't say. The prognosis for people with Stage Four pancreatic cancer was, as my siblings and I had read on the Internet, usually three to six months. That didn't leave much room for hope. But there was no clear prognosis for people with "cancer that has spread."

Stage Four is the end of the line. There is no Stage Five—though there are stages IVa and IVb, which reminded me of my tenure on the "E minus" basketball squad, thusly named because they didn't want to call the grouping of the sixth least talented (or, more charitably, least motivated) players the "F" Troop.

I decided to say nothing more.

Soon it was time to leave chemo. It was then that I witnessed the peculiar dance that takes place at the elevator bank. When an elevator arrives, age may still go before beauty, but illness goes before health, chairs before canes, canes before the caneless, the wobbly before the surefooted. After you, my dear Alphonse. No, after you. No wonder it took so long to get an elevator.

On the way out we usually made a visit, never brief, to the pharmacy on the second floor. I told Mom a joke I'd heard ages before about an Englishman at the time of the Crusades who leaves a prescription off at a pharmacy in London and then goes to fight against the infidels. He's captured, is eventually released, falls in love, and lives for thirty years in Persia. Eventually he decides to come home to England and, once back, finds in his pocket the receipt for the prescription. Miraculously, the London pharmacy still exists, and the same pharmacist is behind the counter. He hands over the receipt; the pharmacist looks at it and says, "It's not quite ready yet—can you come back at five?"

Actually, the joke involves shoes and a cobbler. Mom smiled indulgently. She's never thought my jokes very funny, but she's endured them politely, except during those childhood years when I fell in love with punning. That tried even her patience.

Theoretically, the doctor has called the prescription down at the start of chemo so that it will be ready and waiting at the end. But it usually isn't ready, or it's ready but there's a problem. The problem almost always involves Medicare. Either Mom has exceeded a limit; or she can get only so many of these pills if she is also getting those; or the drug is strictly controlled and needs an extra signature. There are pills upon pills: to stimulate the pancreas, for nausea, for exhaustion, for sleep. Sometimes Mom doesn't have to pay anything at all for pills that cost thousands of dollars. Sometimes it's hundreds or thousands of dollars that she needs to pay. It's impossible to keep track of it all and always a surprise.

Mom's reaction to this chaos isn't a surprise. No matter how high the bill that she is paying or that Medicare is paying for her, she will say to me or herself: "What happens to all the people who can't afford this? It's just not fair."

Universal health care was always an issue Mom cared about, and the more care she got, the angrier she became that good medicine wasn't available for everyone in the United States. The pharmacy almost always provoked a political discussion or diatribe.

On this particular day, there was a woman in line right in front of us. She was in her thirties, smartly but not expensively dressed, wearing dark glasses. When she took them off, you could see she'd been weeping. She was shaking her head. Mom talked to her in a soft voice. Not unusual—Mom talked to everyone and had no hesitation approaching people who were crying, in pain, or in distress. ("If they don't want to talk, they'll tell you so, but how can you ignore them?") The medicine wasn't for this woman, it turned out; it was for her mother. The mother had Medicare yet was in that odd place called the doughnut hole, which meant that the government had paid thousands for medication but now she would need to pay thousands before the government would pay thousands again. (Imagine trying to eat a straight line across a doughnut—you would eat cake, go hungry, and then eat again.) My mother was, at that moment, still in the cake of the doughnut; this woman's mother was in the hole.

My cell phone rang, and I stepped out into the hallway to take the call. When I got back, Mom was in a chair, waiting for her prescription. There was no sign of the woman who couldn't quite pay for what her mother needed.

"Mom . . . you paid for that woman's medicine, didn't you?"

"It wasn't much," she said, a little cross at being caught. "But don't tell your father."

Then, as always, she refused to take a cab. ("The M20 takes me almost to my door; it's crazy to spend money on a taxi.") So I waited with her for the bus that would take her home.

MOM HAD ONE more chemo session before Thanksgiving, a holiday I love because of the pies, because it's pretty secular, and because you don't have the stress and expense of shopping for gifts. Also, if you grow up in Cambridge, Massachusetts, Thanksgiving is huge—it's all the holidays rolled into one. That's partly because the Pilgrims landed and lived nearby. But everything is huge (winters, sports teams, lobsters) when you grow up in or around Boston—a city that calls itself "the hub," as in "the hub of the universe." As a kid, I thought that was a fact and was shocked to discover that people in Paris, Berlin, Tokyo, and New York didn't agree.

I was born, not in Massachusetts, but in New York City in 1962. My dad was working for Fairchild Publications, which put out trade papers ranging from *Women's Wear Daily* to *Drug News Weekly*. He'd been one of the first Jewish kids (albeit not a remotely religious one) at his preppy boarding school. He'd then enlisted in the navy, catching the end of World War II on a boat out of Norfolk, Virginia. After that, he'd gone to Yale and to Harvard Business School and eventually found himself in advertising. While Mom had come from prosperous Jews who had moved to the United States in the seventeenth century and later married other Jews who had either converted to Christianity or who were so assimilated that they celebrated Christian holidays, Dad came from earthier and more recent stock. His father's grandfather came over during the Civil War as a German Jewish mercenary drummer boy and wound up selling vegetables, mostly potatoes, on New York's Lower East Side, living in the Five Points section made infamous by Martin Scorsese's film *The Gangs of New York*. My dad's father did well in the family potato business—expanding the wholesaling dramatically and buying a seat on the Chicago Mercantile Exchange. His wife, Latvian by birth, had great aspirations for my father and his two sisters—all of whom were sent to the best schools and colleges.

Dad had proposed to Mom on their first date—and she'd said yes. They'd met days earlier when Dad had come to visit with a friend. After a few months' engagement, they were married in 1959. Dad was thirty-two and Mom twenty-five.

Dad tells me he looks back on their "courtship" with disbelief. He'd immediately fallen in love with Mom—but it's as though he still can't quite believe she chose him. The wedding was held in Connecticut and was Christian, which was just one of the details of which Dad's mother, a more observant Jew than her husband or children, disapproved, somewhat vocally, until one of Mom's best friends suggested that she keep her opinions to herself, which she then did.

Seven years after the wedding, Mom and Dad decided to move the whole family from New York to Cambridge, Massachusetts, so Dad could take the job working with Bob Chapman, managing Harvard's theater. It was 1966. I was four; my older brother was five (and a half). My sister was about to be born. We rented a house down the street from Julia Child, who had published *Mastering the Art of French Cooking* only three years before we became her neighbors and who had just started appearing on local television. I like to tell people she baked hot cross buns for all the children trick-or-treating at Halloween. This may or may not be true.

My earliest memories involve Mom reading to us—we had a story every night before bed, and then she would tuck us in. Even though my brother and I were just eighteen months apart, Mom never read us the same book. Each of us got to choose our own book every night. My favorite was *The Story of Ferdinand* by Munro Leaf, a classic from the 1930s about a peace-loving bull. (Hitler hated the book and ordered it burned.) My second favorite was Crockett Johnson's *Harold and the Purple Crayon,* a book from the 1950s about how a very artistic child uses his imagination and one crayon to create beauty and adventure—and get himself out of jams. My brother was obsessed with Maurice Sendak's newly published *Where the Wild Things Are;* in its rumpus-loving antihero Max he found a role model. When my sister was old enough to have a favorite, hers was Sendak's *In the Night Kitchen,* with its naked protagonist and slightly slapstick (yet somewhat sinister) bakers. Mom's own best-loved book from her childhood was *Pink Donkey Brown* by Lydia Stone, a 1925 story about two unspeakably polite children who had charge of a pony—a book so saccharine that even when we were tiny, we couldn't bear it.

("Weren't Betty and Billy glad that they had been good children? Waiting didn't seem so very hard now that it was over and they were going to have their ride.")

As we sat in chemo, I asked Mom if she remembered the one night she forgot to read to me. I was seven or eight years old. I remember lying in bed, hearing my parents' voices at a party downstairs. My brother had dropped off to sleep, oblivious that night as to whether we'd been read to or not. I had brushed my teeth and jumped into bed and was waiting for her to read us each a story and tuck us in. She didn't come. I heard glasses clinking and noisy conversation. And I started to get upset.

The more laughter I heard from downstairs and the more time went by, the more hysterical I got. I remember feeling alone, ignored, and abandoned. It never occurred to me to put on my robe and slippers and go downstairs to remind her. She couldn't have forgotten—she'd never forgotten before. It must have been that she no longer loved me. Hearing what a good time everyone was having without me made it that much worse.

Eventually I was wailing so loudly that one of the guests heard me—and Mom bounded upstairs. It took her ten or fifteen minutes to calm me down and reassure me that nothing had changed.

"Do you remember that night?" I asked her.

"Oh, sweetie, how could I forget?" Mom said.

AS SOON AS my brother and I were able, we began reading to ourselves. Sometimes Dad would read chapter books to us while Mom shared picture books with my sister. Dad loved

Ian Fleming's *Chitty Chitty Bang Bang* and Roald Dahl's *Charlie and the Chocolate Factory*. So did we.

There was one sure way to avoid being assigned an impromtu chore in our house—be it taking out the trash or cleaning your room—and that was to have your face buried in a book. Like churches during the Middle Ages, books conferred instant sanctuary. Once you entered one, you couldn't be disturbed. They didn't give you immunity from prosecution if you'd done something wrong—just a temporary reprieve. But we quickly learned you had to both look and be completely engrossed—just flipping pages didn't count.

Almost all the earliest conversations I remember with my parents were about books: Why didn't the men understand that Ferdinand just didn't want to fight? Why is Chitty Chitty Bang Bang's license plate GEN 11? The answers, according to Mom and Dad, were: People can be mean, but they can learn not to be, and Try to figure it out yourself. (The license plate spells "Genii" but with number 1's in place of letter I's—it was, after all, a magical car.)

Mom and Dad spent hours every week reading—and whole weekend days. Mom was always a little amazed at parents who thought their kids should be reading more but who never read themselves. It reminded me of a line I'd heard a Denver newscaster say, in all seriousness, during host chat: "I like books. I don't read them. But I *like* them."

I was an indoors kid: reading, painting, spending endless hours in my room chatting about books and records and movies with my best friend. My brother, also a big reader, was the athletic one.

When I was nine, I fell head over heels in love with *The Hobbit* by J.R.R. Tolkien. I read it when we were on vacation in Morocco. I'd become terribly sick with a temperature of 104, and the Moroccan doctor gave me the only medicine he had, which turned out to be almost pure morphine. Feverish, drugged, and delirious, I lay on a bed in a luminous house in Tangier, mint tea by my side, reading *The Hobbit* for days on end as I drifted in and out of consciousness. I remember the tea, hot and sweet and delicious, and the breeze from the ocean, and the whitewashed walls. I remember the handsome Moroccans who would come in and out of the room to make sure I was okay. And most of all I remember *The Hobbit,* the most phantasmagorical book I could ever imagine. Only years later did I discover that half of what I remembered was Tolkien and the other half the product of my febrile, narcoticized mind.

After I recovered, I went on to the full *Lord of the Rings.* My brother, meanwhile, was reading C. S. Lewis's *The Chronicles of Narnia* while I was blissfully stuck in Tolkien's Middle-earth. We used to argue about which series of books was better, just as we argued, sometimes ferociously, about the merits of Bob Dylan (my brother) versus John Denver (me), or, during the year we were in England, Liverpool (Doug) versus Manchester United (again me, mostly because I liked a soccer player named George Best). As a result, I always believed that Tolkien versus Lewis was just a matter of taste and rivalry. (We had no idea that Tolkien and Lewis, fellow dons at Oxford, had been good friends). Mom believed differently. "I've always thought it was interesting that your brother preferred the Narnia books and you loved the Tolkien. I think your brother liked the Christian symbolism of the Narnia books—you just weren't interested in that."

Ironically, I recently learned that Lewis went to great

lengths to deny that his books were Christian allegory, and that Tolkien, a devout Roman Catholic, insisted that his books were fundamentally religious. To me, Tolkien's series has always seemed wonderfully and purely pagan.

Mom's chemo was now done for the day, but, once again, we had a wait at the pharmacy. Since we hadn't traded any new books or fixed on one thing to read that pre-Thanksgiving week, we were discussing various books we'd read throughout our lives. "Actually," Mom continued, "I'm not sure I've ever met anyone who really liked both Tolkien and Lewis. Everyone seems to like one or the other."

"And which do you like?" I asked Mom.

"The Lewis. But I think your brother and I both envied how much you loved the Tolkien. We liked the Narnia books a great deal—but you were *obsessed* with the Tolkien. You talked about Bilbo Baggins so much, I felt like he was a member of the family. You started writing everything, including your name, in ancient runes. I drew the line when you wanted to smoke a clay pipe. You were nine."

"Did you ever get that obsessed about a book?"

"All the time. Poetry. *Gone With the Wind*. And I would get obsessed with the plays I worked on—especially the ones right around when your father and I were first married and still living in New York: *Five Finger Exercise* by Peter Shaffer and Harold Pinter's *The Caretaker*. Working on a play absorbs you completely. I really missed that when we moved to Cambridge."

In the late 1950s, before she met my father, Mom had worked for the producer Irene Selznick (after an introduction from Selznick's son, a college classmate) and then, both before and during her first years of marriage, for the producer

Freddie Brisson and his actress wife Rosalind Russell. (Mom loved to tell of being sent to Paris to pick up Rosalind Russell's furs and jewelry, which Russell had accidentally left there, and then being instructed to wear them through customs with such aplomb that the agents would be convinced they belonged to Mom so no duty would have to be paid.)

Mom had also been running New York auditions for the London drama school she'd attended after college—and continued to do so while pregnant and right up until we moved to Cambridge.

While casting about for a job after the move, Mom realized that her experience casting plays and interviewing kids for drama school could be put to good use: knowing which person was right for what part made her a natural for the Radcliffe admissions office. Over the next decade or so, she became the director of admissions, first for Radcliffe and then for Harvard and Radcliffe, and she was eventually appointed associate dean of admissions and financial aid.

The job of gatekeeper to the college was a coveted role. Mom was impervious to bribes (although we did not let some amazing Iranian caviar go to waste, nor did we refuse to eat the fortune cookies whose fortune read "You will admit Bella Wong," the daughter of the local Chinese restaurant owner). Mom was also impervious to threats. Once someone showed up at her office with a gun and threatened to kill her if his kid wasn't admitted. His kid wasn't. Bella was.

Dad worked. Mom worked. Several decades before today's crop of wildly scheduled children, we were left pretty much to our own devices, mildly supervised by a succession of exchange students and recent graduates. We did have piano lessons and soccer practice and theater. But we also had bicycles.

It was our responsibility to be where we were supposed to be when we were supposed to be there. We were latchkey kids of sorts—rustling up a snack after school, and then getting lost, often literally, until dinner. On weekends, when Mom and Dad had settled into the living room, each with a stack of books, we had two options: we could sit and read, or we could disappear until mealtime.

As for television, we could, in theory, watch as much as we wanted. But there were only three channels, and there was never much worth watching during the day—other than *Candlepins for Cash,* a uniquely New England show, on which you tried to knock down anorexic bowling pins with a very small ball; *Star of the Day,* a precursor to *American Idol,* of very dubious production quality; and old movies, almost always with Shirley Temple in them, or so it seemed. There's a limit to the number of Shirley Temple movies that even I, who adored her, could withstand.

So when we weren't running around, we read.

I wasn't aware that I was one of the few kids in my class with a working mother—and I think that was partially because even the stay-at-home mothers subjected their kids to a kind of benign neglect back then. It was also because Mom never referred to herself as a working mother. She was a mother. And she worked. "People don't talk about working fathers," she once said to me. She came to as many of our school plays and sports events as she could. "I think parents should do their best not to be unhappy. That's the worst thing for children—to have unhappy parents. If you want to work outside the home, you should. If you can afford not to and you don't want to, then you shouldn't."

"So you never felt guilty?"

"Not for a second."

Long before "take your child to work" days, Mom had her own version—take your work to your children. We were frequently pressed into service—reorganizing the application folders, for example, so that the personal essay would be the first thing Mom would see. Mom wanted to read each applicant's free-form essay prior to looking at anything else so she could get a sense of the applicant as a person before she looked at grades, SAT scores, or even gender.

"But did the other mothers approve of your working?"

"Well, I know some of them thought I must have been neglecting all of you. Remember when your brother decided he wanted to have dog biscuits in his lunch box? And you and your sister did the same? I think one of the other mothers had the school call me about that. I told them I'd checked with your pediatrician—and he said that the dog biscuits wouldn't do you any harm and would probably be good for your teeth. But no, I don't think most of them judged me. Beside, lots of people were doing interesting things. It was the sixties, after all."

When I look back, I do remember that lots of my friends' parents had fascinating lives. We lived in an insular community where almost every family had some connection to Harvard or MIT or Brandeis—so when we thought about our parents, and I'm not sure we thought about them all that much, we were more aware of their connections to the universities than of what job they did or didn't have. And we were very aware of their hobbies and passions, too: this one painted; this one made yogurt.

We also saw a lot of turmoil: the war in Vietnam on television every night; protest riots in Harvard Square; the assassinations of Bobby Kennedy and Dr. Martin Luther King, Jr. The kids with much older siblings told us most of what we knew about the draft, the civil rights movement, and other timely topics, and they introduced us to the music of Woodstock. The rest we learned from dinner conversations and *Life* magazine.

Books loomed large. Every family we knew had bookshelves in the living room. Parents' friends and friends' parents wrote books. And everyone read the same ones, often dictated by Book of the Month Club. *The Family of Man* by Edward Steichen, a book of photography from around the world, with a prologue by Carl Sandburg, adorned nearly every coffee table. John Updike's scandalous *Couples,* a literary novel about adultery, was in every parents' bedroom. Everyone had John F. Kennedy's *Profiles in Courage.* Mystery novelists Ngaio Marsh and Agatha Christie and Erle Stanley Gardner were on the shelves of everyone who loved mysteries. Leon Uris was a staple. Maybe Michener. And when Solzhenitsyn's *The Gulag Archipelago* and Günter Grass's *The Tin Drum* were published, they instantly appeared on the Books That Must Be Read shelf in every house.

I sometimes think Mom had a secret plan to encourage us to read beyond our level. She would announce that certain books were a little old for us. Nothing made us read them faster. I read *The Autobiography of Malcolm X* when I was ten. She was right—it was too old for me, and when I returned to it later, I was amazed to discover how much I'd missed. Zoot suits were about the only thing that had lodged in my mind. We discovered by ourselves other books that were too old for us. *Fear of Flying* by Erica Jong was published when I was eleven and both shocked and fascinated me with its descriptions of anonymous screwing. As did *Everything You Always Wanted to Know About Sex But Were Afraid to Ask*, a book Mom and Dad didn't, as far as we could discover, have. But other parents did and kept it securely tucked away, only for it to be unearthed and pawed over by their little no-neck monsters and us.

At the dining table we could always talk about a book we were reading. I went through a bizarre Paul Revere phase. After reading and loving *Johnny Tremain* by Esther Forbes, a novel about a boy who is apprenticed as a silversmith to Paul Revere and who burns his hand horribly in an accident, I then discovered the same author's 1942 Pulitzer Prize–winning biography of Paul Revere himself, *Paul Revere and the World He Lived In*. I read it eleven times in a row, marking each completion with a check on the inside cover, like a prisoner keeping track of years in captivity.

"Come on, ask me anything about Paul Revere, anything!" I would beg my brother and sister over meals. When they wouldn't, Mom would gamely ask me a question. Sadly, I've forgotten almost everything I knew about Revere, except for the most basic facts and a third of the Longfellow poem fictionalizing his famous ride. (I now suggested to Mom that she and I reread the Esther Forbes biography for our book club so I could say I'd read it a dozen times. Mom nixed that, saying fondly but firmly that she'd heard enough about Revere during my childhood to last several lifetimes.)

As a kid, I also went through an Alistair MacLean phase: *Where Eagles Dare, The Guns of Navarone, Puppet on a Chain*. I don't usually remember flap copy of books I read as a child, but I'll never forget a sentence that described that last title: "From the moment he landed in Amsterdam, he knew he was in Dutch."

My favorite MacLean books were the ones where anything was possible if you pulled together the right team. Sure, someone on the team would betray you. But you'd find out in time and overcome insurmountable odds—including horrific weather or some horrific accident at sea—to achieve your objective. There would be a terrible cost. Someone, usually one of the band of brothers, would have to die. You would grieve—and then move on. Because it wasn't about you—it was about something much larger, like fighting Nazis. MacLean had served from 1941 to 1946 in Britain's Royal Navy—and his World War II stories are by far his best.

I would stay up for hours past my nine P.M. bedtime re-reading by flashlight the Revere book or reading MacLean. Mom knew, but she never busted me or scolded me. Now I realize that Mom must have been exhausted, juggling all she was doing: three children, a husband, a rambling, drafty house, and a big job that required traveling across the country to meet high school guidance counselors and attend conferences. She did have some help—especially from Mrs. Murphy, an Irish grandmother who looked after my sister in the afternoons and who made delicious meat loaf once a week. (Poor Mrs. Murphy would later have a stroke but went on looking after my sister. I used to tell people that my family's move back to New York in 1979, after almost fourteen years in Cambridge, was because Mom couldn't bear to tell Mrs. Murphy that she'd lost the ability to make meat loaf but also couldn't stand the waste of throwing a whole inedible meat loaf in the garbage every single week.)

I remember one day when Mom's endless commitments finally got the better of her. My brother, my sister, and I were sitting in the kitchen in our Cambridge house. I was eating cereal and worrying about the school day. Doug and Nina were probably chatting with or annoying each other. There were just a few moments before we needed to sling on our coats and head out into the cold. Mom came down the stairs, looking a bit harried, which was unusual. There was something that I wanted to tell her, and I tried to catch her eye.

I watched her go to the tap for a glass of water. Surrey, our English setter, lay on the floor. Mom had a pill in one hand, which she shoved into a little ball of hamburger that she'd fetched from the refrigerator, and then put into Surrey's mouth, massaging her neck so that she would swallow it. Then Mom washed her hands, took another pill, and swallowed that.

Finally I was able to catch her eye. Now I could tell her the thing I really wanted to tell her. But before I could speak, Mom's eyes grew wide, and she said a word I'd never heard her say, followed by "I just took a worming pill and gave the dog my birth control."

That was the only time I'd ever seen Mom panic—although she would quickly discover, after a phone call, that the dog would be fine and so would she. Additionally, she'd be wormless. The dog had already been spayed, so puppies weren't a possibility.

But mostly, when I look back, what I remember is not Mom rushing about; it's Mom sitting quietly in the center of the house, in the living room, under the swirling colors of a Paul Jenkins painting; there would be a fire in the fireplace and a throw over her lap, her hands sticking out to hold a book. And we all wanted to be there with her and Dad, reading quietly too.

RECALLING THANKSGIVINGS PAST, and with this first Thanksgiving after Mom's diagnosis ever nearer, we realized how different our lives were now, revolving around such things as the timing of Mom's treatments. She would usually have good days the day of the treatment and for one or two days after; then she would have days that were "not so good." Her new mantra was a piece of wisdom given to her by a friend of my sister who specialized in palliative care: "Make Plans and Cancel Them." But Mom almost always felt compelled to go ahead with any plan she'd made, whether she was feeling up to it or not.

Not a day went by that she didn't keep up with her emails and calls—to her friends and to her brother. She spoke to Doug, Nina, and me almost every day—always with reports on each of us and often on the progress of the Afghan library. She was hugely pleased that a brilliant and charming young *New York Times* reporter named David Rohde had agreed to come on the board. And the timing was perfect—he was just about to take a leave to write a book on the region and therefore would be spending time there.

One of the cruelest things about cancer is the side effects of the treatments. Rodger had warned her that she would feel so awful, she wouldn't be able to get off the bathroom floor and would lie there in misery. That did not turn out to be the case. But the mouth sores she got meant she couldn't eat or drink or speak without real pain. Then came the diarrhea and the constipation and the exhaustion. When it turned out her red-blood-cell count was low, a transfusion helped. But often she was just plain tired. And keeping weight on was a constant struggle—she wasn't hungry, and the chemo made everything taste awful.

Thankfully, Dr. O'Reilly was all over this. She under-stood, in a way that many doctors don't, that a dreadful mouth sore or needing to go to the bathroom five or ten times in a morning needs treatment just as the cancer itself does. Treating a disease that isn't curable is, in essence, palliative—the goal is both to slow the progress of the tumors and to make life worth living while you do. So every visit to the doctor involved an interrogation in which Dr. O'Reilly tried to get Mom to be honest about how much pain she was in (with Mom refusing even to use the word *pain*, preferring to talk about the level of her discomfort) and adjusting the medicine accordingly

Mom had always done a big, festive Thanksgiving, and we'd always invited everyone we knew who lived far away and couldn't get home. In the Cambridge years, we often had Iranian and Pakistani students come—not just for Thanksgiving dinner but to spend the whole week. Perhaps this was where my mother's interest in that region began. After Mom started working with refugees, we might be joined by a family recently settled in New York from Bosnia or some students from Liberia, thousands of miles away from their families and just starting to experience the cold of New York.

But this year Mom's doing Thanksgiving, even for our immediate family, was out of the question. So my friends Tom and Andy said that they would have Thanksgiving dinner at their place. All Mom and Dad had to do was show up.

MOM CALLED ME on Thanksgiving morning. She wasn't doing so well.

"Today's not great," she said. She would play it by ear, but she thought she might not be up for Thanksgiving dinner. What made it especially frustrating was that just a week before she'd had some very good days. She'd gone to two concerts, taken the subway to work a few days in a row, seen friends, caught up on email. She'd even regained some appetite.

Mom was now two months into her diagnosis, and it was nearly impossible to tell how things were going. It was like following the stock market. When the Dow goes down, it could be a minor correction before a surge, or it could be the start of a tumble. So if Mom felt worse one day, maybe it was the chemo—or maybe the cancer. Even when things seemed to be getting better, we couldn't be sure what was going on. It could be genuinely good news (the tumors were shrinking), or it could be what stock market folk call the "dead cat bounce" (a vivid but dreadful metaphor for the appearance of hope when there's none to be had). Correction or crash? Surge or bounce? All we could do is guess a few days at a time until Mom's next scan.

The unpredictability was maddening for Mom. She had many more of what she called the "good days" than she did of the "not so good days" and was very grateful for that: she just wished she could be right more often about which would be which. Mom updated the *Will's Mary Anne Schwalbe News* blog as best she could, trying not to be too hopeful when things went well, and always tempering the bad reports with a sense of hope. We continued to pretend that I was writing the posts about Mom, when in fact she was writing them about herself in my voice ("Today, Mom . . .") and then emailing them to me to post.

For obvious reasons, I avoided referring to Mom as my ghostwriter when talking with her or others in the family about the blog. Actually, I avoided referring to the arrangement at all for fear of making her self-conscious about it. She would send me an email saying, "Why don't you say something like the following?" and there would follow a few paragraphs that I would post verbatim as though I had written them about her, when she had written them about herself from my perspective.

That Thanksgiving morning Mom was also upset that she had neglected to write a condolence note to a church friend whose father had died.

"Mom, I'm sure she understands. She knows you're not well."

"Well, I wrote one just now. Not feeling well is no excuse for forgetting that there are other people in the world."

Mom got worse during Thanksgiving Day—but she insisted that my father go with me and David to our friends Andy and Tom for their celebration. She would stay home and have some soup. That was another set of tea leaves one had to read—when did her *go* mean "go," and when did it mean "stay"? On Thanksgiving, her *go* meant "go."

At the end of a lovely evening at our friends' apartment—in which everyone ate and drank too much, maybe a bit more too much than usual—David and I poured my father into a cab back to his and Mom's apartment, and then we walked the few blocks home. The whole meal had lasted under two hours, and Dad went back to Mom with a full set of leftovers. Still, everyone was trying to deny that it felt like a rehearsal for the first Thanksgiving when Mom wouldn't be alive anymore. When we got home, David went to sleep, and I sat in the living room for a while with the lights off.

I hadn't really allowed myself time for sadness. I'd been keeping busy with my job and also the bills and the dry cleaning and the emails, all the mundane tasks that fill my life. So I tried to just be still and sad—but I couldn't. I could be still.

And I knew I was sad. But waiting for the dawn to come up, I found myself unable to focus on my sadness for more than a minute or two at a time, as much as I thought I'd wanted to. I'd cried far more over David Halberstam's death than I had over my mother's terminal illness. I'd cried more over the Hugh Grant romantic comedy *Love Actually*. I'd cried more over the death of a beloved character in an Alistair MacLean thriller.

To pass the time until morning, until I heard the familiar thump of *The New York Times* being chucked against our apartment door by our local news carrier, until David would rouse and we would put on coffee, I turned on a solitary light and went searching for my copy of *The Hobbit*. I wanted to see if it still entranced me—if I could get lost in it again.

Soon I found my copy—and started reading at random. It had been nearly forty years since I'd more than glanced at it, but it all sprang magically back to life: hobbit houses, silver spoons, runes, orcs, dwarves, spiders. After twenty minutes or so, I stumbled across the part of the book, about halfway through, where our hobbit hero Bilbo and his dwarf companions suddenly find themselves, scattered and separated from one another, in a dark wood.

Bilbo races around in circles, frantically calling his friends' names. He can feel and hear them doing the same. "But the cries of the others got steadily further and fainter, and though after a while it seemed to him they changed to yells and cries for help in the far distance, all noise at last died right away, and he was left alone in complete silence and darkness."

Tolkien continues, "That was one of his most miserable moments. But he soon made up his mind that it was no good trying to do anything till day came with some little light."

◇◇◇◇◇◇◇◇

THE NEXT DAY Mom said she was feeling a little better.

As we sat in the waiting room before her chemo, in our usual chairs, I told her about the dinner and how we all missed her and that I was thinking about her. I didn't mention that I sat for a while in the dark—that seemed a slightly Goth detail. But I did tell her I found myself rereading *The Hobbit* and that it still had the same power over me.

"Why do you think that is?" Mom asked.

"I think it's because it shows that people—or hobbits, as the case may be—can find strength they didn't know they had. In that way, it's not so different from the Alistair MacLeans, I guess."

"I spent some time thinking, too," Mom said. "And I was so grateful that your father was able to get out of the house. It can't be fun for him spending so much time sitting around with me when I'm not feeling great. I did manage to read some pages from a book that's also about how people can find strength they didn't know they had."

"What book was that?"

"The Book of Common Prayer," Mom answered.

"Didion?"

"No, Will." Mom's voice was somewhere between amused and exasperated. "The other one." And then she added, smiling: "Besides, I think the Didion is *A Book of Common Prayer*, not '*The* Book.'"

Daily Strength for Daily Needs

Mom's appointments were usually first thing in the morning—she liked to get them over and done with so she could get on with her day. Even when she was feeling "really not great," Mom always took care with her appearance. I, on the other hand, usually rolled out of bed and into a cab to be there on time and frequently arrived unshaven, wearing yesterday's jeans and whatever frayed sweater was closest at hand. Mom never seemed to notice, but if my father was there, he might make a comment like "Late night last night, son?" Dad is a very natty dresser, known for his bowties.

How can I describe what Mom looked like? She was perhaps five feet four inches tall. She'd had gray hair for decades and never colored it. She loved the sun but had pale skin, beautifully clear when she was younger, freckled and splotchy as she grew older. Some people described her as birdlike—her dark eyes were firmly set back and locked onto yours while you were talking. She wasn't one to fidget when people were speaking to her; she held very still, with her feet curled up under her if she was at home and on the sofa; or leaned toward you if you were at a meal or a meeting, sometimes touching the pearls she loved to wear. People always commented on Mom's eyes, their energy and spark, and on her smile. Mom almost always smiled—but when she was happier than usual she beamed. Her cheeks, just under her eyes, would crinkle, and her smile would encompass her whole being.

Before she got sick, Mom had sometimes felt she could lose ten pounds or so, but didn't obsess about it. She wasn't a big eater—salads and yogurt were her favorite foods. I never saw her overeat—she was that rare person who could restrict herself to one almond even if a bowl overflowing with them was right in front of her and she hadn't eaten for hours; she could have one cookie off a plate (or half, for that matter), one small scoop of ice cream, one glass of wine. She was, I think, somewhat proud of her self-control, a form of mild asceticism; she also wasn't terribly interested in food. When we were growing up, she cooked the things that everyone cooked: pot roasts and pork chops, a tuna noodle casserole recipe (omnipresent in the 1960s) that featured potato chips crushed and scattered over the top, and lemon meringue pie. That was my favorite, and I could down huge slabs of it. But whatever treat we were eating had to be cheerfully shared with one another, or Mom would redistribute it, with the smallest portion by far going to the kid who'd tried to hog it.

Mom also had a slightly socialist streak when it came to our possessions—again, mandatory sharing. My father was given to more Stalinist purges, in which any toy not properly stored was immediately put out with the trash. If the lesson Mom was trying to teach us was that people were to be valued over things, Dad was solely concerned with tidiness.

When I was around six, I was obsessed with my stuffed animals, of which I had a large collection, and I could spend hours happily playing with them. There was a downside to this overabundance, however. As a precursor to my adult manias, I would grow panicked that I hadn't shared my love for them equally and could lie awake at night worrying that I'd spent more quality time with Koala that day than I had with my oldest teddy bear, or with Basil Brush. Tomorrow, I swore, I would do better and be a fairer, kinder, more responsible friend to my stuffed companions. But one stuffed animal I rarely neglected was my turtle—mostly because I stumbled over him on the way to and from bed. He was the biggest stuffed animal I had—the size of a real Galápagos centenarian, albeit somewhat flatter.

And then someone, a relative perhaps, arranged for me to spend a week away. I was excited, packed my bag more or less by myself, and had the difficult choice of deciding which stuffed animals would come with me. This was a chance to redress some of the imbalance, and I took along several smaller ones who had been largely ignored of late.

I recall coming home afterward to find my big stuffed turtle gone. I'm sure I looked everywhere before I went in a panic to Mom.

"Where's Turtle? I can't find Turtle."

"Oh, sweetie. I'm so sorry. Turtle died when you were away," she replied.

I don't remember how long I grieved for Turtle, or how aware I was of mortality, that stuffed animals couldn't actually die in the same way that people could and do. Now, nearly forty years later, it occurs to me that if Turtle had been a real turtle, he might still be alive.

Maybe it was this thought that caused me, one day in early December 2007, during a pause in our conversation as we were sitting, waiting for Mom to be called for chemo, to ask Mom if she remembered the death of Turtle. She did.

"Mom, I've always been curious: Why would you tell a six-year-old that his stuffed animal had died? And whatever did happen to Turtle?"

"One of my students was collecting toys and stuffed animals for an orphanage, and I gave her your turtle. You had so many stuffed animals! I didn't really think about it. But I also didn't give any thought to what we were going to tell you. When the time came, I just said the first thing that popped into my head."

"And were you trying to teach me not to get too attached to things?"

"I wish I'd given it that much thought! I really was just thinking of the orphans."

I can't help but feel sad when I think about Turtle, even if I remind myself to think about the orphans instead.

"I think I was pretty mad at you," I told Mom as we sat there.

"I was pretty mad at myself," Mom said. "Are you still?"

"Maybe a little bit," I said. Then we both laughed. But I was . . . just a bit.

AT FOURTEEN, I left most of my stuffed animals behind and cheerfully went off to boarding school at St. Paul's School in

New Hampshire; my brother, the year before, had gone off to Milton Academy, in Massachusetts. My parents and sister embarked on their own adventure, moving from Cambridge back to New York. My father bought into a small concert management agency, falling in love with the burgeoning early music movement. Mom wasn't sure what she was going to do back in Manhattan, and it was difficult to give up a job she adored, not to mention tenure. But Dad was tired of Harvard and Cambridge, and they were both, by birth and at heart, New Yorkers and had always intended to return. In addition, Mom wanted Nina to go to The Brearley School, in New York, where she had gone. Once back, Mom soon got a job as a college counselor at a school called Dalton and later as head of the high school at Nightingale-Bamford.

"Were you sad to leave Cambridge?" I asked her.

She was, she said. Very sad. But she was also looking forward to being back in New York. "The world is complicated," she added. "You don't have to have one emotion at a time."

MOM HAD RECENTLY reconnected with an old Harvard friend. He would ultimately give her two gifts that would change what was left of her life. The first was a book called *Daily Strength for Daily Needs* by Mary Wilder Tileston. It was originally published by Little, Brown in 1884. My mother's Harvard friend found a worn copy of this little book and sent it over. The jacket, if it had ever had one, was long gone. The book was stained and foxed, and its olive linen boards had turned sickly institutional beige.

The introduction to Mom's 1934 edition, published right after the death of Mary Wilder Tileston, was written by William Lawrence, bishop of Massachusetts, and it explains the book well. The bishop writes:

> For fifty years, ever since its first publication, I have used "Daily Strength for Daily Needs" from time to time and have given away many copies to Confirmation candidates and others; now that Mrs. Tileston's hand is stayed, I count it a privilege as a token of gratitude to commend this Memorial Edition to the younger generation, knowing that however far they have traveled from the habits of life and thought of their elders they have still the same need for a call to courage, faith and cheer.
>
> Since this little book was published empires have fallen, theologies have been rewritten, wars have been fought and standards of life have changed, but men are still men, their yearning in times of disaster for comfort is still keen and the call for courage strong. . . .
>
> If you have a friend who is discouraged, laden with heavy cares or weak of body or faith, give him a copy of "Daily Strength for Daily Needs"; two minutes in the reading, one minute of thought or prayer, and his day will have a fresher note.
>
> The great inventors of the age are those who connect mighty physical resources with the needs of men; Mary W. Tileston, by her love of spiritual literature, her skill in selection and her knowledge of the spiritual needs of men and women, has brought them into connection with eternal truth and spiritual resource. I wonder at the untold influence of a quiet, modest little woman whose skill has given new impulse to millions of men and women through this little book.

Daily Strength for Daily Needs is not designed for the secular reader. Each day's entry gives you one or two Bible quotes, drawn almost entirely from the New Testament; it almost always includes a scrap of poetry as well, usually religious. And every page has one or two or additional quotes—again usually theological in nature, but not always. The day's theme relates to the selected Bible passages. Still, the whole point is brevity. Even reading slowly, it would be hard to spend more than one or two minutes on a day's page.

The first time I examined the book, I found it somewhat ridiculous: it looked stern and pious and certainly dated. I couldn't imagine that Mom would more than glance at it. But the book became her constant companion. It was almost always either on her bedside or in her shoulder bag. When she needed to go to the hospital, as she often did for fevers or bad reactions to chemo, it went with her. She kept her place with a colorful embroidered bookmark, something she'd brought home from one of the refugee camps she'd visited.

The very physicality of this little book provided part of the comfort. I think Mom liked that her copy was at least secondhand, if not third or fourth. The text had been providing wisdom and solace to people for well over a hundred years, and this one particular book had been doing the same for seventy-three of them. It was printed the same year Mom was born. Other people had turned the pages, had put their own bookmarks in and taken them out. Was it crazy to think that all of them had somehow left on the pages traces of their own hopes and fears?

Someone (not Mom, because I asked her) had underlined

passages, but only in the first five pages and only where the book spoke about death: "<u>For this day only is ours, we are dead to yesterday,</u> and <u>we are not yet born to the morrow</u>" (Jeremy Taylor); and "<u>For to know Thee is perfect righteousness; yea, to know Thy power is the root of immortality</u>" (Wisdom of Solomon XV. 2, 3). The underlining was meticulous, in blue pen, and the underliner carefully omitted the word *and* in the first passage and *yea* in the second. This person either ceased underlining or ceased living after January 5. But she or he left an indelible mark.

The owners of the book were born and died; what remained was the physical book itself. It needed to be handled with increasing delicacy and care as the binding grew loose with age, but you knew that it was the exact same book that others had read before you, and that you had read in the years before. Would the words have inspired Mom the same way if they had been flashing on a screen? She didn't think so.

Other books stayed by her bedside, too—like Jon Kabat-Zinn's *Full Catastrophe Living* and Bernie Siegel's *Love, Medicine and Miracles,* two best sellers from previous decades about the connections between mind and body, which we would discuss and which she also loved. But part of the reason *Daily Strength for Daily Needs* occupied a special place in her life was that it gave her solace from a Christian perspective.

I don't know if it would be accurate to say that Mom was *disappointed* that I'm not religious, but I suspect it would be. It was something she wished for me, as in "I wish you got the same comfort from religion that your brother and sister and I do." She'd given up on my father, who would come to church with us but put so much energy into remembering and thinking up Bible jokes that he actually had an engraved leather book in which to write them.

Q: "What time of the day was Adam born?"

A: Just before Eve.

Q: "What Christmas carol mentions Charlie Chaplin?"

A: "O Little Town of Bethlehem." It says "The silent stars go by."

Mom would express great aggravation about these jokes, especially when Dad loudly whispered them to us during the sermon, on those occasions when we all went to church together. But she was also capable of cracking a hint of a smile when Dad told them once church was over. We kids, however, were not encouraged to repeat them or to create our own. One of the times Mom got truly angry at me was when I was making up a story about that famous biblical children's book character "Gladly, the Cross-Eyed Bear."

My brother teaches Sunday school and has always taken his family to church; my sister had always belonged to a church. And when we were little, before my brother and I went off to boarding school, my siblings had both cheerfully gone to Sunday school at Memorial Church, Mom's place of worship. But I never wanted to go and at some point dug in my heels. To this day, I can't remember why. I was quite a malleable little fellow, happy to do what I was told, and rarely expressed a strong opinion about where I should be. But that Sunday school had started to annoy me. I wasn't going.

As liberal as Mom was, she did have rules. We were to eat what we were served (except for one food that we could choose that we never had to eat, no matter who served it, or when); we were to dress nicely for dinner and sit properly at the table until we were excused; we were to write thank-you notes the same day we received a gift; we were to make our bed every day (that, we hardly ever did) and unpack our luggage the minute we got home (we punted on that, too); we were to look people in the eye when they talked to us, and call adults Mr. or Mrs. or Miss unless we were specifically given permission to use a first name ("Ms." came when we were older); and we were to go to Sunday school and learn about the Bible. That last one was especially nonnegotiable.

To deal with my looming insubordination, Mom devised a plan. She would have various friends take me to different kinds of services representing different Christian traditions. I could go to Sunday school at any church—my choice. But I had to choose one. I found it both bewildering and exciting—the way I would feel later during the first weeks of college, when you can shop for courses and try out different majors, imagining different lives for yourself: geologist, accountant, historian. I went to a Catholic service where they had a folksinger and preached what I later found out was liberation theology but at the time seemed a lot like what I was hearing every day at my very liberal grade school. I went to a Quaker meeting, which I quite liked despite the fact that the juice and cookies that they served were clearly substandard—homemade rather than delicious store-bought treats. Logic says I should have chosen the Unitarian Universalist Church, as it's really church for people who aren't committed to one path, but I didn't. What I chose was the First Church of Christ Scientist. A local handyman who did work around our house and looked after us from time to time took me there. I don't think Christian Science was what Mom had in mind—I think she thought I'd ultimately

choose her church, which was Harvard's and decidedly Prot-
estant. But she was a good sport about it. She'd set up the rule;
I'd followed it.

The Christian Science Sunday school was a friendly place.
The cookies were store-bought and of the highest quality.
Tang—the very same drink the astronauts had in space, or so
we were told—was served. We got a good overview of the most
important Bible stories. And as for the principles of Christian
Science—we got a basic grounding in them, and they made a
fair bit of sense to me. But we were also told we were too young
to choose a religion, so it was fine in the meantime just to learn
some Bible stories and stop at that. I liked my independence.
And I also think that I picked up on the fact that there was
something a little bit daring about this religion—that many
people regarded Christian Scientists with suspicion. It was fun
to both follow the rules—I was going to Sunday school—and
cast my lot with the outlaws. I think Mom got a little kick out
of that, too, though not as big a kick as she would have gotten
had I chosen her church.

But religion didn't stick with me, then or later. My boarding school was Episcopal, and we had to go to chapel five times
a week. I enjoyed chapel fine, the organ music and the archi-
tecture, but felt, once I graduated, that having gone to church
five times a week for four years meant I never had to go again.
Also, there are just too many other places I want to be on Sunday morning: if not asleep in bed, then watching television, or
reading, or having brunch with friends. I also developed an
aversion to the part of the service where you're supposed to
turn to those around you, greet them warmly, and wish them
peace. I felt like a phony when I did it. All that hugging and
kissing and handshaking was too much for me.

Mom adored warmly greeting her fellow men and women and wishing them peace. She loved the Scripture and the sermons and the music. But more than any of that, she believed. She believed that Jesus Christ was her savior. She believed in the resurrection and life everlasting. These weren't just words to her. Her religion gave her profound pleasure and comfort. That's what she wished for me.

Quickly, Mom had started to steer our book club toward certain books where Christian faith played an important role. Marilynne Robinson's *Gilead,* which had won the Pulitzer Prize in 2005, was one of her favorite books. Robinson had published a highly praised novel called *Housekeeping* in 1980 but no new novel for nearly a quarter century until this one. I would read it for the first time; Mom would read it again.

Mom said she wanted me to read *Gilead* because of the writing and the vivid portraits of the characters and of the small fictional town of Gilead in 1950s Iowa where the story is set. And maybe also, I thought, because the novel is in the form of a letter that a dying parent, the town's Congregationalist minister, writes to his son—though in the novel the child is just around seven years old. But mostly I suspected that she wanted me to read it because it's a book that almost perfectly described her own faith. Mom was a Presbyterian, but she'd been married and had us baptized in a Congregationalist church. In the minister's stories of the stormy relationship between his father and his grandfather, both preachers; of his battles with loneliness; and of his struggle with forgiveness over the behavior of the son of his best friend, the town's Presbyterian minister, he presents a Christianity that allows him great solace as he contemplates his own death at the age of seventy-seven. It's a book about living as a Christian in an

America where injustice and racial intolerance still had and have sway; and it's a book about grace and faith and what makes a good life. The minister's final prayer for his son is simple but profound: "I'll pray that you grow up a brave man in a brave country. I will pray you find a way to be useful."

Mom said she had the same prayer for all of us.

For Mom, the simple beauty of the prose was like the beauty of choir music or of the church itself. She knew I would appreciate that—and I did. Reading the novel, Mom said, was like praying.

Mom took great comfort from praying—in church and out. She would talk with God and pray for all of us: for those she loved and knew and for those she didn't know; for people who weren't well and for people who had disappointed her—even for world leaders. I know she prayed for me because she told me so. And when people would say to Mom, "I'll include you in my prayers," it gave her great solace. It wasn't a platitude for her—when she knew people were praying for her, it was something concrete and immense.

One of Mom's favorite passages from *Gilead* was: "This is an important thing, which I have told many people, and which my father told me, and which his father told him. When you encounter another person, when you have dealings with anyone at all, it is as if a question is being put to you. So you must think, What is the Lord asking of me in this moment, in this situation?"

She thought about this question, she said, as much as she could—whenever she met refugees, bus drivers, or new colleagues. She thought about it now when she went for chemo and met the nurses, her doctor, the woman who scheduled appointments, other people with cancer and their families. The answer was different for every person and every situation. But the question from *Gilead,* Mom said, was always the thing you needed to ask yourself: "What is the Lord asking of me in this moment, in this situation?" It helped you remember that people aren't here for you; everyone is here for one another.

Mom loved the pace of *Gilead,* which matched the rhythms of a church service, measured and deliberate yet full of passion. It's a book that she felt allowed her to have her own thoughts and communion. Reading the book gave her another chance to talk with God.

Some authors fill every inch of the canvas—everything is described and detailed; anything not mentioned doesn't exist. Like a real-estate-listing writer, if something is worth saying, certain authors say it. (If a real estate listing doesn't say "sunny," you can bet the apartment is stygian dark; if it doesn't say it has an elevator, it's a walk-up; and if it doesn't say "dry," well then, a river runs through it.) Those "say everything" authors are usually more to my taste: Dickens and Thackeray and the Rohinton Mistry of *A Fine Balance.* Mom preferred authors who paint with few strokes. She loved abstract art, and I love figurative.

It had taken me a good six or seven false starts before I was into *Gilead.* I just couldn't, at first, get enough of a picture in my mind. What did the characters look like? How was the house decorated? More important, why weren't there any adverbs! Mom, on the other hand, did not see those omissions as flaws. She had taken to it instantly and passionately and was delighted to be plunged back into it.

The parts of the story I liked most had to do with the

friend's son: what he had done years ago and his situation now. But when we talked about the book, these parts weren't what Mom most wanted to discuss.

"Doesn't the book make you want to have faith?" Mom asked me that day in December, after we had discussed Turtle and once she was settled into her chair and hooked up for chemo, following a long wait for a cubicle to become available.

In *Gilead,* the narrator's friend's son describes himself not as an atheist but in "a state of categorical unbelief." He says, "I don't even believe God doesn't exist, if you see what I mean." I pointed this passage out to Mom and said it closely matched my own views—I just didn't think about religion. "And you wouldn't want me to lie about it, would you?" I added.

"Don't be silly," Mom said, with a flash of annoyance. "That's the last thing I'd want. But just as you can read this novel for the plot and the language, you can also go to church for the music and the quiet and the chance to be with other people and with your own thoughts."

Because we'd exhausted that topic, Mom decided to change the subject. "I had a wonderful time with Nancy," she said. Nancy, my brother's wife, had gone with Mom to chemo the time before. "That social worker, the young woman, came by with the survey again. The one for people with Stage Four cancer. They asked a lot of questions about faith, church, family. I told her how lucky I was—to have them all. And she asked if I was in pain, and I'm really not. Sure, I'm uncomfortable, and there are good days and bad days. But not pain. I'm not sure that's what she wanted to hear."

"I think she just wants to hear whatever you want to say."

"It turns out that I'm going to be in the control group—the

one that gets no counseling. So I'm done for a while. But it made me think—it's time to ask the really big questions. I want you and your brother to come with me when we see the doctor next after the scan. That's when we'll know if the treatment is doing anything at all. If it isn't, well, we'll have some questions, and I want you both to be there when we get the answers—and then I'll want you to call your sister in Geneva right after and my brother and tell them the news, whatever it is."

The one topic my mother and I had been avoiding was her death. Sure, we'd talked about death abstractly. We'd talked about the "death" of my stuffed turtle. We'd talked about Christianity, a religion steeped in death and resurrection; about the impending death of the minister in *Gilead,* how he's very clear about the difference between wanting it, which he doesn't, and accepting it, which he does; and about my friend Siobhan Dowd, a beautiful writer who discovered in her forties that she had an astonishing gift for children's literature and wrote four and a half books before dying of cancer at age forty-seven, just four months earlier, in August of that year. And the news was full of stories and pictures of young men and women dying in Iraq. Sometimes it seemed like all we talked about was death. But the death we hadn't yet discussed at all was hers.

I needed to go back to *The Etiquette of Illness* and see what it had to say about this subject. There's a big leap from "Do you want me to ask how you are feeling?" to "Do you want to talk about your death?"

And even if I was to bring it up, how could I be sure she wouldn't then talk about it because she thought I wanted to, even if she didn't? But it would be worse if it was something she wanted to talk about, but we were all afraid to bring it up. What if our not talking about it was making her lonelier and robbing her of the chance to share not just her fears but her hopes—especially given that her religion is one of hope after death?

I decided not to tackle the subject of death directly right then. Mom's forty-eighth anniversary with Dad would be the next day. We would all have a small dinner together. My partner's fiftieth birthday would be the following week, and we would be having a big banquet for David in a Chinese restaurant; Mom was determined to attend. Both meals were celebrations of the passing of time, sure, but also of life. Still, I didn't want to ignore completely where we were or what was going on.

"Mom, are you worried about the scan?"

Mom's face did display her natural smile, though slightly less than usual, as I think the mouth sores were still giving her a great deal of pain. We sat quietly for a while. She didn't answer. I couldn't tell if she was thinking or just trying not to speak. We'd done a lot of speaking, and it may have aggravated the sores. Her eyes were the same, but just a little duller. She still had that wonderful glow that drew people to her, but it was softer, more diffuse. Her hair was thinning, and her skin was thinner, with more spots, more lines. She was wearing a mandarin-collar shirt, one of many that David, a fashion designer, had made for her, but it now draped like a robe in a Goya court painting, fold on fold.

What did I want to say? Did I want to say that I was desperately worried about the scan, that I feared it would be awful news, that we would need to stop talking about books and characters who died in books and turn to discussions of her dying?

And then I had a brief moment of clarity as I looked over at her.

"I have a feeling it's going to be good news, Mom," I said, lying. "But you know what I'm going to do to make sure?"

She looked at me inquiringly.

"I'm going to pray," I said. "Well, not in a church. But I am going to pray."

I don't know if Mom believed me, but she beamed. She'd been so pleased that my nonreligious cousins had prayed for her. And if heathen prayers were indeed the best of all, then mine should count big-time.

That night and in nights to come, I did pray. For my text, I used something I'd read in Anne Lamott's *Traveling Mercies: Some Thoughts on Faith,* a book of autobiographical essays that's funny and heartbreaking whether you're a believer or not. Both Mom and I had read it when it came out in 1999 and had recommended it to each other simultaneously. In the book, Lamott says the two best prayers are "Help me, Help me, Help me" and "Thank you, Thank you, Thank you." Sometimes I alternate. Mostly I use both. But I'm also not above asking for specific things—like a good scan and more time with Mom—whether anyone is listening or not.

People of the Book

It had been just over two months since Mom's diagnosis, and we were sitting waiting for the result of the first scan she'd had after starting chemo, and I couldn't for the life of me figure out how to live her dying. Mom had indeed attended her and Dad's anniversary dinner and was thrilled to be at David's fiftieth-birthday banquet, even though she was feeling "not great" that day and had to leave before the toasts. Still, we didn't know if she would have three months or six or a year or, if we were amazingly lucky, two, or if we we were miraculously lucky, five.

Imagine that you had a book set aside for a long plane trip, but you didn't know how long the book was. It might be as short as Thomas Mann's *Death in Venice* or it might be as long as his *The Magic Mountain,* and you wouldn't know until you came to the end. If it was *Death in Venice,* you might find that you'd raced through it and now had nothing to read for the rest of the flight. But if it was *The Magic Mountain* and you'd read sparingly so that the book would last the whole trip, you might discover you'd barely made a dent—and who knows when you would have the time to scale it again?

We were going to have to learn how to pace ourselves—which routines we could keep and which we had to jettison; what we could try to cram in and what we had to give up; which occasions we would be sure to celebrate no matter what and which we would ignore; which books we were still going to read and which we would abandon; and even when we would focus on her dying and when we would talk about anything but.

Of course, we are all dying and none of us knows the hour, which could be decades away or tomorrow; and we know that we need to live our lives to the fullest every day. But I mean, really—who can play that mental game or live like that? And there's a world of difference between knowing you could die in the next two years and knowing that you almost certainly will.

WALKING TO GET a second mocha, passing the television quietly thrumming with CNN's latest news, I realize we will need some rules—or I will, at least, to help me navigate. When I get back to my seat, I pull out my iPhone and email myself a note: "Celebrate Whenever Possible." We are soon joined by my brother, Doug, who has just come from yoga. He is holding his trademark fedora hat, which he passes nervously from one hand to the other.

"Greetings, Mr. Will," he says, which is how he almost always addresses me.

"Greetings, Mr. Doug," I answer. "How are you doing?"

"Excellent," he says. "Yourself?"

Doug and I, especially around Mom and Dad, tend to address each other less like brothers and more like two boarding school masters who have worked together for decades: a hearty blend of fond and formal. Mom smiles. I think there's something reassuring about any family dynamic untouched by changing circumstances.

Doug has morphed over the years from an easily excitable child into a much calmer adult. But like my father, sister, and me, he's particularly talkative when anxious. It's only Mom who grows quiet in times of stress. So Doug and I chat, mostly nonsense, filling airtime, and Mom listens.

Then it's time to go and see Dr. O'Reilly and get the results of the scan.

WE LEAVE THE comfortable waiting room and walk through the white doors into an alternate universe, a sterile world where the comfortable chairs and sofas give way to plastic and metal, where the warm pine yields to polymers and laminates and steel, and where the lighting subtly shifts from incandescent to fluorescent.

"Left or right?" Mom asks, as she always does.

"It's this way, Mom, to the right." My mother usually had a pretty good sense of direction, but this turn is always to the right, and she always needs to ask me.

A nurse, one of Mom's favorites, leads us into an examining room and tells us that Dr. O'Reilly will be with us soon. Usually "soon" is a minute. Sometimes it's more like ten or fifteen. Although Dr. O'Reilly is a doctor who rarely keeps you waiting long—she clearly does her best to wait to summon you from the land of the blond wood and upholstery until she's ready—any delay is always tough. Nowhere else does Mom look quite so old or tired or sick as she does while waiting here. The light draws harsh attention to the lines on her face and to her mottled hands. I look down; her ankles are swollen again. She rubs her thumbs against the tips of her other fingers.

She has a list of questions she wants to ask, and she's given me a copy. She'll also give a copy to the doctor. We rehearse the questions.

"So you're going to ask her about the numbness, right?"

"Yes, the numbness. And the stomach problems."

"Yes, we'll make sure to ask her about those."

"And whether it's okay for me to plan a trip to Geneva," Mom adds.

"Yes, that too," answers Doug.

"And about going to Vero Beach and getting chemo down there. I really want to skip some of the winter and spend time there when it's horrible here."

"We'll make sure to ask," I say.

The final item on the list is just a simple phrase: "Other questions."

"And you have other questions, right?" I ask. Mom had said she wants to ask how much time she has left.

"Yes, I have a big question."

And then Dr. O'Reilly enters. She's Irish and is indeed tiny, as Mom promised—about five feet three or four, and very thin. Her coloring is fair, bordering on transparent. I'm struck by her handshake—it's the quickest firm handshake I've ever experienced. She talks in soft, staccato bursts and fixes you with an intense gaze. She makes me nervous, but she conveys tremendous authority.

The news is good. Some of the tumors have shrunk dramatically, and there are no new ones. The chemo is working.

Before any of us can really absorb this great turn of events, there's Mom's physical exam (she is behind a curtain drawn across the room; Doug and I sit on the far side of it) and then the questions, both from Dr. O'Reilly to Mom (tiredness? nausea? numbness?) and from Mom to Dr. O' Reilly. But Mom stops short of the last.

"Do you have any other questions you want to ask Dr. O'Reilly, Mom?" I prompt.

I look over at Mom. She seems lost in thought. Everything's silent as we all wait for the last question.

"Yes I do," says Mom. "Are you taking a holiday this year, Dr. O'Reilly? I hope you're getting home to Ireland to see your family."

THE TUMORS HAVE shrunk. The tumors are shrinking. Amazing. Those extraordinary chemicals, with their remarkable names, now sound totally different: Gemcitabine. Xeloda. Before they sounded like harsh detergents. Now they sound cool and magical, like a new rock band you've come to love. So there's more time for Mom and all of us with her, and more time before Mom wants to ask how much more time there is. I can go on with my busy life of meetings and drinks and dinners. She can go on making plans for hers: concerts and visitors and movies and trips.

And we now need a book for our book club. Being an optimist, I've brought with me a new book by Geraldine Brooks, the author of *March,* a Pulitzer Prize–winning novel that invents a life for the absent father in Louisa May Alcott's *Little Women*. It was one of Mom's recent favorites. The new Brooks novel is called *People of the Book,* and I've managed to score two advance copies from a friend who works for her publisher. Mom has brought a book for me, too: *The Lizard Cage* by Karen Connelly. With the good news from the doctor, we exchange books. Everything is back to the new normal again. There will be more meetings of the book club.

FOLLOWING OUR VISIT to Dr. O'Reilly, Mom sent me a new entry to post to the blog, as always written in the third person by her as if by me. I added the last paragraph.

> After two great days on Friday and Saturday, Mom had two bad ones on Sunday and Monday. Today is looking better.
>
> She read an amazing book about life in prison in Burma called THE LIZARD CAGE by Karen Connelly, which, Mom says, makes one forget any problems here. She is looking forward to going to The Messiah. Dad's conductor, Nic McGegan, is leading the New York Philharmonic at Avery Fisher Hall.
>
> I (Will) am about to venture out and try to start and finish my Christmas shopping. Thankfully, it's just beautiful outside.

I'd read *People of the Book* but had been so busy shopping that I hadn't had time to start *The Lizard Cage*. Then Christmas, with all its parties and obligations, was in full swing. Soon it was New Year's Eve. And though the news had been good and there were so many reasons to be hopeful, there was no ignoring the fact that Mom was terribly ill. Her hands were numb; she was weak, nauseated, and exhausted from the chemo; and worse, she had more of the terrible mouth sores, which made speaking painful and eating difficult.

The holiday made things worse. Of course, you can tell yourself that New Year's Eve is just a day like any other. But there's the ball dropping in Times Square and the relentlessness of the papers and television and everyone asking what you are doing and where you are spending your time and what your resolutions are for the coming year.

The plan was to stop by Mom and Dad's in the early evening for a glass of champagne. When David and I arrived, Mom was in her usual spot on the sofa. On the Chinese coffee table in front of her was Geraldine Brooks's *People of the Book*. She'd just finished it.

"I think the Brooks is amazing," she said. "It reminds me so much of the time when I was an election monitor in Bosnia." Brooks, who was born in Australia, had been a *Wall Street Journal* correspondent in Bosnia, among other global hot spots. "But it's so rich—it's like many books in one. You know I don't usually read thrillers. But the story Brooks makes up about the creation of the book—the Sarajevo Haggadah—and how people risk their lives to protect it is really a thriller. I adored Hanna, the rare-book expert. And so many other characters. But the Haggadah itself is a character, the main character. Did you feel the same?"

I sat down on the sofa beside Mom. "I know just what you mean about the Haggadah being a character. I started by thinking: Well, it's only a book. But as you get to know its history—all the sacrifices people made for it—you start to care for it desperately. The wine stains, the insect wing, the saltwater—it was so cool to see how each of these is a clue to how the book survived, but each tells the story of some person from history who cared enough to save it."

"Don't forget the white hair," Mom added, referring to the clue about the book's creation. Her own hair, gray and white, was definitely continuing to thin—but still very much there. She tucked some errant strands behind her ears. "But I did think Hanna's mother was just horrid."

The main character's mother is a distinguished doctor, and when she isn't ignoring her daughter, they get along dreadfully. Part of the mystery in the book is Hanna's paternity—something her mother doesn't share with her until near the book's end. And part of the suspense revolves around whether Hanna and her mother will ever find common ground.

"I don't know. I mean—I felt quite a lot of sympathy for Hanna's mom."

"I didn't," Mom said.

"But she was a working mother at a time when that was very unusual." I suddenly felt self-conscious that I was pointing this out to Mom.

"That's not really a good excuse, Will, for not being kind."

"But do you think people are more forgiving of male doctors when they aren't nice? That people expect women doctors to be more, well, nurturing?"

"I don't know what other people think—but I know what I think," my mother replied. "I think everyone needs to be kind—especially doctors. You can be a very great doctor and still be kind. That's partly why I like Dr. O'Reilly so much more than the first oncologist I saw—not because she's a woman but because she's kind."

"But you always taught us that sometimes people aren't nice because they aren't happy."

"Yes, but maybe those people shouldn't be looking after other people. And I'm also talking about kindness, not just about being nice. You can be gruff or abrupt and still be kind. Kindness has much more to do with what you do than how you do it. And that's why I didn't have much sympathy for Hanna's mother in *People of the Book*. She was a doctor and a mother and she wasn't kind."

"But did that make you like the book less?" I asked.

"Of course not! That's one of the things that made it interesting. But the thing that made it most interesting is what it had to say about books and religion. I love how Brooks shows that every great religion shares a love of books, of reading, of knowledge. The individual books may be different, but reverence for books is what we all have in common. Books are what bring all the different people in the novel together, Muslims and Jews and Christians. That's why everyone in the book goes to such lengths to save this one book—one book stands for all books. When I think back on all the refugee camps I visited, all over the world, the people always asked for the same thing: books. Sometimes even before medicine or shelter—they wanted books for their children."

Just then Dad, who had been chatting with David, interrupted us. Given that it was New Year's Eve, though still early in the evening and hours away from the end of 2007, he wanted to create more of a party atmosphere, so he put on a lively CD by one of the artists he represents. He didn't quite have the volume under control, and the first notes blasted through the living room. It startled Mom, and a burst of panic crossed Dad's face. Before Mom's illness they'd developed the ability to selectively ignore each other, a habit I've witnessed in most long-term couples. But after Mom became sick, Dad grew watchful, keenly aware of how everything affected her: if the air-conditioning was too cold, the sun too direct, her tea out of reach, Dad would struggle to fix it. When he fussed too much, Mom looked a little irritated. But she was also clearly touched by his attentions.

While I was listening to the music, now at a pleasant volume, I noticed something else on the table: Mom's copy of *Daily Strength for Daily Needs,* with the marker on the last page.

Mom soon excused herself for a minute. (How much pain was she in? She wouldn't say.) Dad went to get champagne for us and other family and friends who would be stopping by, but not for Mom and himself. He had given up drinking, fearing that alcohol would make him less alert to her needs. For the two of them, he'd bought sparkling apple cider—not something either of them liked but having the necessary bubbles. I flipped open to read the marked passage in *Daily Strength*:

"It is not by regretting what is irreparable that true work is to be done, but by making the best of what we are. It is not by complaining that we have not the right tools, but by using well the tools we have. What we are, and where we are, is God's providential arrangement,—God's doing, though it may be man's misdoing; and the manly and the wise way is to look your disadvantages in the face, and see what can be made out of them."—F. W. Robertson

When Mom came back, I was still reading. The passage got more religious after that. Mom saw me reading it and smiled. She said nothing. I said nothing. But I think she knew that I thought she'd left the book out for me to read. The coffee table was a staging area for things to be discussed. Just then I noticed another item there, a form letter. Mom saw me looking at it. "That's the letter we sent out for the Afghan library."

"How did it do?" I asked.

"We got some contributions—but not as many as I would have liked. We finally got a letter of support from President Karzai. That was amazing. But there's so much more that needs to be done. And I'm just so worried about it all." After a while she added: "If Afghanistan doesn't have books, the people there don't have much of a chance. So that's my New Year's resolution. I'm going to get this library built."

"Are you sure you feel up to that?" I asked.

Mom frowned at me. "If I'm not, I'll stop." A reminder—not dead yet. She did not feel well that day, but the scan had been very good news. We weren't to count her out. She then turned her attention back to my life.

"And I have a New Year's resolution for you, Will," she said. "You need to stop complaining about your job and just quit it. I've told you this before. Not everyone is lucky enough to be able to do that."

I helped myself to more champagne and looked around at all the things surrounding Mom and Dad. The music was Mozart's *Exsultate, jubilate*. Paintings and drawings were on every wall. There was also Mom and Dad's collection of pots by English and Japanese potters. The pots, grouped by potter and by color, took up a few of the shelves that lined the near wall. On most of the rest of the shelves were books. She also had, just to her left, an elegant mahogany table she'd inherited from her grandfather, which was crammed with framed photos of family and friends and students: us at all ages and in various groupings; countless babies and smiling couples; sepia pictures of her grandparents; black-and-white photos from her and Dad's childhoods; and an exploding universe of pictures of her grandchildren. From where Mom loved to sit, she could look at her pots, and her books, and her paintings, and her photographs.

Mom rarely sat still, though: the perch was also her command center, with the coffee table serving as a desk and the phone within easy reach. This evening she wanted me to look at some new pictures she'd received—from three Liberian refugees she'd helped come to the United States to study, and from a Laotian refugee who'd settled in Minneapolis and was married and working in medicine. All of them had become family, and all of them had made special trips to visit her when they heard she was sick. Mom wanted me to see the latest photos of them and their children and tell me how they all were doing.

I thought then about whether I was indeed going to quit my job. Looking at the new pictures Mom was so proudly showing me, I was reminded how much she had gained by quitting one of hers.

"I Am Sorrow"

Almost twenty years earlier, in the spring of 1988, when my mother was head of the high school at Nightingale, a postcard arrived one day in the mail. It simply said: "Dear Mary Anne Schwalbe. I am a nun from the Philippines working in a refugee camp in Thailand and I need your help." It was signed: "Sister Mater, Daughter of Charity."

It would be years before my mother would find out how Sister Mater got her name and address. It turned out to be through either a complete fluke or an act of God, depending on your religious beliefs. What happened was this: A student of Mom's had been wandering through northern Thailand. He had a stack of postcards and a wad of small bills and couldn't find a post office and didn't speak Thai—so when he literally bumped into a nun on the street, he figured he could trust her to mail them for him. She was not only a good Daughter of Charity but also, Mom liked to say when she told this story, a great fund-raiser. The nun mailed the cards—but copied down the addresses first.

Mom replied to Sister Mater of the Mysterious Post-card, and Sister Mater then wrote a long letter to her. They wound up writing to each other for years. In her letters, Sister Mater would include pictures of the handicapped Hmong children with whom she worked at Ban Vinai, the largest camp in Thailand for refugees from Laos. There were 45,000 refugees at Van Binai, and 80 percent of them were women and children. Hundreds of the children were severely disabled.

Soon into the correspondence, Sister Mater began send-ing Mom marked pages from various catalogs. Mom would pay for the items and have them shipped to the camp. It was twenty dollars here and thirty dollars there. A book or two. A magazine subscription. Mom enlisted her students to collect books and paper and crayons to mail to the children of Ban Vinai. Then one day Sister Mater wrote Mom a letter more or less the same as all her others—except in one respect. Instead of asking Mom for a small amount, she asked for thousands of dollars. Mom wrote right back and said she couldn't afford that kind of sum. Mom's letter must have sounded a bit cross, as the nun replied immediately and apologetically, saying that as a nun she had no idea whatsoever about money.

They continued as before, but then Sister Mater men-tioned in a letter that one of her friends from the Philippines was coming to volunteer at the camp. If Mom couldn't afford to give more money but wanted to help more, perhaps she could come work at the camp too?

My mother was an incredibly orderly and careful person, but she also had that impulsive streak. So when Sister Mater's suggestion arrived, Mom decided to take a semester's leave from her school and move to the refugee camp.

It was just then that Nina was getting ready to graduate from college.

My mother and Nina have always been tremendously close, but they were, at that moment, going through some minor mother-daughter agita and weren't able to agree on a variety of things. Somehow they both agreed on one thing: Nina should go with Mom to work in the refugee camp. I remember thinking, *This is either the best idea in the world or the worst.* I suspected the latter. So did my father and brother.

But off they went. By plane to Bangkok. Then there was a terrifying, careening ride in the back of a truck over mud roads at night for twelve hours. *What have I gotten Nina into?* Mom thought. Only then did she realize that she'd never even bothered to check out whether the nuns and the camp were real. And then they arrived—at the grimmest place they'd ever seen.

Here, from Mom's journal, are some of her first impressions of Ban Vinai: "Everything covered in swirling dust— thousands of almost naked children who screamed and/or ran when they saw foreigners—hundreds of mangy dogs—runny noses everywhere—scalps that looked singed—sores all over bodies."

The first children Mom and Nina met at the Rehab Center, where they would be working, were four deaf-mute girls, who did all the cooking and who instantly adopted my mother and sister. The girls were delighted to have more help and had naturally sunny personalities. Many of the children at the Rehab Center could not crawl; some could barely move at all. Many had severe developmental problems. On the first morning, Mom spent time with a young woman named Mang Quan, who was twenty but looked twelve and had dozens of medical challenges, including incontinence. Mang Quan seemed to take to Mom immediately. She was able to feed herself with her one functioning hand; the other she wouldn't remove from around Mom's neck. She couldn't walk, was heavy, and had to be carried everywhere. She and Mom formed a close bond. Or so Mom thought.

But Mang Quan didn't come the next day, or the day after that. So Mom went to visit her tent when another day had almost passed. Mom soon discovered why Mang Quan hadn't returned to the center. Mang Quan's parents did love her—but they were old and couldn't tend to her. So they housed her outside their very basic tent in a bleak shed, where she lay naked on a slab of wood with a dish of rice beside her. Her parents had been ill and unable to bring her to the center. She was now filthy and ashamed. She didn't want Mom to see her like that. She threw rocks at Mom to keep her away.

That was day four.

Mom and Nina persevered and grew quite proud of their ability to weather the atrocious conditions. The latrines were a horror show, but one that soon made them laugh.

One hundred children aged three to eighteen showed up at the center every day. Mom and Nina would feed them breakfast, help them brush their teeth, bathe the ones who had soiled themselves, and try to engage and entertain them. As time went by, Mom and Nina started to make progress. Resources were extremely scarce. They taught them games—at first with pebbles. Then Nina found macaroni at the local Thai grocery store and showed the youngest ones how to string necklaces. Mom did more of the bathing; Nina, more of the games.

Eventually Mang Quan came back. Mom later wrote in her journal:

Two weeks later: Total disorganization in our unit today. One of my little girls—a Down syndrome child whom I called The Dancing Girl, Chong Thao, had fallen and bitten through her tongue. While I was cleaning up the blood, Mang Quan, who was jealous when I was with other children, made a total mess of herself on the concrete floor. Nina and I were so desperate that we decided to teach the children a song. The easiest one we could think of was "If You're Happy and You Know It, Clap Your Hands"—and the children who could clap, did, and we arranged for some of them to have their arms around children who could not clap. And we sang this every day till we left.

Every afternoon Mom and Nina would teach English to a group of nine young men who had sought them out. These were older teens who had nothing to do all day and were desperate to learn something. They had no books, but Mom and Nina found a stack of ancient *Reader's Digest*s in town. It was among this group that my mother and sister made a great friend named Ly Kham.

The very first day Ly Kham met them, he'd given them a composition he'd written that began as follows: "There is nobody in the world like to be a refugee. They have to move from one place to another place. The refugee is hated by all people in the world." But Kham had been born with optimism that never stayed buried for too long.

At night, Mom and Nina would go back to the room they shared in a Thai village an hour from the camp. Nina tended to go out at night for beers with local friends and other aid workers, while Mom more often stayed in to read books by flashlight.

When the three months were up, Nina knew what she wanted to do with her life and stayed on in the camp. Mom had a new direction too. She would work one more year at her school before quitting that job to take a new one as the first director of the Women's Commission for Refugee Women and Children, running the organization in its early years and devoting herself to the cause of refugees. As for Kham, who as a five-year-old had walked days from his home in Laos to Thailand, and had seen many members of his family killed, Mom would help bring him to the United States, where he would get a scholarship to college and go on to have a career and family. Well, two families—his own and ours. He was one of the former refugees who'd recently visited Mom and whose pictures she'd proudly shown us.

I'VE ALWAYS LOVED telling this story and will do so at the slightest provocation. Many people have told me that it inspired them to find an unusual way to connect with an adult child, or with a parent. It changed Mom and Nina, but it also changed the rest of us. It was a challenge of sorts—and I think we're all a bit more fearless and, I like to think, we try to be a bit more selfless thanks to their example.

Mom was often asked to give speeches about why she felt so committed to the cause of refugees. She would say, "Just imagine that you are awakened tonight by someone in your family who says to you, 'Put the things you treasure most in one small bag that you can carry. And be ready in a few minutes. We have to leave our home and we will have to make it to the nearest border.' What mountains would you need to cross? How would you feel? How would you manage? Especially if across the border was a land where they didn't speak your language, where they didn't want you, where there was no work, and where you were confined to camps for months or years."

And she would also explain it with a poem called "I Am Sorrow," written in 1989 by a sixteen-year-old Vietnamese girl named Sindy Cheung, who was living behind barbed wire in a refugee camp in Hong Kong. At one meeting of our book club—I can't remember exactly when, but it was while Mom was getting chemo, and in winter—I asked her to name some of the writers who had changed the course of her life. "There are so many," Mom said right away. "I wouldn't know where to start. Really, whenever you read something wonderful, it changes your life, even if you aren't aware of it." She paused for a few seconds and then added: "But I'd certainly put Sindy Cheung near the top of the list."

I AM SORROW

> Who will listen to my feeling?
> Who will listen to my useless land?
> After the war, my skin had been damaged,
> There are craters in my body.
> Although I was sad, sorry, and suffering,
> Who will listen to my feeling?
> I am sad, sorry, and suffering,
> Who will know my feeling?
> I am not sad about my harmed body,
> I am sorrow because of the people who can't use
>   me rightly.
> Who will know my feeling?

The Uncommon Reader

At the start of January 2008, Mom was looking forward to traveling to London, her first trip out of the country since she'd learned of her diagnosis. She had a wretched week before going but toughed it out and felt strong enough to fly. Because Mom hadn't been well, Dr. O'Reilly had to reschedule a chemo treatment from the Friday a whole week before her trip to the Tuesday right before her departure. This made Mom anxious about whether she would feel well the week she was there. But ultimately I'm not sure anything could have kept her from going.

Mom had fallen in love with London as a drama student in 1955. I think it was the first place she really felt like an adult. Mary Anne had been twenty-one, and seven years away from being my mother. She wrote to a friend, who shared the letter with me: "I really am completely happy over here, and don't ever want to relinquish my freedom again. It's quite wonderful to be completely on one's own, especially for my kind of sheltered, spoilt brat variety. But I do wish some of my friends were here too. When one sees something especially wonderful, it's always nice to have someone to share it with."

In another letter, "London is a magic kind of city, at least I think it is. One doesn't mind the cold or the terrible weather, and people always smile at you in the streets, and when you ask someone directions, they not only tell you where to go, but if they possibly can, they take you there, and no one is in a hurry, and everyone is fantastically polite, and there are so many marvelous places to go, and concerts that you would adore, and so many art exhibits every week, and I've been going to church regularly on Sundays, because the services are so beautiful, and the choirs are so well trained, and there is a real peace and quiet about it."

There's something extraordinary about the first city you love, and many things brought Mom back to London again and again. That Dad loved it too certainly helped. We spent a year there when I was nine and my parents were on sabbatical, and the family vacationed somewhere in the British Isles almost every summer, always with time in London.

In addition to the pleasures of the place, it was partly nostalgia that drew Mom back there. There was, it seemed, a fair bit of romance involved on her initial visit—and her feeling that everyone was friendly there may have been owed to good spirits on the part of Londoners but also thanks to Mary Anne being a pretty twenty-one-year-old woman.

This trip, more than fifty years after her first, had a rocky start. The minute she got to London, she spiked a ferocious fever. Dad took her right to a hospital, but as soon as she got there, the fever vanished. Mom was glad but also frustrated when a fever disappeared before the doctors could take her temperature. Even though this isn't unusual for people undergoing chemo, Mom was afraid that people would think she was a hypochondriac. We discussed it once, and I tried to tell her that having a terminal illness pretty much excuses you from accusations of hypochondria. But she'd placed so much stock for so long on not complaining that it still irked her when there was any chance that someone might think the few things she did complain about weren't real but were in her head.

The rest of the London trip went better. Nina and Sally and the boys flew over from Geneva. Mom was also able to attend a friend's seventieth-birthday party and see there dozens of people she loved. She sent me back two enthusiastic posts for the blog—happily noting that she was meeting with a colleague from the International Rescue Committee in London. She'd founded the IRC-UK a decade earlier, and it now contributed more than thirty million pounds a year to the IRC's overall budget, as well as having programs of its own.

WHEN MOM RETURNED to New York, it was time to pick a new book for the club. We decided it should be set in the British Isles. We settled on *Felicia's Journey* by the Irish short-story writer and novelist William Trevor. In this disturbing novel from 1994, a young woman, pregnant and broke, flees her small town in search of the handsome man who got her pregnant. She finds herself wandering through the English Midlands, desperately searching for the lawn mower plant in which he said he worked, and unwisely trusting the kindness of a stranger, an overweight, unctuous, lonely fifty-year-old whose mind keeps spinning back to a series of women he befriended and who now live only in his Memory Lane.

We both read it in one sitting.

"When you go to towns, you see people all the time," Mom said, as we met back at the hospital, just a few days after her return from London. "And you don't give them a second thought: maybe a homeless woman, or people going door-to-door trying to convert people to their religion, or a man having tea with a younger woman. What I find so remarkable about this book is that Trevor not only introduces you to these people, he explains exactly how they came to be where they are."

Mom showed me a page she'd dog-eared: "Hidden away, the people of the streets drift into sleep induced by alcohol or agitated by despair, into dreams that carry them back to the lives that once were theirs."

"I found the book terrifying," I said. Then, forgetting briefly Mom's odd reading habits, I asked: "And I was very surprised by the ending. Were you?"

"Of course not—I'd read it first. I don't think I could have stood the suspense if I hadn't known what was going to happen. I'd have been way too worried."

For obvious reasons, Mom wasn't a big mystery reader—but the series she liked were the ones that were set in one place. She loved Donna Leon's Venice and Dennis Lehane's Boston and Colin Cotterill's Vientiane and Alexander McCall Smith's Botswana and his Edinburgh. (I wish he'd written his London series a few years earlier.) In each case, the location becomes an active participant in both the crime and its solution and therefore demands that the writer have a deep knowledge of its surprises and idiosyncracies. My mother delighted in the ways great mystery writers could turn a city or town into a character and reveal its hidden corners—where you might hide, where you go with money, where you slink to when you have none, where a certain person would blend in and where he would stick out like a bloody thumb.

Keeping with our British theme, we next chose *The Uncommon Reader,* a novella by Alan Bennett that had been published six months earlier. It was fate that Mom would fall in love with it. How could she not? It was written by one of her favorite writers. (Bennett was born two months after Mom—and she'd avidly followed his career as a playwright, novelist, screenwriter, and memoirist since seeing him do comedy on the London stage in the early 1960s.) It was set in London. It even involved the Queen of England. But what really captured Mom was the cast of supporting characters: especially the young page, a "ginger-haired boy in overalls," who gets the queen to start reading, and Sir Claude, who sets into motion the queen's new life, the revelation of which makes for a very unexpected (if you haven't skipped ahead) and charming ending to the book.

Also, how could anyone who loves books not love a book that is itself so in love with books? The day after we both finished the novella, I saw Mom at her home and she pointed out to me her three favorite passages. Whenever we were together and she came to a passage in a book that she liked, she wouldn't read it to me—she would hand the whole book to me, with her finger pointing to a line and instructions where I was to start and where to stop. There was a certain amount of shuffling involved. As always, she lifted her finger only when she was sure my eyes had found their way to the right portion. It was like the passing of a baton in a relay race:

> "Of course," said the Queen, "but briefing is not reading.
> In fact it is the antithesis of reading. Briefing is terse, fac-

tual and to the point. Reading is untidy, discursive and perpetually inviting."

*

"Pass the time?" said the Queen. "Books are not about passing the time. They're about other lives. Other worlds. Far from wanting time to pass, Sir Kevin, one just wishes one had more of it. If one wanted to pass the time one could go to New Zealand."

*

The appeal of reading, she thought, lay in its indifference: there was something undeferring about literature. Books did not care who was reading them or whether one read them or not. All readers were equal, herself included.

In the Bennett, a very high-profile character winds up quitting a very high-profile job. I'd wanted to start a website for months and had, in the first days of January, just before Mom went to London, finally gotten up the courage to quit my day job, even though I wasn't sure what kind of website I wanted to start. Up until the last minute, I debated whether to say to my boss that I was thinking of leaving, or to say that I was indeed leaving. I found myself saying the latter.

"That's the best news," Mom had said, when I told her.

"Yes," I said. "I'm scared but excited. And the ironic thing about quitting book publishing is that now I'll have more time to read."

"And maybe even write?" suggested Mom.

"I don't think so," I said.

DAYS AFTER CHATTING with Mom about the Alan Bennett, I saw her again at my niece's fourth birthday. By the time David and I arrived, it was full-fledged happy chaos. There was a Cubist pin-the-tail-on-the-donkey—which was particularly thoughtful because the children couldn't help but get it right/wrong and screamed with laughter wherever the tail landed. There was plenty of alcohol for the adults. There were crafts and the usual complement of New York parents hanging around, sipping wine or Dunkin' Donuts coffee and either encouraging their children to join in or allowing them to stand, thumb-in-mouth, draped around their mother's legs.

In the midst of it stood Mom. Her hair was definitely thinner. And even though the studio was hot, she was wearing two layers of sweaters. Lucy, the birthday girl, was a little feverish—but was trying her darnedest to have a great time at the party. And her grandmother was doing the very same thing. Everyone had warned Mom that as someone undergoing chemo, she shouldn't be around people with colds and shouldn't kiss or hug people hello or ride the subway or bus. But Mom wasn't going to live like that. So there she was in a scrum of children—about half of whom had runny noses and hacking coughs—completely in her element.

After a while, though, I could see that she was getting tired. She'd told me on the phone about the sores on her feet and how standing and walking weren't great. She broke away from the pack and came to join Dad and David and me.

We talked plans, as ever. She was preparing for her trip to Vero Beach and could hardly wait. I was to join her at chemo and her doctor's appointment that coming Friday. We also talked more about London.

She and Dad had walked as much as she could to visit places she loved, she said. She'd even gone back to see the house where she'd lived in the fifties, 20 Courtfield Gardens. She'd seen her oldest godchild and his family, and his father and mother, friends from that first year she lived there. Her godson's mother was in an advanced stage of Alzheimer's, and Mom said she was amazed at the love and attention her family was giving her—as difficult as it must be.

"I feel so lucky," Mom said to me. "I can't imagine what it would be like not to be able to know the people I love, or to read, or to remember books I've already read, or to visit my favorite places and remember everything that happened there, all the wonderful times."

We watched Lucy play for a while and also chatted with her seven-year-old brother, Adrian, who was taking a brief break from his duties as the party's entertainment director.

"The only thing that makes me really sad," said Mom, once Adrian had returned to the scrum, "is that I won't see the little ones grow up. I really wanted to take them all to Broadway musicals and on special trips and to London."

Mom had recently seen on television the film *Auntie Mame,* starring her former boss Rosalind Russell and her lifelong friend Pippa Scott, who played the ingénue at the end. I think it had rekindled in her the fantasy of being Auntie Mame, the woman who took her nephew on a glorious trip around the world and taught him that "life is a banquet and most poor suckers are starving to death."

I realized then that for all of us, part of the process of Mom's dying was mourning not just her death but also the death of our dreams of things to come. You don't really lose the person who has been; you have all those memories.

I would always have the summer in Godalming when I was six and learned to tie my shoe; and the year in England when Nina drank so much Ribena blackberry currant syrup that we dubbed her Nina Ribena; and the performance of *Giselle* in London I'd seen with Mom, my first ballet ever, when Baryshnikov and Gelsey Kirkland danced so brilliantly they got seventeen standing ovations, and Mom and I stood side by side with tears rolling down our faces because it was so thrilling; and all the plays we'd been to together—Janet Sussman in *Hedda Gabler* and Paul Scofield in *Volpone*. I would even have the times that seemed awful then but looked hilarious now: when we arrived in Wales with no hotel reservation and it was impossible to get a room and we'd driven for hours with me vomiting prodigiously all over my siblings in the backseat; the car ride through the Ring of Kerry with my sister spewing her guts over my brother and me.

But we were all going to have to say goodbye to Mom taking her youngest grandchildren to a Broadway show or to the Tate Modern or to Harrods to marvel at the Food Hall and visit the pet store puppies. We were going to have to say goodbye to the little ones remembering their grandmother beyond a fleeting image or an imagined memory prompted by a photograph. We would need to say goodbye to Mom at their graduations and to her buying them clothes and to them bringing home boyfriends and girlfriends to meet her.

We would also have to say goodbye to the joy of watching this next generation soak up the massive quantities of love their grandmother would have given them, and seeing them learn that there was someone in the world who loved them as much as their parents did: a grandmother who was delighted by all their quirks and who thought they were the most amazing creatures on earth. It was an idealized view of the future—but it was the one I carried in my head, and I don't think it was far off from the one my brother and sister and father and mother had.

I was learning that when you're with someone who is dying, you may need to celebrate the past, live the present, and mourn the future all at the same time.

Yet I had a thought then that made me smile. I would re-member the books that Mom loved, and when the children were old enough, I could give those books to them and tell them that these were books their grandmother loved. The lit-tlest ones would never see the British Isles through her eyes, but they could see it through the eyes of the writers she ad-mired; they would soon be old enough to read *The Railway Children* by Evelyn Nesbit and *Swallows and Amazons* by Arthur Ransome, and eventually Iris Murdoch and Alan Bennett. They could all be readers, and maybe even uncommon ones.

The Lizard Cage

The roller coaster continued, good days flowing into bad days, bad into good. At each appointment, we learned when the next would be. And one book made way for another.

Every time I talked to Mom, she asked me if I'd yet read Karen Connelly's *The Lizard Cage,* the novel she loved about Burma, which had been published the previous year.

On a cold and damp day at the very end of January 2008, I was finally able to say that yes, I had.

"I can't get it out of my head," I said.

The book starts with a little boy, an orphan, and tells the story of his interaction with a political prisoner, a songwriter named Teza. The novel has harrowing scenes in prison. Teza, a Buddhist, must capture and eat raw lizards, breaking his faith by killing and consuming something that lived in order to survive himself; this is just part of his torment, though a potent symbol of it. It's a tremendously powerful book that also speaks to our need to connect with each other, to tell stories and to pass them on, especially through writing.

Early on you come to a passage where the little boy talks about his friends in the prison. He names them and then says, "And books . . . My friends were books." Even though he couldn't read them, because he didn't yet know how, their very existence gave him comfort.

Soon you learn that Teza is hoarding cigarettes because they are wrapped in newspaper and thus have scraps of words, odd little accidental modernist poems that are a lifeline to civilization. Soon, too, a single pen enters Teza's life and then seemingly disappears. The search for this pen drives the plot, bringing both disaster and salvation of sorts—for Teza, the orphan, and a prison guard who befriends them. As for life outside the prison, where all dissent is forbidden, Connelly writes, "As long as there is paper, people will write, secretly, in small rooms, in the hidden chambers of their minds, just as people whisper the words they're forbidden to speak aloud."

In an era of computers, there's something deeply poignant about a political prisoner with his scraps of paper, about a prison convulsed in the hunt for a pen, and about Connelly's recognition of the importance of the written and printed word. It's easy to forget in our wired world that there are not just places like prisons where electronic text is forbidden, but whole countries, like Burma, where an unregistered modem will land you in jail or worse. Freedom can still depend on ink, just as it always has.

"What did you think of the amazing prayer Teza says to himself after that horrible beating?" Mom asked me as we sat together, chemo flowing into her arm. "I xeroxed it and put it in my copy of *Daily Strength*. It's in my bag."

I gave Mom her bag, which was propped up on the chair beside me. Mom carefully, with her free hand, fished out the book and handed it to me. Neatly folded inside was a copy of the page from *The Lizard Cage,* with the incantation that made such an impression on Mom. It's a Buddhist meditation that Teza uses to calm his mind, to put aside not just the physical pain but the sadness and rage he's feeling:

> He starts to whisper a prayer. "Whatever beings there are, may they be free from suffering. Whatever beings there are, may they be free from enmity. Whatever beings there are, may they be free from hurtfulness. Whatever beings there are, may they be free from ill health. Whatever beings there are, may they be able to protect their own happiness."

"I particularly like that last phrase," Mom said. "About protecting your own happiness."

"But how can you protect your own happiness when you can't control the beatings?" I asked.

"That's the point, Will. You can't control the beatings. But maybe you can have some control over your happiness. As long as he can, well then, he still has something worth living for. And when he's no longer able, he knows he's done all he can." In my mind, I replaced the word *beatings* with *cancer.*

"It's very inspiring," I said.

"Yes, but *The Lizard Cage* shouldn't just inspire you. It should also make you furious."

Often we feel the need to say that a book isn't just about a particular time or place but is about the human spirit. People say this of *Anne Frank: The Diary of a Young Girl,* or *Night* by Elie Wiesel, or *A Long Way Gone: Memoirs of a Boy Soldier* by Ishmael Beah. But it's one thing to feel that a book can speak beyond its particular time and place to something universal, and another to ignore the circumstances and time in or about which it was written. Mom felt that we were all too quick to do that—for those books and for *The Lizard Cage*. Sure, it's about human courage. But it's also about human rights in Burma. And at the time of our reading, and the time of this writing, the situation in Burma was and is indeed something that should inspire fury and action. Connelly, a Canadian poet and nonfiction writer, had been to Burma many times until she was denied a visa by the military regime; she'd also lived for nearly two years on the Thai-Burmese border. She not only knew the situation intimately; she had committed to doing something about it.

When I went to visit Mom and Dad's home a week after my conversation with her about *The Lizard Cage,* I noticed an envelope waiting to be mailed. It was for the U.S. Campaign for Burma. This wasn't Mom's first engagement with this country. She'd traveled there in 1993 on a mission for the Women's Commission. And she'd even met with Aung San Suu Kyi, the lawfully elected leader of Burma, in one of the brief periods where Suu Kyi was free from house arrest. They'd talked about women's rights, health issues, and refugees. Always refugees.

IF *The Lizard Cage* reminded Mom to send a check to the campaign for Burma, it also inspired her to redouble her efforts for Afghanistan. It was, after all, a book about the importance of books and reading and writing. The Afghan library had added a sixth board member in January, a prominent Afghan diplomat. Things were moving. What was needed now was money—and lots of it. Not thousands but millions. Otherwise, ground would never be broken in Kabul; the books would remain in storage; no roving libraries would reach the children of Afghanistan's villages.

Mom was always spreading the word about the library to anyone who would listen.

This was another lesson I learned from Mom over the course of our book club: Never make assumptions about people. You never know who can and will want to help you until you ask. So you should never assume someone can't or won't because of their age, or job, or other interests, or financial situation.

"I was once giving a talk to some high school students during the war in Bosnia," she told me. "And the next day one of them called me. It turns out that she was the daughter of a big executive, and over the previous night's dinner, she'd convinced her dad to get his company not just to donate a huge amount of supplies but also to pay to fly them to Bosnia. That's why I tell everyone about the library. You never know who will help."

Even the doctors at Memorial Sloan-Kettering who were treating Mom heard, in the middle of the treatments, about the Afghan library—and so did the nurses, cabdrivers, friends at dinner parties, and strangers in delis.

I teased her one day. "Mom, I sometimes think if your apartment was burning down and the firemen rushed in, you'd tell them about the Afghan library before you let them put the fire out."

"I'm not that bad," Mom replied. "But I might tell them after they put it out."

Brat Farrar

J ust before I left my job in book publishing, a remarkable
opportunity had arisen for the company to publish a book
called *The Last Lecture* by Randy Pausch, a forty-seven-year-old
computer scientist and professor who himself was dying of
pancreatic cancer. It started with an article by the *Wall Street
Journal* staff writer Jeffrey Zaslow about Pausch, who'd been
asked by his university, Carnegie Mellon, to deliver what used
to be called a "Last Lecture," the idea being that you would
speak about the things you would speak about if you were giving the last lecture you would ever give. The irony in the case
of Randy Pausch was that he knew that it would, indeed, be
that—and he used the speech to impart lessons he'd learned,
not just for the people listening, but for an audience that was
extremely important to him: his young children. I'd told my
former colleagues about Mom's illness, and they gave me a
typescript copy to read as soon as the last word was written,
which was right before I was to leave for Florida to spend two
weeks with Mom. I'd brought the copy with me.

Mom was to be in Florida for the whole month of February. Dad had been there the first two weeks but was on his way back to New York to look after his business. My brother and sister and their families had also been there. So now I flew down to West Palm Beach the same day Dad returned to New York. Mom arranged for a driver to pick me up and bring me to Vero Beach—I would use the car she and Dad had rented there for getting around.

Mom loved almost everything about Vero—the weather, the beach, the house she rented from a friend, the rituals and rhythms, the small but excellent museum, the lectures at the library, and even the supermarket, with its luxuriously wide aisles. The town also has one of America's great independent bookstores, the Vero Beach Book Center. Immediately after I'd thrown my suitcase into what would be my bedroom, I sat down with Mom as she went over the schedule.

"First off, I want to get some new books for us to read. I also really want to spend some time rereading authors I've loved—more Jane Austen—and also poetry—T. S. Eliot and Wallace Stevens and Elizabeth Bishop." New and old. Mom always kept these in balance, constantly introducing her childhood friends to people she'd just met, always adding a stopover in a new place on a journey to a more familiar city or town, reading the latest authors in counterpoint to her favorites.

As Mom was talking, I looked at her closely. Her hair was much thinner, wispy, flatter, the grayish-white color of chicken bones left in the sun. And she'd continued to lose weight, something you couldn't help noticing even though she was always bundled up in several layers—to protect her from the sun outside and the fierce air-conditioning of Florida's shops and homes and restaurants. Yet she did look well, especially in comparison to how tired and drawn she'd looked when I'd last seen her, a few weeks earlier, on a freezing day in New York.

Mom told me about a lunch that the Women's Commission staff had given her right before she left for Vero Beach. She'd come in to tell everyone about the Afghan project, but the staff turned it into a celebration of Mom's contributions, from the years when she ran the organization and since. They'd presented her with a scrapbook of photos of her various missions to refugee camps and of all her friends at the commission. Mom had been very moved.

Oh, and she had one more thing to show me. I was to wait right there. It was a surprise.

I sat at the kitchen table in her Vero condo, waiting. Mom had left the kitchen for her bedroom. Many minutes went by. And then more.

"Mom, are you okay? Is everything okay?"

"Yes, just wait there. I'll be right out."

Mom was not usually a fan of surprises, so I couldn't imagine what this one was. And then finally she emerged, and I saw it. She was wearing a wig—a large, almost Jacqueline Kennedy bouffant, in several different shades of gray and also with strands of black. It was perched awkwardly on her head; she'd been trying to get it right, but it sat uneasily, more like a hat.

"Not bad, is it?" said Mom.

I was determined not to cry.

"Not bad at all," I said.

"Maybe it needs a little more styling—it's too big—but I think it will be the difference between me looking sick and looking okay. I feel so lucky that I still have some hair, but it gets thinner and thinner—so I have this now. Still, keeping my hair for six months after starting chemo was more than I'd hoped for. So I'm not complaining. Your sister thinks the color isn't quite right, but I'm sure they can do something with that."

"It is a little dark. But it looks great. You look great, Mom."

"I'll go put it away. Then we'll do the errands and have fun being together."

One of the problems about lying to my mother when I was growing up was that I almost always got caught. This was partly due to Mom's formidable memory. "Where are you going?" she would ask me as I was sneaking out of the house, at age twelve, for a forbidden trip on the subway from suburban Cambridge to louche downtown Boston to visit Jack's Joke Shop, where I could buy fake vomit, joy buzzers, and other such things. "To Jim's house," I might lie. "But I thought you mentioned a few months ago that Jim and his parents were going this weekend to visit Jim's grandmother in Asheville." Arrggh.

It would be months before Mom would try the wig again.

THAT AFTERNOON, ACCORDING to plan, we did indeed go to the Vero Beach Book Center. Whenever I went to a bookstore with Mom, we would first split up—doubling our recon ability. We'd wait maybe fifteen minutes before finding each other—then each of us would give the other a little guided tour of what we had discovered. Just as you might wander a bit by yourself when visiting a garden outside a historic home, but then feel the need to show your companions the treasures you'd found—*Look at these lilacs, the hydrangea, the rose garden*—so we would point out to each other what we'd stumbled upon.

"Did you know this author has a new book? What do you think?" Mom might ask.

"I didn't love his last four or five," I might answer.

"Well then, why did you keep reading him?"

"I edited them."

Or: "Have you heard anything about this one?"

"Yes, I'm sure I read something—but I can't remember what—it's either supposed to be terrific or terrible."

There are all kinds of serendipities in bookstores, starting with Alphabetical: while looking for one novel, you might remember that you'd always meant to read something by another author whose last name shared the same first two letters. Visual: the shiny jacket on this book might catch your eye. Accidental: superstitiously, I almost always feel the need to buy any book that I knock over. And Prompted: both Mom and I gave very serious consideration to any book placed in the "staff recommends" section, particularly if it sported a yellow stickie (aka Post-it note) or a handwritten shelf talker—a bookstore neologism I love, because it conjures such a vivid image of a shelf talking to you, or of a person who talks to shelves.

This trip I wound up with *Brat Farrar* by Josephine Tey (a Vero Beach Book Center Staff Favorite) and the second volume of W. Somerset Maugham's *Collected Short Stories,* which I'd clumsily knocked off a shelf. Mom bought *Three Men in a Boat* by Jerome K. Jerome, an 1889 account of a comical boat trip that one of our friends insisted she read. (I'm pretty sure she did, but we never discussed it.)

"Mom, there's one book I brought with me from New

York," I said as we headed out the door and toward the car. It was quite cool for Florida. I'm terrible at parking and so had avoided spaces near the store that a normal driver could have squeezed into in favor of one far away that a Mack truck driver could have sailed into drunk. "It's actually a typescript of the book I told you about—*The Last Lecture*—the one by the Carnegie Mellon professor, the man who has pancreatic cancer."

"How is he doing?" Mom asked.

"I think he's hanging in there. I spoke to him on the phone once, a few weeks ago, right before I quit. He's incredibly nice."

"That's what my friends at Lustgarten say. They love him." Mom had recently been in touch with people at the Lustgarten Foundation, an organization devoted to funding research related to pancreatic cancer and raising awareness of symptoms and treatments, which was founded in memory of an executive at Cablevision who'd died at age fifty-two of the disease.

I wasn't sure if Mom wanted to read a book that so baldly stated from the outset that the author knew he had only a few months left to live. As soon as we were back at Mom's house, I decided that I would just leave it on the breakfast table—my own little "staff recommends." That way she could come across it and decide whether she wanted to read it or not.

"Why don't you have a walk on the beach?" Mom suggested. "I'm going to put my feet up for a bit."

So I left Mom sitting on the couch, and out I went, Tey in hand.

I stayed out far longer than I'd meant to, sitting on a bench overlooking the ocean. Usually beach reading is better in theory than in practice. The sun is too bright and my sunglasses aren't progressives, so I need to take them off to read; people walk by and stir up mini-sandstorms; I get too hot; I need a drink; I should really swim, as the water is great. Sometimes I just have the wrong book—something too serious to compete with the hysterical shrieks of children all around, or too silly to match a darkening mood.

But today was perfect for beach reading, and *Brat Farrar* grabbed me from the start. Written in 1949, it reminded me a great deal of Patricia Highsmith's breakout book *The Talented Mr. Ripley,* published six years later: in both, there's murder, lies, and an imposter. Tey's clever twist is that the murderer is the only one who knows for sure that the imposter can't possibly be who he says he is, and yet he can't reveal this fact without incriminating himself. Beyond the plot is the sheer fun of life in a British country estate—the descriptions of which you never tire, if you never tire of that sort of description—the silver service, the horses, the drawing room drinks, the dressing for dinner.

Tey had died in 1952 of cancer at the age of fifty-five. Her real name was Elizabeth MacKintosh, and she was born in Inverness, Scotland, the daughter of a fruit dealer and a former teacher. She never gave interviews and wasn't known to have close friends. Not only had I never read her, I'd never heard of her. But I found myself whipping through *Brat Farrar.* I was excited to give it to Mom.

Every now and then I would force myself to pause, put down the book, and think. What my mind kept fixing on was lies. Would it have served Mom better to tell her that the wig wasn't great? Probably not. And yet I had a hard time remembering a single time Mom had lied to me. There was my stuffed turtle, of course, which she'd given to the orphans, though no Brat Farrar–like mock turtle had appeared in its place. And there were the lies when she said something was really no problem and of course it was. Was she lying now? She said she wasn't in pain, yet we all caught her, in private moments, grimacing, or taking a sharp breath, or biting her lower lip.

Eventually it was time to leave the beach and walk back to the condo. Mom was still on the couch, back to me, when I came through the door. There was a stack of papers on the coffee table in front of her. It was *The Last Lecture*.

"What did you think?" I asked her.

"It made me feel so very, very lucky."

"Really?" I felt then the need to state the obvious. "But you have exactly the same thing he has."

"Of course. But he's got three small children and will never get to see them grow up, and he'll never know what it's like to have grandchildren."

Continental Drift

Plenty of people are willing to talk about death but very few about dying. Mom, on the other hand, made it clear to all who asked her that she knew she had an incurable disease that was eventually going to kill her. Any mention of something a year off—the wedding of the child of a friend, for example—brought the subject to the fore. Mom would usually say that she would love to attend, if she was still here and well enough. Sometimes she'd candidly say that she didn't think it likely that she would be around.

Some people continued to ignore the way Mom talked about her cancer. "I'm sure you'll get better," they would say. Or "You'll beat this." Or they would volunteer the story of a friend or relative or entertainer who had a miraculous recovery from something everyone had deemed hopeless and fatal.

When we talked about it, Mom occasionially expressed frustration. People weren't listening. She wasn't going to get better. But sometimes I think she was genuinely comforted and did consider that there could be a miracle. There were days when she wanted to talk about her death, and days when she didn't. It could even switch minute to minute. It felt like being in a car with a driver who abruptly changes lanes without ever signaling. One minute we'd be talking about aspects of her funeral, then suddenly she'd be onto the television film of Alexander McCall Smith's *The No. 1 Ladies' Detective Agency,* and then, barely pausing to take a breath, she'd be right back at the funeral—no flowers in the church; Doug was to be in charge of all aspects of the service (they'd had extensive discussions already about what prayers would be read and what hymns would be sung); it should definitely not go one minute over an hour.

Years before Mom was diagnosed, after she and Dad had discovered the hospice movement and the concept of palliative care, they'd talked to us about their Do Not Resuscitate orders and their Living Wills and other legal paperwork they'd executed. They were emphatic that they wanted to die at home; no heroic measures were to be taken to save their lives once their bodies started to fail, if it was clear they did indeed have a terminal condition. Perhaps this helped explain why Mom was so comfortable discussing all aspects of her death and what needed to be done.

A FRIEND OF a friend of mine from London had once visited New York and gotten sick. She spent her whole time in New York City cooped up in our friend's apartment. At the end of a week watching U.S. television day and night, she announced she had finally gotten Yanks all figured out. "The thing about Americans," she said, "is that you're very concerned about everything all the time."

Mom wasn't. Part of what made her effective was that she worried about things sequentially. She did what she could for everything that concerned her but devoted the bulk of her attention to one major project at a time. In her last years, the one thing was to be the Afghan library. So every day was filled with phone calls and meetings to advance this cause. Brochures had to be designed and distributed and people invited to benefits. There were proposals to look over, and architectural concepts for the library building to assess, and questions about governance and the logistics of the traveling libraries to consider. Safety was always a priority. Mom told me that she was especially concerned about her friend and fellow board member David Rhode, the *New York Times* writer, as he was reporting for his book from Kandahar and was not embedded with the U.S. troops. "Mom," I said one day, when she seemed particularly tired. "Everyone said it's fine if you want to relax and stay at home and listen to music."

"I know that," Mom said. "And I really am going to slow down—just as soon as everything is set on the library. I'm just going to do a little more work trying to raise money for it, and then I'll hand it all over."

ON MARCH 16, 2008, now back in New York, we went in for the results of Mom's second scan since she'd been diagnosed. She had started to react badly to Xeloda, one of her chemo drugs, and had been taken off it. Therefore the results of this scan, we were warned, might not be as good as the first.

Mom was feeling better, had gained some weight, and had more energy. So she said she didn't think it could be terrible news but was ready to hear anything. I thought back to a dramatic story I'd been told at college by a man who'd spent more than twenty years in a Chinese prison. I always pondered it (or, rather, my probably not-entirely-accurate recollection of it) when I needed to remind myself that good news and bad news are often relative to your expectations, not anything absolute.

This man had joined the CIA right out of Yale, during the Korean War, and then been shot down over China during his first mission and captured. He'd fully come to terms with the fact that he might be sentenced to several years in jail there and was praying that his sentence would be less than five years. That he could handle. But he would be devastated should it be more. After two years in solitary confinement, he was called into a courtroom with a whole bunch of prisoners. They would all have their sentences read, one after another. He described hearing the first sentence: death. Then the second: death. Then the third: death. And all of a sudden, he found himself praying for life in prison. He could handle that. Life in prison was indeed the sentence he got—and he was delighted.

I told Mom that story and she smiled.

"No new tumors would be great news," she said.

SOON DAD ARRIVED, and then we were called into the examination room to wait for Dr. O'Reilly, who joined us minutes later. She was in her usual white medical coat—but this time I noticed that she was wearing a delicate gold necklace. Her eyes sparkled more than usual—they're robin's-egg blue and jewel-like against her pale skin. Her hair, as always, was in the mop-top style of teen boy idols. I may have imagined it, but her step seemed lighter, as though she were bursting to tell us something, and she seemed to rush through her initial questions. (*How was Florida? How did the treatments there go? The blisters and mouth sores—much better? The constipation and diarrhea?*) Now it was time for the scan results.

"Well, I have to tell you," began Dr. O'Reilly, "that the news is very good. There are no new tumors and the ones that are there have shrunk. It's significant improvement. And you've put some weight back on. And your energy?"

"Much better," said Mom.

"It's hard to believe you're the same person," Dr. O'Reilly said.

"How much smaller are Mom's tumors?" I asked.

"Well, about thirty percent of the liver was involved when you first came in," she said, as always addressing Mom, no matter who had asked the question. "Now it's much closer to fifteen percent."

I thought of the CIA agent, thrilled with the sentence of life in prison. Only when you've had 30 percent of your liver filled with cancerous tumors does it qualify as great news that you are at 15 percent. Though if the number kept falling, of course, it would be great news no matter how one viewed it. When I looked over at Mom, I saw that color had returned to her face. Dad was smiling broadly, whereas minutes ago he'd been smiling, but nervously. As soon as we were back out in the waiting room, I called my sister and brother and uncle to give them the report.

There would be more time.

DAD LEFT, AND Mom and I went to sit together during her chemo. "I guess everyone's prayers really made a difference," she said, settling down into the chair in one of the curtained rooms. "I'll have to let Fred know." Fred was her minister at Madison Avenue Presbyterian.

"Do you have the Wodehouse?" she then asked me, without missing a beat.

"Yes, right here in my bag. It's just so much fun."

P. G. Wodehouse's Jeeves novels were turning out to be a joy: tales of a butler of uncanny abilities and his sweet but hapless employer. My oldest godson, a classicist turned lawyer, is a huge fan of the Jeeves novels; his parents, great friends of Mom and Dad and mine, had insisted we both give Wodehouse another try.

"I'd never had much patience for Wodehouse," Mom said, "until now. But I think the stories are wonderful. And more sweet than silly. Certainly not as silly as *Brat Farrar*. I still don't understand why you liked that so much." The Josephine Tey book I'd read in Florida was one of the few books about which Mom and I disagreed. She'd argued that the surprise ending would have been entirely predictable even if she hadn't already read the end and that she didn't find the characters very interesting. I got a bit huffy about it.

"I just liked it," I said, realizing that I wasn't making a very good argument. "And don't you sometimes feel like reading something silly, just to distract you, to take your mind off things?"

"I think it's much harder for me now to read very silly things when there are so many wonderful things to read and reread. And if the book is too silly, I find that it's often because the writer doesn't really have anything to say—or there are no values. Or because the whole book is just a lead-up to a trick at the end. If you read the ends first, you have much less patience for wasting time with that kind of book. Even a well-written book can be silly and a waste of time. But most of the Wodehouse is different. I don't find the stories silly. I like his people—Bertie and Jeeves and Psmith. They're slightly ridiculous but also endearing. And I like the odd things that Wodehouse characters collect, socks and silver and monocles. It reminds me of so many of our friends who collect strange things, like jewelry made from mahjong tiles or postcards of all-female marching bands. He's clearly having fun with that world of dinners and engagements and dowager aunts. That's my point, Will. The books are fun, not silly. There's a difference."

"But what about a book like *Alice in Wonderland*? Is that silly?"

"Lewis Carroll is definitely not silly. It has silliness, but it's a wonderful, fascinating, complicated book. I'm talking about those novels where the characters aren't really interesting and you don't care about them or anything they care about. It's those I won't read anymore. There's too much else to read—books about people and things that matter, books about life and death."

"But"—I looked at the floor, because I was about to bring up a subject I hadn't intended to discuss here and now—"isn't it hard to read books about death?" I paused. "Especially books where a character has cancer?"

Mom shook her head. "It's not hard to read about death abstractly. I do find it tough when a character I love dies, of course. You can truly miss characters. Not like you miss people, but you can still miss them. I don't think I'll ever get over Melanie's death in *Gone With the Wind*. But I'm still so glad I got to know her. As for books about cancer—" She paused to consider the question. "Well, I don't think it's any sadder to die from cancer than from a heart attack or another disease or an accident or anything else. It's all just part of life, real life. If we ruled out books with death in them, we wouldn't have much to read."

"So you don't mind if we read depressing books?" I asked.

"No—not at all. It's cruelty that gets to me. Still, it's important to read about cruelty."

"Why is it important?"

"Because when you read about it, it's easier to recognize. That was always the hardest thing in the refugee camps—to hear the stories of the people who had been raped or mutilated or forced to watch a parent or a sister or a child be raped or killed. It's very hard to come face-to-face with such cruelty. But people can be cruel in lots of ways, some very subtle. I think that's why we all need to read about it. I think that's one of the amazing things about Tennessee Williams's plays. He was so attuned to cruelty—the way Stanley treats Blanche in *A Streetcar Named Desire*. It starts with asides and looks and put-downs. There are so many great examples from Shakespeare—when Goneril torments King Lear or the way Iago speaks to Othello. And what I love about Dickens is the way he presents all types of cruelty. You need to learn to recognize these things right from the start. Evil almost always starts with small cruelties."

I was reminded that Mom had spent years teaching high

school English after moving back to New York. I asked Mom if there'd been books that were too depressing for her to teach or read.

"I don't think so."

"Even books where the characters are not just dying but in pain?"

"Even those."

"And even ones where really bad things happen to people?"

"Yes."

"Okay. Well then, here's our next book." I'd heard great things for years about *Continental Drift* by Russell Banks, and the book had been on my shelf for ages. I'd also heard that it was savagely depressing. I gave Mom my copy and then bought another.

OVER THE COURSE of *Continental Drift,* you watch a life fall apart. There's something very *Appointment in Samarra* about it, as one bad decision starts to unravel everything. As with the O'Hara, it's not just the bad decision; weakness and stubbornness also contribute. Fate sometimes lives in character—there are people who can't change who they are any more than they can change what happens to them. Banks chronicles the deterioration of a flawed but sympathetic man, a hockey player, who moves from New Hampshire to Florida with his wife and children to pursue the classic American Dream—to get a better life for himself and his family. The book tells in parallel the story of a young Haitian woman and her infant and nephew, and their journey as refugees—also to Florida—as she tries to make a new life for the three of them. Things go horrendously badly—both on an illegal boat and long before, on their journey to it. There's horrific sexual violence, of the kind used as a weapon of war against so many around the world. There's other violence too. And rage and cruelty. It's a book filled with missed opportunities, chronicling lives where people could have caught breaks but didn't; where if anything could go wrong, it did.

Banks was born in 1940 in Massachusetts, making him six years younger than Mom. He got to college on a scholarship but dropped out and started to travel toward Cuba, stopping in St. Petersburg, Florida, where he married at age nineteen, having a child and then getting divorced in 1962, the year I was born. *Continental Drift*, published in 1985, was his second book and a major critical success.

We both read *Continental Drift* right away—but had no opportunity to discuss it. It would be a few weeks before Mom's next chemo appointment. Mom's birthday was coming up soon after, so our immediate task was to figure out how to celebrate it, and this, along with the usual updates about the grandchildren, occupied all our calls. The scan had changed our lives yet again. Mom was still dying but not, thankfully, as quickly as we feared. She would be dying for some time to come. Or to put it more cheerfully, living. No matter what, we would have celebrated her birthday; what had changed was how we would celebrate it.

For someone who had little appetite for food, Mom had expressed a very odd wish for this birthday. A year or so before, she'd discovered a restaurant called Daisy May's that delivered delicious barbecue. The actual restaurant is in what was then a desolate area of Manhattan, a stretch of Eleventh Avenue that is home to auto dealers and body shops, the occasional bar, parking lots, and industrial buildings. Not dangerous, just derelict. This was where Mom wanted to celebrate her seventy-fourth birthday. She didn't want anything fancy or fussy or expensive, and she wanted the meal at the actual restaurant itself—so no one of us would have to do any cleanup.

The party would be small—the immediate family, my dad's two sisters, and a few friends. I'd arranged for a thirty-pound barbecued pig and lots of sides: macaroni and cheese, sweet potatoes, creamy corn with cheddar cheese, bourbon peaches, coleslaw, baked beans, collard greens, Texas toast. With barbecue, you need to go big or go home, as they say. The pig was ordered two days in advance. I kept Mom up-to-date during our morning calls about various details and asked her advice: Who should sit where? Was it necessary to have mashed potatoes in addition to the sweet potatoes? What time should the dinner start?

As the day of the party grew closer, however, I could tell Mom was feeling worse and worse. After the euphoria from the scan results wore off, we went from "much better" to "not great." She was to have a treatment four days before her birthday, with a friend accompanying her. She was hoping that the steroids they gave her with the chemo would carry her through. They usually gave her a lift. But this time they didn't.

The morning of the party, I called Mom to consult on the final details. If it sounds like I was being a little crazy with all the questions, well, I was. But I just wanted it to be flawless. I wanted the pig and sides to be delicious, the seating to be perfect, the timing to be right. I wanted the weather to be good, and people to be able to find cabs afterward. (There is no subway anywhere nearby.) I wanted it not to be too loud or too quiet. What I really wanted was for Mom not to be dying so that I wouldn't have to feel that I only had one or two more shots at throwing a birthday party for her. But that wasn't an option. I felt I needed to get every little thing perfectly right.

But that's quite a tightrope act. Who can stand the pressure? Still, I couldn't help myself. I was reminded of visiting Disneyland, The Happiest Place on Earth, and seeing some families ready to tear one another's eyes out—the kids sobbing inconsolably from greed and exhaustion and the stress of it all, the parents looking daggers at each other, the older children rolling their eyes or clearly stoned out of their minds. Every now and then you even heard someone say a variation of the following: "We traveled all this way and paid all this money, and you are going to have fun, do you hear me? You will have fun right now, damnit, or I'll pack up the whole family and drive us home this instant, and we'll never come back again."

So I asked my nutty questions, tried to think out every detail, and prayed that it wouldn't rain and that the god of taxicabs would smile upon us.

It didn't rain. And all the details were falling into place. Except for one. On the day of Mom's birthday, she was feeling worse than "not great." She was feeling "rocky."

I GOT TO Daisy May's early. Mom was already there. She looked small and frail and tired. In the minutes before everyone arrived, I updated her on the evening and the drill. She then went to meet Junior and his dad, both of whom are key parts of Team Daisy May. As I was fussing with the coolers of wine and beer, I watched her do as she always did. She introduced herself to them and asked questions about where they were from, and before my eyes I saw her get a little better, a little stronger. So when everyone arrived, she seemed back—if not to herself, then to a pretty good imitation of herself.

MOM PERCHED ON the edge of her chair, too unwell to eat, with an enormous pig laid out in front of her, flayed. My job was to wear the thick rubber gloves the restaurant provided so I could stand the heat of the pig meat as I ripped out great chunks of it with my fingers—the bacon, the ham, the shoulder—and deposited flesh on everyone's plates. Very primal.

Perhaps unsurprisingly, the conversation quickly turned to *Lord of the Flies,* the 1954 novel by William Golding, about kids fending for themselves on an island. A pig features heavily in the novel as a target of the boys' ferocity, as does a character unkindly called Piggy. As the meal got under way, though, the conversation turned to other books.

Mom and I hadn't yet announced to anyone in the family that we had a book club. It was just something special between us that we barely acknowledged, even to each other. After all, what kind of club has only two members? Still, no one thought it odd that Mom and I both started talking, more or less simultaneously, about *Continental Drift;* we couldn't wait any longer to discuss it. Almost everyone else had heard of the book, but my brother, who reads as much if not more than anyone in the family, was the only other person there who had read it.

"What did you think of it?" I asked both Doug and Mom.

"Brilliant," said my brother.

"Yes," said Mom as I ripped out a juicy bit of bacon and

dumped it, dripping with gorgeous fat, onto my sister-in-law Nancy's plate right beside her. "Brilliant. But so depressing. I think it may be the most depressing thing I've ever read."

The most depressing thing Mom had ever read? I was shocked. Had I been insane to include *Continental Drift* in our makeshift book club? Maybe I'd made a terrible mistake.

Meanwhile, all around me, the party went on—lots of laughter, lots more pig. One of the great things about Daisy May's is that there can be only one pig a night, and you don't have it in a private room—there are no private rooms. You have it at a big gingham-covered picnic table at the far end of a room with two other giant picnic tables, both of which are filled with an assortment of people eating food, cafeteria style, that they buy from the counter up front. It's a popular place among cops and firemen, and the pig is an event that involves the whole restaurant. Everyone who is new to the place wants to stand over it and have a look and find out how you get one.

So throughout the evening, a small parade of people came up to say "Sorry to interrupt" and ask about the pig. True to form, Mom talked to everyone who approached.

I could see the others in our group checking on Mom periodically, and it was obvious that she was growing less and less animated. My brother, when he wasn't deep in conversation, kept the sides moving. Doug has a remarkable ability to engage fully in conversations while also being attuned to the comfort of everyone around him.

We hurried through the rest of the meal to make sure that it reached its conclusion before whatever adrenaline Mom had been able to muster evaporated or did whatever it is adrenaline does when it's done.

For dessert, we ate red velvet cupcakes. They put a candle

in Mom's. We sang "Happy Birthday" quite quietly—Mom had never liked it when we were loud in restaurants. But everyone at Daisy May's joined in nonetheless. David took pictures. Then we packed up the leftovers and divvied them up, insisting that others take them, or begging off with elaborate politeness, not because we didn't want more pig meat in the days ahead but simply because there was so much of it.

Almost before we knew it, Mom was in a cab on her way home with Dad. It was a clear night and there were plenty of taxis. David and I walked home down Eleventh Avenue.

Though it had actually been a fun evening, I was suddenly overcome with anxiety and sadness. Yes, people had enjoyed themselves. Yes, the pig had worked, not just because it was delicious but also because it had given everyone a distraction—something to laugh about and discuss. Mom had been right about the mashed potatoes (not needed) and about the placement. Most important, she had felt well enough to be there.

But what had I been thinking, giving her *Continental Drift* to read? Mom had said she liked serious books, even depressing ones, but was this one too depressing? Had I given her not more than she could take but, perhaps, more than she'd wanted to take? Should I have read it first, before suggesting it—or just known from the description on the back that it might be too dire, too depressing, for someone dying?

Soon enough, David and I were home, but I couldn't sleep. How could I have been so stupid as to suggest that book? David slumbered while I paced, quietly, around our apartment, racked with remorse. It doesn't take a genius in psychology to know, and I did, that I was behaving like a crazy person. I hadn't given Mom the wrong medicine or made her stand out in the cold or left her feverish to fend for herself by the side of the road. Okay, so I'd suggested a book that might have been a bit dark. This was not even a particularly big offense in the pantheon of book club crimes, where the worst sin one could commit was not to read the book in question— or, even worse, to lie about having read the book when, in fact, you'd simply seen the movie, a lie usually uncovered when you used the actor's name by accident. ("I love the part when Daniel Day-Lewis . . .")

Many people who have my kind of insomnia have various behavioral strategies for dealing with it. One technique involves keeping a notepad by the bed. We write down our worries—to get them out of our perseverating brains and onto paper so we can sleep knowing that they will be there, in black and white, for us to worry about when we awake, and also knowing that we'll likely find those same worries inconsequential or even ridiculous when the morning does come. I tried that. It didn't work. I was still awake.

It was too late for an Ambien. I had to be up the next morning for my eight A.M. chat with Mom. And so I did what I was to do so many times that year: I sat in the dark and berated myself. Then I watched some television—episodes I'd taped of *The Real World,* a reality show I loved about seven kids picked to live in a house and have their lives taped. Then I tried unsuccessfully to read. At about four A.M., I finally fell asleep for a few hours. When I awoke, I remembered being awake most of the night, but at first I had only the vaguest memories of what had kept me up—maybe it was too much pig, too much beer, too much stress? After serving as the human snooze alarm for David—the king, every morning, of "five more minutes, five more minutes"—I finally glanced at the "worry pad" I kept next to my bed. It said:

YOU MUST CHOOSE MORE CHEERFUL BOOKS FOR THE BOOK CLUB.

AT EIGHT FIFTEEN A.M., I called Mom. She'd had a wonderful time at her birthday, she said, and was very grateful to David and me and to Doug and Nancy, who'd shared the tab and co-hosted.

"I've been sending lots of emails this morning," she added.

"What about?" I asked.

"Mostly arrangements for the trip your father and I are taking to England and Geneva this spring. And I also wanted to send lots of emails to people about *Continental Drift*. I kept waking up and thinking of people who should read it."

The Painted Veil

Prior to getting this sick, Mom hadn't been big on seeing doctors. When her previous one had retired, she told
the new doctor that she would come and see him only if she
was dying. So it was indeed very strange that the first time
she went to see him after her initial physical, when she was
just back from Afghanistan, she had indeed been dying, even
though she hadn't known it.

She'd been relatively healthy since the gallbladder operation a few years before, other than constantly picking up, as
I've written, a cough or a rash or a stomach bug on her trips.
And though she didn't take part in walks for the cure, or ever,
in my hearing, refer to herself as a breast cancer survivor, she
did consider it one of the major experiences of her life, again
framing it in terms not of bad luck that she'd had it but of
good fortune that she'd survived it.

Now she was seeing doctors all the time: Dr. O'Reilly, and
her GP, and the doctor who'd put in the stent and would re-
place it when it got infected, and the doctors at the urgent-care

facility where she would go when she got a sudden fever, and various specialists for various things.

In early April 2008, she would have her only treatment of the month, so that would be our next book club meeting. She was now more than six months past her initial diagnosis, during which time she'd been undergoing chemotherapy without pause. She'd been feeling increasingly "not great," and Dr. O'Reilly decided to give her body a few weeks to recover after this treatment.

Given that we were at Sloan-Kettering, Mom and I often found ourselves talking about doctors and books. But during this meeting, we talked of doctors *in* books, something you wind up doing frequently when you talk about Somerset Maugham, whose collection of short stories I'd picked up at the Vero Beach Book Center. I'd read the volume and then given it to Mom.

The Maugham stories had brought us back to his novels. Maugham wrote brilliantly about doctors, having trained and worked for six years as one. We didn't reread *Of Human Bondage,* his first major success, but we did decide that it was time to visit *The Painted Veil* again, the story of a doctor and his unfaithful wife, Kitty, who go, for very different reasons, to rural China to battle a cholera epidemic. He wrote it in 1925 when he was fifty-one years old, inspired in part by a story he came across in his travels about a woman in Hong Kong who had been involved in a scandal for cheating on her husband; but also, he said, by a scene in Book V of Dante's *Purgatorio,* in which a man who suspects his wife of adultery takes her to his castle, hoping the "noxious vapors" from the surrounding bogs and marshes will kill her.

The Painted Veil is one of those big-themed books that also tells a great story. It's about infidelity and forgiveness and goodness—and also courage. One of the great pleasures of the book is watching Kitty discover her courage and seeing her realize that it's not something you have or don't, like height, but something you can develop.

"I want to show you my favorite passage," Mom said, handing me her copy of the book. She was in her usual position on a comfy chair in the treatment room, pillow under her arm, Dixie cup of juice by her side. She had her finger on the part where Kitty is describing the nuns she's been working for in a Chinese orphanage:

> I can't tell you how deeply moved I've been by all I've seen at the convent. They're wonderful, those nuns, they make me feel utterly worthless. They give up everything, their home, their country, love, children, freedom; and all the little things which I sometimes think must be harder still to give up, flowers and green fields, going for a walk on an autumn day, books and music, comfort, everything they give up, everything. And they do it so that they may devote themselves to a life of sacrifice and poverty, obedience, killing work, and prayer.

I remembered noting that passage, but I also recalled what came after. I said to Mom: "But Kitty also wonders if maybe the nuns have been duped. What if there is no everlasting life? Then what was the meaning of all the nuns' sacrifice?"

Mom frowned. Just as another character corrects Kitty, so she corrected me. In the novel, Kitty is first told to consider the beauty of the nuns' lives as perfect works of art, no matter what comes after. Then she's asked to consider a symphony concert, where each musician plays his own instrument, content to add to a symphony that's no less lovely whether or not there is anyone to hear it. And finally she's told to contemplate the Tao: "Mighty is he who conquers himself."

Mom said, "Kitty admires the nuns' courage—but she's every bit as brave as them, braver. The nuns do what they do without fear; she does what she does in spite of it. I think that's what her friend means when he quotes from the Tao. And besides, the nuns' reward is in this life and in the life after. They haven't been duped at all."

Thanks to Maugham, or thanks to Kitty, we continued to talk about courage in general and Mom's in particular. It was something I wanted to discuss, but usually Mom would dismiss instantly anyone's efforts to portray her as brave; people were always asking her where she got the courage to go to Darfur or to Bosnia while it was being shelled, or to a leper colony.

"That last question always makes me cross," Mom said. "Everyone should know that leprosy is very hard to get and completely treatable. Visiting someone who has the flu requires far more bravery."

"Is that why you're always giving people crafts made by lepers—so you can take the opportunity to teach them that?" I asked. My brother and I would gently tease Mom about this proclivity.

"No, that's not it at all," Mom said, just a little indignantly. "I give people crafts made by people with leprosy because they're so beautiful."

And now people were constantly complimenting Mom on her courage in the face of her illness. "You are so brave," they would say to her. And they would say it to us, too. It became the second c-word. "You mother has so much courage."

"Well, how about when people compliment you for being brave fighting cancer?"

Mom didn't even pause. "The brave people are the ones like that young woman who was trying to figure out a way to buy medicine that she couldn't afford—without letting her mother know how much it was costing." That would be the woman for whom Mom had bought the medicine—they'd kept in touch. "I'm getting the best and most expensive care in the world, and I just don't think that's brave. If I were really brave, I'd do without it, so that the money could go for preventative care or for research."

As much as I tried that day, I couldn't get Mom to admit that she'd ever been courageous. The people she thought were brave were the people she sought to help and serve.

Mom would often talk about a refugee boy she'd met in a hospital in Afghanistan. He was the victim of a land mine and had lost a leg. She said to him that she brought greetings to him from schoolchildren in New York. "Tell them not to worry about me," this little boy told her from his hospital bed. "I still have one leg."

She'd talk, too, of John Kermue, a Liberian refugee she'd met in a camp where she'd taken his photo. A year later, when he'd heard from Mom that she was returning to Liberia for another fact-finding trip, he realized she wouldn't be able to locate him because he'd been moved to a different camp. And so he sneaked out and traveled to Monrovia in order to meet her at the airport, managing to convince a cordon of soldiers to let him into the heavily guarded terminal by saying he was there to meet his mother. They told him that if he was lying to them, they would kill him. When Mom got off the plane, she heard a voice shout, "Mom!" and instantly realized what was going on. "Son!" she shouted, embracing him. With her help, he would later come to America to study criminal justice.

She reminded me about the bravery of a Bosnian family she had met while she was in their country as an election monitor. They had to walk through a heavily land-mined area to get to their polling station but were willing to do so just in order to vote. To accompany them, Mom had been paired with a very young Dutch volunteer—the oldest monitor, Mom, with the youngest one. Mom and her fellow monitor wanted to walk ahead. "No," the family insisted. "We should walk first. You came to help us, not the other way around. So if anyone gets blown up, it should be us."

Then there was her friend Judy Mayotte, who'd had polio in college, taught herself to walk all over again, been a nun for a decade, and then become a world expert on refugees. She was the chair of the board of the Women's Commission for several of the years when Mom was the director.

In 1993 Judy was in southern Sudan, helping a community that desperately needed food. An airdrop was planned, and the planes were supposed to come in from one direction. They came in from another. A two-hundred-pound sack of food that was dropped from the sky missed its target and landed on Judy's leg, crushing it in ten places. Miraculously, a doctor doing relief work was right there: Judy was bleeding so much that at one point she had no pulse.

First, Judy's lower leg was amputated in Africa. Then, at the Mayo Clinic, most of the upper leg had to be amputated too. But Judy survived and continued to work with refugees.

"Fortunately, the leg knocked off was my polio leg," Judy would tell a *Chicago Tribune* reporter. "I've always been lucky."

All of them Mom considered brave.

"I understand, Mom, and I agree. Those are all amazing stories of courage. But didn't you need courage to go over the Khyber Pass, that time when you were shot at, when Afghanistan was all but closed? Or to take that Russian helicopter to get out of Darfur with all those unsecured logs rolling around inside?"

"No, that really isn't courage," my mother insisted. "I wanted to go to all those places, so how could that be brave? The people I'm talking about, they did things they didn't want to do because they felt they had to, or because they thought it was the right thing to do. The courage of that little boy, or the Bosnian family, or John, or Judy—that's very difficult to fathom."

"Okay, what about when you shared a hostel in Afghanistan with those twenty-three mujahideen warriors?"

"It was much braver of them," Mom said, laughing. "I think they were terrified of me."

It was growing late and a little cold. The chemo was taking a very long time. We both glanced up to make sure that there was enough saline left. Like two streams coming together, the saline had to drip into the same tube as the chemo so that they both could flow into Mom together. If the saline ran out before the chemo did, the nurses warned us—well then, the fluid might burn. That never happened, but it gave us something else to think about and was a merciful distraction. I felt that I was doing something if I simply glanced every now and then at the plastic saline pouch. Just as good kindergarten teachers give each kid a small job—cleaning the chalkboard duster, making sure the rabbit is fed—so, I think, the nurses

168 THE END OF YOUR LIFE BOOK CLUB

THE END OF YOUR LIFE BOOK CLUB

give family members little things to do so we can feel useful. Watch the saline. Check. Almost done. But so was the chemo.

"I think the other people who are really brave," Mom continued, "are people who take unpopular stands. Physical bravery is one thing. And sometimes, of course, physical bravery isn't bravery at all but people being foolish—especially when they put other people in danger who need to rescue them. Wherever I went on refugee missions, I always checked with the local staff to make sure we weren't taking unnecessary risks or making them do anything that made them uncomfortable. That's very important."

Soon the saline and the chemo were both gone. The nurse came in to unhook Mom. Usually Mom popped right up after that and gathered her things, and we were on our way. Today she remained in the chair.

"Are you okay, Mom?" I asked. She looked very tired.

"I'm feeling a little sad. I know there's a life everlasting—but I wanted to do so much more here."

I didn't know what to say. So I just said, "I know."

"Still," Mom said, "I have a strong feeling I'm going to have some very good news soon."

MOM HAD BEEN increasingly in touch with her old Harvard friend, the one with whom she'd recently reconnected, the one who'd given her *Daily Strength for Daily Needs*. That was his first great gift to her. As they'd talked over the next few months, he was moved by her stories of Afghanistan and her passion for education. He also loved books as much as she did, maybe more so. Then one day, out of the blue, he told her that he hated seeing her work so hard. So he had a deal to propose:

If he gave some money to build the Afghan library, would she promise to take it a bit easier? Yes, she promised him. She would.

A FEW MORNINGS after the book club meeting when we'd discussed *The Painted Veil*, my phone rang. Usually I called Mom, but this time she couldn't wait: she had something urgent to tell me.

"You'll never believe it," she said to me on the phone that morning. "You'll never believe it. And you can't say anything. But that friend who doesn't want me to work so hard on the library . . ."

"Yes," I said.

"Well, he just told me he's donating one million dollars to build it."

Murder in the Cathedral

For days after the news of the million-dollar gift for the Afghan library, Mom was as happy and optimistic as I'd seen her since she got sick. By the middle of May, though, she was running high fevers that not even several courses of antibiotics could tame. And a week before she was to leave for Geneva to see my sister and her family, one of Mom's friends died.

Of course, Mom would be at the funeral and the memorial service. As we stood in her kitchen, me nursing a tiny, tepid espresso, I asked her if it was depressing going to funerals and memorial services when she herself had a limited amount of time left.

"Funerals and memorial services are just part of life. And I do know that there is life everlasting." Usually Mom said *believe*. Recently, I noted, she said *know*.

"And how do you decide if you should go to a service or not? I mean, what if you didn't know the person well, or maybe at all, but only knew the spouse or a child?"

"If you need to think about whether you should go or not, you should go. But if you can't go, you can't. Then you write a nice note as soon as you can." Mom looked distracted for a second. "Darn, there was something I wanted to tell you and now I've forgotten."

This wasn't chemo brain. Mom always had an impossibly long list of things she wanted to tell us. No one could be expected to remember them all. We talked awhile longer, and then her face lit up—she'd remembered the thing she wanted to tell me.

"Oh, yes. Let me show you something." She left the kitchen but returned almost immediately, with a printed note card in her hand. It said, "At this very sad time, our family thanks you for your kind expression of sympathy." Mom had crossed out *very sad* and inserted the words *the Schwalbe* in place of *our* before *family*.

"I think this is a really nice way to thank people for their condolence notes," she said. "But do take out 'very sad,' as it sounds a little gloomy, and you should also make it more personal with our name. You'll want to write something on the inside of your note that acknowledges something they said in theirs. And I know this one is in black ink, but I think you should use blue ink—both for the engraved words and for what you write. The black is too somber."

So that's what Mom had forgotten to tell me and then remembered—how to answer the condolence notes we would be receiving after her death.

MOM AND DAD went to Geneva in April 2008. She shivered from fever and chills all the way over. While she was there, she was in and out of the hospital, but she was determined to spend time with Milo and Cy—even though her body wasn't up to it. She had to fly back early. Mom and Dad loved their travels together—seeing new places, going to museums and concerts, meeting friends and friends of friends. It was one of the great passions they shared (though Dad preferred to go only on the more comfortable trips, leaving the refugee-camp and developing-world travel entirely to Mom). So they were both disappointed to be returning home, although not yet willing to give up on the idea of more trips abroad in the future.

Once home, Mom immersed herself in planning a board meeting for the Afghan library. The million dollars had turned the project from a mad dream into something that would almost definitely happen: it was a third of the money they needed and would allow them not only to break ground on the main library in Kabul but also to fund some of the traveling libraries. Mom, of course, hadn't held up her end of the bargain. She wouldn't stop working on it—perhaps she was working even harder than she had been before.

We had chosen as our next book club selection Jhumpa Lahiri's new collection of short stories, *Unaccustomed Earth,* as we'd both loved her 2003 novel *The Namesake* and her first book of stories, *Interpreter of Maladies,* which had won the Pulitzer in 1999. Born in London in 1967, Lahiri had moved as a child with her parents to the United States. Lahiri's immigrant characters often have experienced the same kinds of dislocation that Mom had seen in her refugee friends; many of them grapple with balancing two cultures, trying to preserve the known while embracing the new.

Lahiri makes the connection between immigrants and

refugees explicit as she describes, in the new book, one character who has become a war photographer: "He was reminded of his family's moves every time he visited another refugee camp, every time he watched a family combing through rubble for their possessions. In the end, that was life: a few plates, a favorite comb, a pair of slippers, a child's string of beads."

The collection begins with a story of a man whose wife has just died, and his visit to his adult daughter and her family. It ends with a cycle of stories about two characters, one of whose mothers dies of cancer. We talked about those stories, but not more so than all the others and not focusing on the deaths or the cancer. In the first tale, the death has taken place before the story begins; in the story nearer the end, the mother, for the longest time, doesn't want anyone to know she's ill. The emphasis in both tales is on the survivors—a father and his daughter; a father and his son—and how their changed or changing circumstances bring to center stage their inability to communicate.

Mom and I discussed the jumbo-size gap that exists between generations in so much of Lahiri's work, and how tough life can be for the children of immigrants and refugees. We discussed the Lahiri characters as though they were friends of ours, or even relatives. Why didn't this one say this, or tell someone that, or let anyone know she or he was so unhappy, so lonely, so scared? Lahiri's characters, just like people all around us, are constantly telling each other important things, but not necessarily in words.

WHEN WE TALKED about what book to select next, Mom again said that she really wanted to go back to something she'd already read and loved. After some thought, she decided it should be T. S. Eliot's 1935 verse drama *Murder in the Cathedral*. Mom had been in the chorus in a joint Harvard and Radcliffe production of this play when she was at college.

Ever since I could remember, Mom and Dad kept a handsome slipcased copy of *Murder in the Cathedral* on a special part of the bookshelf, in the center, along with other cherished volumes, including the leather-bound collections—Thoreau, Dickens—that Mom had inherited from her grandfather. The reason this stuck in my mind was that I first encountered it as a child in Cambridge while searching their shelves for a mystery to read. At the time, I was still obsessed with Alistair MacLean but had run through everything by him that I had on hand. *Murder in the Cathedral* sounded like just the thing to follow *Force 10 from Navarone*. I read several incomprehensible (to me then) pages before roughly putting it back on the shelf, judging it a work of very limited appeal—akin to a book titled *Eton Repointed* about fixing the grout in Eton's stonework that my father loved, which sat near it.

A FEW WEEKS after choosing *Murder in the Cathedral,* Mom and I found ourselves sitting in the not-so-nice environs of the urgent-care waiting room, as she had spiked a fever. We were waiting to learn if she would be able to take some antibiotics and go home, or if she would need to stay in the hospital. We'd both finished *Murder in the Cathedral.* I asked her whether it had been nostalgia that made her want to read the Eliot play again. She said it wasn't that at all. She'd wanted to revisit it for two reasons: the beauty of the language and the character of Thomas à Becket, a man who accepts martyrdom rather than ignore his conscience. "I find the play very inspiring," she said.

As we waited for her to be called to the examining room, Mom told me that when she'd recently been talking about the courage to take an unpopular stand, it was Becket she'd had in mind. Then, as we continued to sit there, with all the urgent-care activity around us—people pacing or quietly moaning, nurses rushing in and out—she added, "He's also able to accept death. He's not happy about it, but he's perfectly calm. When I stop all this treatment, it will be because it's time to stop."

"Are you worried about how you are going to make that choice?"

Mom shook her head. "Not at all. I'm sure the doctors will let us know."

I wasn't so sure of that. Mom had phenomenal doctors, the best, but this was the trickiest area of all. How does a doctor tell you that it's over, that there are things they could do but probably shouldn't, and that if your aim is quality of life and not quantity of life, there simply are no good next treatments? Many doctors simply avoid this conversation.

I know that doctors have some patients who beg them for the truth, no matter how grim the prognosis, and who assure their doctors that they can take the harshest news, and who say they have no desire for heroic and painful measures that will allow them to eke out a few more weeks or months. But many of these same patients end up being the ones who can't bear to hear the truth, and who, near the end, want to do everything possible and even painful to postpone death, if only by days. What could be more human than to want to live?

Dr. O'Reilly had never given Mom a timetable. She listened to what Mom wanted, prescribed the best treatments she could, and adjusted them, balancing their efficacy and side effects according to Mom's desire to have as much good time left as possible, not as much time as possible regardless of whether it was good or not. Our visits with her were confined to discussions of how Mom was feeling and whether the treatment was working. We only looked ahead far enough to schedule new scans and to plan Mom's treatments around trips she wanted to take—London, Geneva to see the grandchildren, Florida. Dr. O'Reilly would help her take as many of these trips as possible.

Soon it was time for Mom to see the urgent-care doctor who would evaluate her; I was left in the waiting room, wondering whether the doctor would tell us Mom needed to stay or could go home. There would be no ambiguity. It would be one or the other.

My thoughts returned to *Unaccustomed Earth* and Lahiri's skill in capturing the subtle ways that people communicate or don't. As a reader, you're often inside one or more characters' heads, so you know what they're feeling, even if they can't exactly say it, or they say it so obliquely that the other characters don't catch it. Readers are frequently reminded of the gulf between what people say and what they mean, and such moments prod us to become more attuned to gesture, tone, and language. After all, we each reveal ourselves through a dizzying number of what poker players call "tells"—verbal and visual clues that display true intention to anyone observant enough to notice them.

Mom was a reader and a listener. When would it be time for Mom to stop the treatments? I thought back to her exact words. She hadn't answered me by saying that she was sure the doctor would "tell" us. What Mom had said was that she was sure the doctor would "let us know." The important thing was to pay attention.

AS IT TURNED out, Mom would spend six days in the hospital with a raging infection. The good news was that a recent scan had shown that the tumors, though no longer shrinking, weren't growing. The other good news was that it was now spring. The return of warm weather had a salutary effect on Mom, even if she could only glimpse it from a hospital window. The infection had been caused by a blockage in the stent that kept bile flowing between Mom's pancreas and liver; to fix the problem, they needed to slip a plastic sleeve inside the stent; and it took IV antibiotics and two blood transfusions before Mom was well enough to leave.

It would be one of many such hospital stays, each one frightening for a variety of reasons. When you're sick, just about the last place you want to be is in a hospital. We were constantly worried that Mom would pick up an infection there, and several times she did: a staph infection a few times and a case of C. *diff.,* a horrible bacterial infection (full name: *Clostridium difficile*) that would recur.

When Mom was in the hospital, Dad would stay by her bedside as long as visiting hours allowed. Doug and I (and Nina when she was in town) would visit as much as possible, with Mom always suggesting at some point that we take Dad out for a burger to give him a break from the place. Over lunch, we'd chat breezily with Dad about our work and lives and try to figure out how many days Mom would need to remain in the hospital this time around. Following Dr. O'Reilly's lead and our own inclination, we never went near a discussion of a timetable beyond that: how many more days, or weeks, or months, or years we might have with Mom—not just because it was impossible to know but because it was too painful.

I remember this stay well because Mom was fixated on getting out by a particular date, and she grew more and more anxious as that date approached.

On May 16, Marymount Manhattan College, where Mom had been a trustee, was going to be giving her an honorary doctorate of laws, alongside the religious historian Elaine Pagels and the philanthropist Theresa Lang. It would be at the Marymount commencement ceremony at Avery Fisher Hall in Lincoln Center. Mom would be introduced by a refugee whom she'd helped attend Marymount; she was then to give a short speech. Mom was tremendously moved by this honor and desperate to be there.

I'd been anxious about the birthday party, but I was even more anxious about the honorary degree. Once again, however, I needn't have worried. Mom was, in her own words, incredibly lucky—again. She was out of the hospital in time. Nina had been home with Mom for a week and was not just a great help on things medical but gave a huge boost to her spirits. So now, though weak and hovering around one hundred pounds, Mom felt strong enough to stand up in Avery Fisher Hall and speak.

I've been many times to this enormous concert hall, but always to hear one orchestra or another. Now the auditorium was packed with graduating students, in cap and gown, and their families, draped with cameras. Mom looked tiny behind the podium on the vast, brightly lit stage. She started her speech by calling Marymount her favorite institution of higher learning in the United States, which got a big whoop from the audience, who knew that she'd held positions at Harvard and Radcliffe. She then told the story of the boy who had lost a leg and of the Bosnian family who insisted on walking ahead of her through the field of land mines to get to the polling station. And also an anecdote I hadn't heard before—about a boy in a refugee camp who begged her to start a school there because, he said, "boys get in trouble when we have nothing to do all day."

Most on Mom's mind was the upcoming presidential election in the United States. She ended her remarks with a story of a pamphlet that she'd been handed when she was visiting an African country where people were able to vote freely for the first time. The pamphlet was called *The Ten Commandments for Voters,* and she read aloud to the graduates just a few of them. There she was, almost disappearing behind the podium. Her hair looked thinner, but the robes she wore hid just how much weight she'd lost. Her voice, however, was loud and clear. She read:

1. You have nothing to fear. Remember that your vote is secret. Only you and your God know how you vote.
2. People who promise things that they never give are like clouds and wind that bring no rain: do not be misled by promises.
3. Your vote is your power: use it to make a difference to your life and your country.

Most of the students were, like her, passionate supporters of Obama. They knew just what she was talking about and cheered.

Then she continued: "I have learned from the refugees I have met over the last eighteen years to have hope for the future—and that is what has helped me through my life, and I know that has been important to the Class of 2008. I wish you all that for yourselves, and so much more."

I couldn't stop crying, and I was surrounded by a thousand proud parents, most of whom were also crying, but with tears of joy to see their children graduate. I thought about Mom's instructions for the acknowledgment cards we would need to print after her death, and I looked around at the rows of our family and friends who had come to support Mom, and I knew that before too long they would be sending me condolence notes and letters, and I would be sending them back these printed cards—personalized, of course, just as Mom had instructed. In blue ink, not black.

What's odd about commencement is that so many people think of it as the end of something, the end of high school or college—but that's not what the word means at all. It means the beginning, the start of something new.

Wherever You Go,
There You Are

The wig reappeared in August 2008. Mom hadn't worn it at all, as she still had enough of her own hair not to feel too self-conscious in public, but now that she was having more chemo, she thought she'd try to improve the wig in case she lost more hair. Mom's yoga teacher, who had become her friend and guide in various holistic therapies like biofeedback and meditation, knew someone who could make the wig better, make the color a little truer to Mom's, and make it less big.

We'd spent the early part of the summer reading various books about current affairs, the upcoming presidential elections, and Obama, whom Mom loved and respected more each day. But for our August book club meeting, Mom wanted a change of pace, so we decided to discuss Jon Kabat-Zinn's books on mindfulness and meditation. The first Kabat-Zinn book we'd read was *Full Catastrophe Living,* which details how meditating and finding ways to handle the stress in one's life can aid in healing. Kabat-Zinn has a Ph.D. in molecular biology from MIT and is the founder of the Stress Reduction Clinic at University of Massachusetts Medical School. The book, originally published in 1990, cites studies he and other scientists had done to show the ways the mind can help heal the body. We now read his 1994 book, *Wherever You Go, There You Are,* which is more of a guide to meditation and mindfulness, of being present in your life, not just to reduce stress and aid in healing but to live more fully every minute. "Mindfulness means paying attention in a particular way: on purpose, in the present moment, and nonjudgmentally," writes Kabat-Zinn. "This kind of attention nurtures greater awareness, clarity, and acceptance of present-moment reality."

"You should do yoga and maybe even try meditation. I think it really makes a difference," Mom said to me when we met.

"I know," I replied. "But I don't have time." As soon as I said it, I realized how ridiculous it sounded. Compared to Mom, I had a lot of time. "Still, just reading things like this helps, I think," I added hopefully. "Maybe reading this book is a form of meditation."

"Maybe," said Mom. "But it's certainly not the same as yoga."

There was a passage in Kabat-Zinn's most recent book, *Coming to Our Senses,* that I'd marked to show Mom. Unfortunately, I couldn't remember what I'd marked, why, or where I'd put the book. It was a book I'd helped edit, so it was particularly irritating not to be able to get my hands on my copy. I was sure I would eventually find it under one of the piles of papers scattered around our apartment. But I was just too wrecked to search for it. Which perhaps proved Mom's point.

"You look exhausted," Mom would say to me whenever I saw her. I'm sure I did. I had decided that my new venture should be a cooking website. So I was racing around town from meeting to meeting, usually soaked in sweat due to the heat and my nerves, trying, with two partners, to get the website designed and funded and built, rushing in and out of a shared fourth-floor-walk-up office that I'd rented from friends, pausing just long enough in their wine shop below to have a quick chat and to grab a bottle to take home or to a dinner. I spoke to my brother and sister about our busy lives: much as we wanted to, we all felt that if we slowed down dramatically to spend more time with Mom, we would communicate to her that we thought she was dying very soon. And it was also clear that Mom didn't want us hovering. While she was relatively well, she had people to see and things to do.

THE EARLY AUTUMN passed with many good days for Mom, but also plenty of not-so-good ones. It was now almost a full year since she'd been diagnosed. Fever brought her to the hospital several more times in quick succession, and again she sometimes had to stay over. It was during a hospital over-night in September 2008 that we saw, for the first time, Mom experiencing what even she would describe as pain. It was terrible to watch. She bit her lower lip, closed her eyes, and doubled over. When the spasm subsided, Mom asked for a painkiller. Up to that day, she hadn't taken anything stronger than an Advil. They gave her a Percocet, and that seemed to do the trick.

"I feel like such a whiner and complainer," Mom said as she took the pill.

I was there with my father, and we shouldn't have, but we both burst out laughing. Mom looked annoyed.

"Mom. You have cancer. You can ask for a painkiller every now and then. It's okay."

"I know that," Mom said, a little sharply. "I just haven't needed them." She paused. "I've also been thinking a lot about that first time Rodger and I talked and about how much pain he said I'd be in." She and Rodger had chatted many times since that conversation and had seen each other on one of his visits to the city. Rodger had moved to Denver years before, leaving behind his best friends and busy life in New York, to take a challenging job running a gay rights foundation, after nursing both a brother with AIDS and the friend with pancreatic cancer through the last stages of their illnesses. Neither Mom nor I ever told him how much that initial call had upset her, and both of our friendships with him had continued undiminished and unabated. "I think that scary conversation with Rodger was actually really a blessing and maybe something he did on purpose," she continued. "No matter how uncomfortable I am, I keep thinking, *Well, it's not nearly as bad as Rodger said it would be.* And that's been a real gift. But I'm worried about Rodger—he's in terrible pain from his back problem, and I don't think people realize what it's like for him to be in pain all the time, not to have good days and not-so-good days, like I have, but constant pain."

When we went to Dr. O'Reilly for Mom's next checkup, we got a full report from her last hospital stay. Mom's colon was inflamed—that was almost certainly thanks to C. *diff.*, the tough-to-treat bacteria she'd picked up during one of the previous hospital overnights. The pain was from the infection, not the cancer. Mom was also to take a second break from chemo before they started a new treatment—the most recent course of chemo had been too hard to tolerate and not as effective as they had hoped.

As for the tumors, they were still smaller than a year ago when Mom had her first scan. While Dr. O'Reilly spoke, I scribbled down notes and asked questions. I did this every time. If I didn't write down everything, I'd remember nothing.

Dr. O'Reilly then had a topic she wanted to approach gingerly. She sat down and asked Mom how she was dealing with all the needle sticks. Mom had started to look like an IV drug user, with all the track marks up and down her arms. The endless blood testing and chemo had taken their toll, and the search for a usable vein had become an increasingly brutal game of hunt and peck. Dr. O'Reilly said she wanted to implant a port under Mom's skin, just at the top of her breastbone. This would make everything easier and allow for a new treatment, during which Mom would be hooked up to a little bottle, like a water bottle, but full of chemo—she'd carry it around for a few days until it was empty. The process is called a Baxter infusion; they would teach her and me how to hook it up and unhook it, though Mom could always go to the clinic and have it done there.

She felt Mom's best option was to try 5-FU, a chemotherapy that's delivered this way, along with Leucovorin, a kind of folic acid that makes it more effective. She warned of side effects that included the return of the dreaded mouth sores, fatigue, diarrhea, and sensitivity in Mom's hands and feet. But she thought the side effects would be far less severe than those the first chemo had eventually caused.

There was literature on it, if we wanted.

I always love that use of the word *literature*. So our book club now included information about drugs written by folks at pharmaceutical companies. Mom took the literature, thanked Dr. O'Reilly profusely as always, and started to head out.

I reminded Mom that she had one more question she wanted to ask.

"That's okay, Will," Mom said.

Dr. O'Reilly wanted to know what.

"Don't bother the doctor with that," Mom said, now exasperated that I'd ignored her hint.

"Mom has an important dinner on November twelfth," I said.

"It's the annual dinner of the International Rescue Committee," Mom said.

"And she really wants to feel well for it," I added. "I've heard that Ritalin can help. Is that right?"

I'd done enough drugs in high school—and had enough friends who still did them—to know these things. Ritalin is a form of speed. It calms kids down but increases energy for adults.

"Yes, that's a good idea," said Dr. O'Reilly. "Many patients think it helps. I'll give you a prescription for it," she said to Mom. "You may want to try one first on a day where you don't have something important to do—just to see how you react to it."

MOM LIKED THE Ritalin. And she found it had a terrific and unexpected side effect—it helped her read. The day she first tried it, she was tired and uncomfortable and having trouble concentrating. She popped the Ritalin right before she sat down with Thomas Mann's *Joseph and His Brothers,* a fifteen-hundred-page book that she'd been attempting to read after a friend gave it to her. Mann spent a decade's worth of work on the book, on and off, between 1926 and 1942, during which time he also wrote *Death in Venice, Tonio Kröger, The Magic Mountain*, and *Mario and the Magician*. With the Ritalin, Mom found herself well into *Joseph* before she needed to come up for air. I, meanwhile, was still tearing apart my apartment looking for the Kabat-Zinn book I'd misplaced. When Mom finished the Mann, she gave me her copy as our next book club pick. What she didn't give me was any Ritalin to go with it.

I TRIED TO read the Mann several times but always gave up. I finally admitted this to Mom.

"It's not easy," she said. "But it's amazing. It's like a catalog of every behavior and dilemma you could ever imagine. And it's quite funny, too."

"Really?" I asked. I'm sure I sounded dubious.

"But did you read the foreword? Because even the translator doesn't suggest beginning at the beginning. He says you should start about one hundred pages in and then go back to the beginning when you're done."

Everything should have been great for the next few weeks—Mom was on vacation, as it were, from the chemo so that she would be in better shape when she started the newest treatment. But she still kept getting fevers and needing to go to the hospital. Another staph infection had Dad hurrying around their neighborhood on a Friday night, he told us the next day, trying to find some pharmacy that had the six-hundred-dollar antibiotic that could cure it. Fevers tended to pop up after hours, when the Memorial Sloan-Kettering pharmacy was closed.

Mom was trying to keep up with all her friends, through a barrage of emails and also visits, which she loved and planned her days around. She would time her medicine, and her energy, with someone's expected arrival. She'd be ready and sitting on her favorite part of the sofa; she'd have some snacks on the table, ice in the ice bowl, coffee or tea during the day, soda and wine in the evening. When the appointed time came, the clock would tick by heavily until her guest arrived. But after a half hour or so, the visitor could see the energy draining from Mom's body, her face becoming increasingly clenched as she tried to stay focused on the conversation.

By the end of October, Mom started to feel better. The new antibiotic was finally working. Dad went with Mom when they installed the port in her chest. I spent the day with her when they gave her the first treatment with it, hooking up the bottle. They showed me how to unclip it once it was empty. I'm not very mechanically inclined, but I was determined to learn how and did.

That day was a long one with lots of waiting. I had many cups of mocha over nearly eight hours. And we had lots of time to talk. We'd both just read *Home,* the latest book by Marilynne Robinson, the author of *Gilead.* Thomas Mann would have to wait, mostly because I'd yet to return to his fifteen-hundred-page book. *Home,* a retelling of the prodigal son story using many of the same characters from *Gilead,* presented its own challenges to us. The tale of the prodigal son, both in its original Bible version and the Robinson update, is an unsettling tale for any child to discuss with a parent.

"The thing about the prodigal son story that's always bothered me," I told Mom, "is that the son is welcomed back so enthusiastically because of all the trouble he's caused, not in spite of it. I mean, what if he'd returned prosperous and well fed, not broke and starving? Would they have given him a party and slayed the fatted calf? I don't think so."

"I think they would have," Mom said. "The point of the story is that he was lost and then came back. It's about salvation, not hunger."

"I wonder," I said, unwilling to cede the point.

My brother was hardly a prodigal son. He always had a job and was raising three terrific kids. And yet he is wilder and freer than I am—more demonstrative and probably more honest. With his thick dark hair, he was always a bit more Rhett, and I tended more toward Ashley. (Okay, he's not Clark Gable and I'm not Leslie Howard, but the point is in the contrast.) So at times he's been further out than me. He occasionally had arguments and points of friction between him and our parents that I never had. And when he returned—hours or days later, as affectionate and voluble as ever—there was a relief and joy that made me feel, well, jealous. Prodigal son. Other son. After Mom and I had discussed *Home,* I joked with my brother that I wished I could be a little more prodigal. He assured me that it wasn't all it was cracked up to be. He also pointed out to me something I'd missed about the book club: Mom had finally succeeded in getting me to talk about faith and religion and even Bible stories, something she'd been trying to do for years.

⋄⋄⋄⋄⋄⋄

NOW THAT MOM had a port installed in her chest, it meant that instead of hours of chemo every few weeks, she would for a few days every fortnight wander around her apartment and the city with a bottle strapped to her midriff. She jokingly told everyone she felt like a suicide bomber. "But no complaints!" she was always careful to add.

She was also jumpier than I'd ever seen her—but this wasn't due to the new treatment; it was anxiety in the last weeks leading up to the presidential election. Mom was beside herself. One of her friends, a renowned psychologist who is active in the Democratic party and who had a son working for the Obama campaign, spent hours with Mom analyzing every fluctuation in the polls and was usually able to reassure her when the numbers didn't look good. But if it wasn't for Ambien, I don't think Mom would have slept at all. She told all of us that if Obama didn't win, she was leaving the country, cancer or no.

"Have you read Obama's memoir?" she asked me during one of our morning calls.

I hadn't yet.

"You have to," she said.

I promised I would.

"I mean it, Will. I can't believe you haven't. You'll love it."

In the months leading up to the election, to an extent I freely admitted to myself, I'd come to place tremendous significance on a connection between an Obama victory and Mom's prognosis. It wasn't superstition—I was desperately worried about Mom's mood if he lost the election. I thought particularly about Kabat-Zinn's research and the proven links between depression and health.

As soon as I heard Obama had won, I was filled with hope. I knew Mom wouldn't get well, but now I allowed myself to believe that she would have months where she would be better. Maybe it was superstitious after all.

MOM WAS ON an incredible no-Ritalin-necessary high for the next week. A trip to the hospital didn't even dampen her spirits: she was just dehydrated, a side effect of all the pills she was taking. The annual International Rescue Committee Freedom Award dinner was now days away. She was going to be well for that, she was sure.

The day before the dinner, I finally discovered, hiding under the bed, the Kabat-Zinn book I'd been trying to find for weeks: *Coming to Our Senses: Healing Ourselves and the World Through Mindfulness.* It's another massive book.

The page I'd marked, and wanted to show Mom, was about interruptions. It's a section where Kabat-Zinn points out that we all know it's wrong to interrupt each other. And yet we constantly interrupt ourselves. We do it when we check our emails incessantly—or won't simply let a phone go to voicemail when we're doing something we enjoy—or when we don't think a thought through, but allow our minds to fix on temporary concerns or desires.

In however much time I had left with Mom, I realized, I needed to focus more—to be careful not to interrupt our conversations with other conversations. Every hospital is, as I've noted, an interruption machine—a flood of people come to poke you and prod you and ask you questions. But modern life itself is an interruption machine: phone calls, emails, texts, news, television, and our own restless minds. The greatest gift you can give anyone is your undivided attention—yet I'd been constantly dividing mine. No one was getting it, not even me.

The morning of the IRC dinner, I called Mom to find out when she planned to arrive. "Just before the food is served," she said. "To preserve my strength. I don't think I can stand around through the cocktails." Held in the cavernous gilded ballroom of the Waldorf Astoria Hotel, the dinner and award ceremony were powerful and moving as always. Throughout the evening, I watched Mom greet people, dozens and dozens of people.

How do you do that? How do you talk to fifty or a hundred different people without interrupting them or yourself? And I understood suddenly what Kabat-Zinn means about mindfulness—it isn't a trick or a gimmick. It's being present in the moment. When I'm with you, I'm with you. Right now. That's all. No more and no less.

Before dessert they showed a video called *Refugee Journeys,* which ends with a montage of a refugee mother embracing her children as she is reunited with them. One thousand people in the ballroom of the Waldorf Astoria Hotel wept as they watched it. Friends at our table were sobbing. It was a very emotional night.

Kabat-Zinn writes, "You can't stop the waves, but you can learn to surf."

OBAMA HAD BEEN elected president. The Freedom Awards dinner was a triumph, and Mom had been there to enjoy it. The

C. *diff.* seemed genuinely gone. And, after months of work, and with a lot of help, my website partners (a digital-guru friend from college and a more recent pal from publishing) and I had even launched the cooking site, without a glitch. Now Thanksgiving—still my favorite holiday—was almost upon us.

The information my siblings and I had gleaned from the Internet had said people with metastatic pancreatic cancer usually didn't make it past six months. Mom was well past a year. That Friday I would accompany her on a visit to the doctor for another installation of the "suicide bomber" bottle, and so our book club would have its next meeting. She was eager to tell the doctor how well she was feeling—she knew Dr. O'Reilly would be pleased. And to thank her for the Ritalin—it had made a difference, Mom thought, in helping her enjoy the IRC dinner.

Her appointment was set for eleven fifteen. I arrived at ten forty-five, in case they could see her early, as they sometimes could. When I got to the waiting room, Mom was in her usual seat. But she looked just awful. Something had gone wrong.

"Have you heard about David?" she asked me. I had so many Davids in my life, I had to ask her which one. "David Rohde, the young *New York Times* reporter," she said. "My friend and fellow board member on the Afghan project."

"No, what's wrong?"

"He's been kidnapped in Afghanistan. He was there researching his book. It's just hideous and everyone is frantic. But you can't say anything to anyone. They need to keep it completely secret. They feel that's the only chance they have for getting him out."

"How did you hear?"

"From other board members who heard from Nancy." Mom was referring to Nancy Hatch Dupree, who was still in Afghanistan, working on plans for the library. "David and Nancy had dinner in Kabul just a few nights ago. She says she told him she didn't think it was safe for him to go where he wanted to go. But he said he needed some more information for his book. And he had a lot of trust in the people who were helping him. Damn," she said. My mother never said "damn."

We sat in silence. She bit her lower lip.

"I'm sorry," she said after a while. "I really wanted to talk about the Obama book today and the Mann. But I'm afraid just now I can't concentrate on anything else. You know, David was just married a few months ago—Kristen must be beside herself. I'll send her a note as soon as I get home. And I'll ask Nancy if there's anything we can do. And when I'm done with all that, I'll pray."

Mom had prayer. I would have to try to make do with mindfulness. It didn't seem like there was going to be anything else we could do to help. But that wasn't the way my mother's mind worked.

"The worse it gets in Afghanistan," she added, "the more convinced I am that we need to see this library project through. It may not be the biggest thing we can do, but it's something. And we've just got to do something."

This, I finally realized, was how Mom was able to focus when I was not. It was how she was able to be present with me, present with the people at a benefit or the hospital. She felt whatever emotions she felt, but feeling was never a useful substitute for doing, and she never let the former get in the way of the latter. If anything, she used her emotions to motivate her and help her concentrate. The emphasis for her was always on doing what needed to be done. I had to learn this lesson while she was still there to teach me.

Kokoro

That autumn, right after the election, in between everything else we were reading, we found ourselves turning
back, from time to time, to short stories—ones that ran in *The
New Yorker,* anthologies, and the Somerset Maugham stories
I'd picked up in Vero Beach.

There was one Maugham story in particular that we loved:
"The Verger."

Like so many of Maugham's stories, "The Verger" makes
you smile. It starts with a humble man being suddenly fired
from the only job he's ever known when a new job require-
ment is imposed from above. I think part of the reason Mom
loved this story is that it's about fate and the surprisingly
happy turns that life can take, financial and otherwise; after
losing his job, things go fantastically well for the protagonist.
Because Mom had deeply involved herself with people whose
lives had been turned upside down, she found that stories of
people whose lives were then turned right side up held enormous appeal.

"The Verger" had a special irony in November 2008: the financial world was crumbling around us, the stock market was a disaster, Lehman Brothers had just failed, and the U.S. car industry was on the verge of bankruptcy. At the end of the story, a banker urges our now rich hero to take all his cash deposits and put them into "gilt-edged securities," which fortunately he both won't and, in a sly twist, *can't* do.

We spent a fair bit of book club time talking about the market and the global financial collapse. It was hard not to, as the paper was filled with news of it every day, and both of us were avid newspaper readers. The collapse also had particular resonance for me, as I was still trying to get funding for the newly launched but barely funded website. Needless to say, there was no one at the time writing checks, and I began to doubt my wisdom and sanity as I poured more and more of my own savings into the venture.

Sometimes as we sat there, me drinking my mocha, staring out at the gray November sky, when we ran out of things to talk about, I would check the little stock ticker on my iPhone and announce the bad news to Mom (and several other people around us, who were curious). The market was down 100 points, or 200, or 300. Mom had a grim fascination with it. She certainly wanted to know the news, but it couldn't help but depress her. She wanted to leave money behind for us, for the grandkids' college funds, and she wanted money to go to her favorite charities. She had given me a list of charities to receive money in lieu of flowers that I was to mention in her paid obituary. But she'd been on so many boards, in addition to the worthy places where she'd worked, that she found it difficult to narrow down the list, so periodically she would give me an institution or charity that she wanted to add, and then another, and then another—and then think twice and take the number back down to four or five, but always trying to feature a mix of different types and include ones that hadn't received her full attention over the last few years.

Because my venture was a cooking website, I found myself talking a great deal about cooks and cookbooks and recipes. And all this around Mom, who had increasing difficulty finding anything she could bear to eat. One friend had brought her hot chocolate from Venice. She'd liked that—so we searched the city for similarly rich chocolate for her. She also liked Jell-O. And soup, so long as it was broth soup and not cream soup. But she continued to have dinner parties, at which she would eat as much as she could. And she was determined to have Thanksgiving dinner. It would be small. Family and a few friends. But unlike last year, when she hadn't been well enough to go to Tom and Andy's, she would host it. My brother's first wife, Fabienne, with whom we'd all stayed very close—Mom had even traveled to Europe for her wedding to her new husband two years before—had come from Paris just to see Mom, and she would be there. (Fabienne is the mother of Nico, the oldest grandchild.) We'd start early and end early. But there would be turkey, and pies, and Brussels sprouts, and sweet potatoes.

"Are you sure you're up to hosting this, Mom?" we all asked her.

"If I don't feel well, I'll just go in the back. But I have so much to be thankful for this year. I wasn't at all sure I would still be here. And I think of other people who can't be here. I've been praying David Rohde would be home for Thanksgiving, but it just doesn't look like that's going to happen. So now I'm praying for something different. I'm praying for him to be back with Kristen for Christmas."

Mom had continued to be in touch with Nancy Hatch Dupree about David, but as everyone was still convinced that the best thing for David was to keep everything quiet, she couldn't talk to anyone else. Nancy had received word through her channels that he was probably, for the moment, as okay as you can be when you've been kidnapped by the Taliban. But whatever could be done for him would take a very long time. Whenever Mom mentioned David to me, she reminded me that I couldn't tell a soul. She even started to refer to him as "our young friend" to avoid saying his name. Nancy was remarkably confident that he would eventually come back—but she told Mom that the situation in the whole region had gone rapidly downhill. Peshawar, where she lived much of the time, she called the capital of kidnappings—and said she went out only when it was completely necessary.

Nancy's optimism gave Mom a great deal of hope—and now she checked her email every few hours for news of David. She'd also added him to her daily prayers—and to the weekly church prayers, so that the whole congregation could pray for him, though just as "David" to preserve his anonymity. Obama's election had preoccupied Mom for the better part of a year, and now David's kidnapping began to play, in some way, the same kind of role in her life. It wasn't that David and Mom had known each other all that well or for all that long. But she considered him a new and fast friend and, as she did all old-fashioned reporters, a great force for good in the world.

I DON'T REMEMBER Thanksgiving dinner very well. I do remember that right before dinner, Mom told me that she'd gone with Dad to see the columbarium in the church where she wanted her ashes and where he wanted his. I remember it was cold and that Mom was excited about food for the first time in a long time, although mostly about the leftovers—she told me she was going to make turkey soup with the carcass of the bird and combine the leftover meat with mushrooms, peas, and cream for a turkey à la king.

She seemed remarkably well at dinner, but I do recall looking over and seeing her fade, noticeably, several times. The color would drain from her face, and her eyelids would droop heavily, even as she struggled to keep them open. Then it would be as if a jolt of electricity went through her, as if someone flicked a switch. The color would come back, her eyelids would open, and her posture would strengthen. She had been gone for a second or two—but now was back. And her smile would come back too.

AFTER THANKSGIVING, MOM was even more surrounded by family and friends than usual, and she was usually surrounded by them. Earlier in her illness, she'd wanted a certain amount of time alone. Now she was almost never alone. That was fine with her.

Once, when I was fourteen, I decided to go to Lincoln Center and sit on a bench. Some image of romantic loneliness was swirling in my head, me on a bench beside the stilled fountain. I remember that day as both brisk and sunny, so that if you sat still, you could stay warm off your own body heat trapped inside the various layers of your clothing. There I sat.

I was terribly impressed with myself. I was watching people. I was gloriously alone. Then someone else sat down on my bench, a woman with gray hair, perhaps in her seventies or maybe eighties. She looked somewhat disheveled. I prayed she wouldn't talk to me. She did.

"Do you have any friends?" she asked.

I said I did, lots of them.

"Well then, what are you doing sitting all alone? You should be with your friends."

I thought back to that as I sat with Mom, waiting to see Dr. O'Reilly. Most people around us were there with a son, a daughter, a spouse, a friend. But there were also those who came alone, who had to take their coat with them when they went in to have their blood drawn, or ask a stranger to keep an eye.

I was thinking a lot about loneliness, because we were now reading *Kokoro,* a remarkable novel by Natsume Soseki, which was published in 1914 and was one of fourteen novels Soseki wrote after retiring from a professorship at Tokyo's Imperial University. It was a book I'd read once before, in college, when I'd taken a course from its translator, Edwin McClellan. I'd been struck by Soseki's exploration of the complex nature of friendship, especially among people who aren't equals, in this case a student and his teacher. I wanted Mom to read it, and to read it again myself.

When we talked about the novel, we discovered that we both had been startled by the same quote, an explanation of loneliness the teacher tells to the young man. The teacher says: "Loneliness is the price we have to pay for being born in this modern world, so full of freedom, independence and our own egotistical selves." The young man can't think of anything to say in response. The truth of the statement is too stark for him.

Had Mom ever been lonely? I asked her. No, she said. There were times as head of the Women's Commission when she grew sick of the traveling and wanted to be home, such as when she'd found herself stuck in a remote refugee camp in West Africa for weeks longer than planned. But missing people and being lonely, she pointed out, are two separate things.

I told Mom how lonely I was when I first moved to Hong Kong (I'd gone on a whim), right after college, before I met David there. And how I woke up one day and realized that I'd traveled across the world expecting people to meet me, instead of trying to meet them.

How can you be lonely, Mom said, when there are always people who want to share their stories with you, to tell you about their lives and families and dreams and plans? But now she couldn't stop thinking about David Rohde and how lonely he must be, separated from his wife, from his books, and, she feared, from anyone who wanted to share their stories with him or hear his.

The Price of Salt

The Price of Salt, by Patricia Highsmith, first appeared in 1952 under a pseudonym and would sell more than a million copies. Highsmith (according to her afterword), then age thirty, wrote it after her first novel, *Strangers on a Train,* a novel of suspense, was bought for film by Alfred Hitchcock. Her publisher wanted another book exactly like her first; *The Price of Salt* is a suspense novel, in a way, so she fulfilled the essential task, but it's also a lesbian love story. It was rejected by her original publisher and picked up by another house. Highsmith would soon go on to write the Ripley novels for which she's now best known. I'd seen the movie made from *The Talented Mr. Ripley* but never read a word of Patricia Highsmith. Mom loved her work but had never read this one.

In December 2008, I had the book with me while we waited for Dr. O'Reilly. Mom had already finished it. Every time I put the book down to go grab some mocha, or check my email, or make a call, I returned to find Mom rereading it, sneakily wolfing down passages as though I'd left behind a bag of cookies, not a book, and she was scooping up crumbs behind my back

The Price of Salt begins with a young woman named Therese who wants to be a theatrical set decorator but is instead working as a temporary saleswoman at a department store, in the doll department—just as Highsmith herself had. She's lonely and listless. She has a boyfriend she doesn't love. She spends a depressing evening with an older woman who is also in sales at the store, which gives her a sad glimpse of what her life might become.

"When you walk around New York," Mom said when we started to discuss it, "or really anywhere, you see so many people like that young woman—not desperate but still sad and lonely. That's one of the amazing things great books like this do—they don't just get you to see the world differently, they get you to look at people, the people all around you, differently."

In the novel, customers come and go, but suddenly one says to Therese two words that will change both their lives: "Merry Christmas." None of the other patrons have bothered to greet her: she's just a shopgirl behind a counter. But a beautiful, charismatic married woman utters these two kind words of greeting—"Merry Christmas"—and sets Therese on a journey—and a road trip—where she'll find herself and, actually, love.

After reading this passage, I put the book down and started to think about the way Mom acknowledged people. Everyone who came into her little chemo cubicle got a warm look-you-in-the-eye greeting or thank-you—the nurse who brought the juice, or fetched a shawl, or remembered the pillow Mom liked under her arm, or checked the chemo to make sure that the numbers matched, or just came in to brusquely fuss with a machine; the same went for the receptionist who scheduled the appointments, and the gentlemen stationed outside the building who opened the door for everyone who came in or went out.

The thank-you thing had been drummed into us intensely when we were growing up. We had three great-aunts, on my mother's side, who believed that when they dropped a present in the mail, your thank-you note should essentially bounce right back out of the mailbox at them. If it didn't, the whole family, cousins and second cousins and all, knew about your lack of gratitude (and, come to think of it, common sense, as the threat was always that no more presents would be forthcoming, ever), and you heard about it from multiple sources. The notes couldn't be perfunctory, either—you had to put real elbow grease into them, writing something specific and convincing about each gift. So Christmas afternoon meant laboring over thank-you notes. As children, we hated this task, but when I saw Mom beam as she thanked people in the hospital, I realized something she had been trying to tell us all along. That there's great joy in thanking.

In *The Price of Salt,* the Christmas at the start of the novel turns out to be a momentous time for Therese. In our family, Christmas was always a big deal, and appropriately joyful, but not without stress. I remember vividly the year there almost was no Christmas.

I think I was eight, which would have made my brother nine and my sister four. We were living in a bulbous shingle-style house on a handsome Cambridge Street. Very Currier & Ives. I'm sure it was snowing, because it seemed like it was never not snowing in Massachusetts in December. (The song "I'm Dreaming of a White Christmas" was a mystery to me growing up, as I knew nothing else.) We almost certainly had a fire. Stockings would have hung in front of it. And we would have been sitting in the living room, surrounded by books and the tree, which towered over the presents that were already there, with more to come from Santa later.

We were probably a little cold whenever we moved away from the fire, as Dad believed in sweaters in lieu of heating and kept the house somewhere between freezing and frozen.

Every year Mom would read the Christmas story to us right before it was time for bed. She would sit in an armchair by the fire, her legs tucked up underneath her, Nina beside her, and Doug and I on a low bench with a needlepoint cushion. (She had done the needlepoint.)

This year, as always, Mom began to read: "And so it came to pass that in those days there went out a decree from Caesar Augustus . . ."

Because of my decades in publishing, I've been to a lot of readings. I loathe most of them. I loathe the phony, singsong reading voice that most writers adopt, a kind of spooky incantatory tone that implies they are reading a holy text in a language you don't understand. (Of course there are exceptions—Toni Morrison, Dave Eggers, David Sedaris, Nikki Giovanni, John Irving reading *A Prayer for Owen Meany,* one of Mom's and my favorite books, pure magic.) And what's worst about most literary events—almost no author knows when to stop reading and sit down.

But Mom had a lovely reading voice, both because she was my mother and because she really did, and actually spoke when she read. Maybe it was her training in London as an actress. I think she was proud of her reading. Her voice became a bit more mid-Atlantic. She read loudly and clearly.

So Mom was reading; the fireplace was glowing; we three children were all around her. And then one of us started to giggle. I'm not even sure which one of us it was. Well, truthfully I am, but even after all these years it would seem like ratting out a sibling to name a name. Mom continued. It wasn't even clear that she'd heard or noticed, but maybe she had and was determined not to break the mood.

Then another of us started to giggle, and then the third. We knew we shouldn't and thought we couldn't help ourselves. We weren't laughing at anything in particular. We were just laughing from high spirits, silliness, anticipation—who knows, probably all three. The more we tried to stop, the more we giggled. Then we were laughing simply beca\use we were laughing.

And then we weren't. The Bible was slammed closed. The air went out of the room. We'd almost never seen Mom so mad.

"Maybe this year there won't be a Christmas."

THERE WAS INDEED a Christmas that year, as there always had been, but I recall an extremely anxious and suspenseful night—not just over presents, though I'm sure that I worried they would all be gone, but over genuine regret at having ruined Christmas Eve and fear of the anger we'd brought out in our mother.

"Do you remember when we laughed at the Christmas story and you sent us all to bed?" I asked this of Mom while we were discussing *The Price of Salt*.

Some memories evoke smiles. This one didn't.

You piece together your parents' child-raising theories by

analyzing later why they did what they did. One of the many great things about having siblings is that you get to do this in a communal, Talmudic way. After my sister and I talked about it as adults, we came to some conclusions:

1. Mom thought that even small children needed to be taught the responsibility that comes with speech and to learn that words, laughter, and even glances can have consequences.
2. Mom thought that religion was not something to mock, even though she believed that there should be no prohibition from doing so.
3. Mom was not a big fan of silliness.
4. The written word, on the page or read aloud, was to be accorded the utmost respect.

I remember one of the few other times I saw Mom that furious. It was when I, at age nine, at the urging of a mischievous older child and not understanding what it was, gave myself a Magic Marker tattoo of a swastika on my arm. Mom was shaking with anger as she struggled to get me to understand the history behind it and what the effect would be on our friends who had lived through the Holocaust, or had family who died in it, should they see me with this evil symbol on my skin. Mom scrubbed my arm down to the bone, or so it felt—there was no way I was leaving the house until every trace of it was gone.

"ARE YOU SPENDING the holidays with your family?" strangers would ask me this December, as strangers do. People who knew me would ask, naturally, both that question and also inquire how Mom was doing. When faced with the query about my mother, I could refer people to the blog—still written in my voice by Mom. But usually I just said, "Not bad at all, all things considered," or something like that. And then I added what was true: "And she's just thrilled to have all the grandchildren around." If people knew me even better, they might ask, "And how are you doing?" That always stumped me, so I'd answer the way I thought Mom would want me to answer. "We're just so lucky—to have such great care, and to have more time than anyone would have dared hope for."

I did start to notice something, however: a difference in tone when this last question was asked by someone whose mother or father or both had recently died, especially of cancer. It was as if we were reading the same book, but one of us had gotten ahead of the other: they'd made it to the end, and I was still somewhere in the middle. The "How are you doing?" was really "I think I may know how you are doing."

Most of the time, however, even the simplest exchange around the topic of how I was feeling about Mom's health seemed forced and awkward and uncomfortable, so I found myself changing the subject as quickly as possible. The awkwardness had lots of causes: She was dying but not dead—so allowing or expressing too much grief made me feel and sound as though I already had her in the grave, prematurely, and had given up all hope of more time. She wasn't the first person to be dying, nor was I the first adult to be losing a parent, so on top of not wanting to sound prematurely morbid, I felt unseemly if I thought I was talking excessively about it. And more than anything, we are a pretty awkward society when it comes to talking about dying. It's supposed to happen off-stage, in hospitals, and no one wants to dwell on it too much.

There's also still a schoolyard stigma to being perceived as overly attached to your mother. I think it's far less pronounced today than it was when I was growing up, but it's still there. Most of the men I know freely admit to loving books about sons coming to terms with the lives and legacies of their fathers—books like *Big Russ and Me* by Tim Russert and *The Duke of Deception* by Geoffrey Wolff and *The Great Santini* by Pat Conroy. But those same men are a little more embarrassed about loving books like *The Color of Water* by James McBride or *The Tender Bar* by J. R. Moehringer, maybe talking about the first in terms of what it says about race and the second for its depiction of the joys of bar life, when both books, really, at their hearts are about the fierce bond between a mother and a son. The subject is regarded, frankly, as a bit gay—the terrain of a writer like Colm Tóibín or Andrew Holleran. Maybe some of that, too, was at work and kept me from feeling comfortable discussing my emotions, my grief.

So I tended to answer yes, I'm spending the holiday with family; Mom is doing remarkably, all things considered; and I'm just fine.

THE NIGHT BEFORE Christmas 2008, Mom took her grandchildren to her church (they were all in town for the holidays), where the youngest ones sat transfixed on the floor in front of the altar as the minister told the Christmas story. No one, thank God or goodness, laughed. My brother and Nancy hosted the Christmas Day dinner. We had, as always, homemade plum pudding for dessert. For more than one hundred years, every single year, all the women in Mom's family had gathered to make plum pudding using the precise instructions in a handwritten family recipe. Mom had participated more than sixty times in this ritual and had done so again this year, but with a difference: this year, at Mom's suggestion, for the first time ever, the men had been invited. She'd wanted her grandchildren there, and if the boys were coming, then the men could come too.

New Year's Eve was quieter than Christmas, celebrated early in the evening at Mom and Dad's house with a big tub of caviar sent by friend who had been a student of Mom's; we were her host family when she arrived from Iran to attend Harvard. Mom had always told her students that she would look after them in high school and college—but that they could buy her meals when they were adults. They were doing all that and more, and the apartment was filled with cards and presents from her former students.

It was natural on New Year's Eve for Mom to talk about how miraculous it was that she was here for a second New Year's Eve following her diagnosis, how lucky she was, and how grateful. Then she said something I hadn't heard her say before:

"I don't want any of you to be sad when I'm not here anymore. But I do want you to look after each other. I'll be very cross if I hear that any of you are fighting. And if anyone causes trouble, I'll come back from the grave and get 'em."

AS USUAL, MOM had given a lot of Christmas presents, including bags made by Burmese refugees to the doctors, nurses, and staff at the hospital. For me, she and Dad had chosen vintage Steuben lowball glasses for the Dewar's I like to drink at cocktail time. When the holidays were over, I sat down to write them a thank-you letter—not on Christmas afternoon, as I had been trained, but soon after. I found it more difficult than I had anticipated: I wanted to thank them for so much more than the glasses that the letter kept ballooning out of control. Each draft sounded more and more like a eulogy for my mother. Mom had made it very clear that she was living while dying and that whatever time she had left was not to be turned into a rolling memorial. And yet how many more chances would I have to thank her for what she'd done for me and taught me and given me?

What I suddenly understood was that a thank-you note isn't the price you pay for receiving a gift, as so many children think it is, a kind of minimum tribute or toll, but an opportunity to count your blessings. And gratitude isn't what you give in exchange for something; it's what you feel when you are blessed—blessed to have family and friends who care about you, and who want to see you happy. Hence the joy from thanking.

Kabat-Zinn's books and the concept of mindfulness sprang to mind—but so did a book by David K. Reynolds, who had, in the early 1980s, come up with a system he called Constructive Living, a Western combination of two different kinds of Japanese psychotherapies, one based on getting people to stop using feelings as an excuse for their actions and the other based on getting people to practice gratitude. The latter therapy has its roots in a philosophy called Naikan, developed by Ishin Yoshimoto. Naikan reminds people to be grateful for everything. If you are sitting in a chair, you need to realize that someone made that chair, and someone sold it, and someone delivered it—and you are the beneficiary of all that. Just because they didn't do it especially for you doesn't mean you aren't blessed to be using it and enjoying it. The idea is that if you practice the Naikan part of Constructive Living, life becomes a series of small miracles, and you may start to notice everything that goes right in a typical life and not the few things that go wrong.

I pulled out a fresh piece of paper and began my thank-you note anew with the following words: "Dear Mom and Dad. I am so lucky . . ."

The funny thing was, the more I thought back on all the blessings, the more grateful I felt, and the less sad. Mom, like David K. Reynolds, was a Japanese psychotherapist at heart.

While I was writing this book, I came across my copy of *The Price of Salt*. And I found a piece of writing paper with a letter Mom had written: "We all owe everyone for everything that happens in our lives. But it's not owing like a debt to one person—it's really that we owe everyone for everything. Our whole lives can change in an instant—so each person who keeps that from happening, no matter how small a role they play, is also responsible for all of it. Just by giving friendship and love, you keep the people around you from giving up—and each expression of friendship or love may be the one that makes all the difference."

I have no idea how that letter got there.

The Reluctant Fundamentalist

Many people dropped off books for Mom. She'd already read most of them, but she never said so to the gift giver; she thought that was impolite. If someone gave her any gift that was a duplicate of something she already had, she would give it to someone else, not tell the generous giver that the thing was redundant. Certain ARBs (Already Read Books) came in multiples over Christmas. She would write a nice thank-you and pass the duplicates on—to a friend, to a nurse—or leave them on a book-swap table in her building.

Books that she hadn't read also came in multiples. Then she would give one to me and keep one for herself—or at least for herself until she'd finished it and could give it away.

We started January with *The Reluctant Fundamentalist,* a novel by a thirty-seven-year-old author, Mohsin Hamid, who had been born in Pakistan but spent some of his childhood and then his college years and young adulthood in the United States—at Princeton and Harvard Law and working as a management consultant in New York—before moving to London in 2001. Two people had given Mom this book for Christmas, even though it had been published a year before; clearly, it was a book for her. Mom raced through it in hours and we talked about it for hours, wrestling with the enigmatic ending. It's a novel about a young Princetonian, originally from Pakistan, who makes every attempt to fit in to New York City but winds up returning to Pakistan. It was just the kind of book Mom loved—a monologue that allows you to get to know a character in his own words. The events of September 11 also play a major role in the book. Everyone is looking for a return to something—a dead boyfriend, a land where he'll be accepted—but it's clearly impossible to go back. Too much has happened in our time, our lives, and our countries.

As for the novel's troubling ending, Mom and I had totally different opinions of it. We were back in the outpatient center at Memorial Sloan-Kettering when we discussed it, and the waiting room was packed; the only seats we could find were in the television section. We talked in whispers so as not to disturb the people around us who were watching—and occasionally glanced at the screen, which was mostly filled with bad financial news from around the world.

We argued about *The Reluctant Fundamentalist* as much as we argued about anything that year. At the end of the novel, it's pretty clear that one of two characters is going to die. It's just hard to figure out which one. I thought that there was one ending and that I just couldn't parse it. Mom thought the author intended the ambiguity, and which ending you chose betrayed something about you. I've now come to believe that Mom was right, but at the time I got somewhat sulky about it.

Even if it took a while for me to accept that I would never

be certain about how it concluded, Hamid's novel immediately made me reevaluate whom I could believe and what I could trust, my own prejudices and those others had about me—on a personal level, but also globally. Reading it while David Rohde was still missing was particularly poignant. David would not, Mom told me, have gone off with someone he didn't trust. He wasn't foolish. And his knowledge and instincts about the region were both first-rate. Even with that, someone could make a terrible mistake simply by being insufficiently paranoid. How then were the politicians to know whom to trust in the region? Or the military commanders? And how could the people in the region know which of us to trust—which countries? The Russians? The Germans? The French? The Americans? And even then—which Americans?

I reminded Mom of my second-grade homeroom teacher, Mrs. Williams. It was 1969, and she would say to us when we were noisy or aggressive, "Boys and girls, if we can't get along with each other, then how are we ever going to get along with our brothers and sisters in North Vietnam?" Even as a second grader, I thought it sounded a bit naïve. But of course she was right.

I asked Mom if she really had any hope at all for Afghanistan and its neighbors. "Of course I do," she said. "The thing is, you can't just talk to people. We learned that. You have to work with people—that's how you find out more about them. You can still be wrong. But you just know a lot more that way. That's true no matter where you are."

"But how do you know which people are the right ones to work with? How do you keep from making a mistake right from the start?" I thought of all the trips Mom had made

as head of the Women's Commission—to Monrovia while
Charles Taylor's rebel forces were attacking; to Sierra Leone
and Guinea and Côte d'Ivoire and all the choices she and her
colleagues had needed to make about whom to trust.

"You don't always. And sometimes you think you do and
you're wrong. But you travel with them, you continue to work
with them, you see their humanity, and you pay attention to
the stories they seek out. Do they talk to people? Do they listen? And then you use your judgment—do they make sense?
And if you still don't know enough, you learn more. But you
can't do nothing."

BAD NEWS CAME in Dr. O'Reilly's examining room in the
middle of January 2009. The tumors were again growing
rapidly. Though they still weren't as big as they were when
Mom first started treatment, the new chemo was no longer
holding them back. It was time for yet another combination.
There's not much furniture or decoration in those examining rooms—nothing to distract you. The floors are linoleum;
the chairs, plastic. There's the tub for used "sharps"—it has
the biohazard glyph on it. Steel sink, paper towels. Examining
table. Curtain. When she heard the bad news, Mom looked at
Dr. O'Reilly as if to assure her that it was okay, that Mom was
okay, that she knew it wasn't the doctor's fault.

They would start the new treatment that very day. Dr.
O'Reilly recited the side effects, which sounded pretty much
like the side effects of most of the previous treatments: numb
fingers, maybe a rash, diarrhea, mouth sores, hair loss. Mom
made a note to get her wig back from the fellow who was supposed to be fixing it.

"But we're going to make sure to adjust the dose, and I don't think the side effects will be difficult for you. Certainly nothing like the mouth sores you got from the Xeloda. And there's no reason you can't go to Florida as planned. I know how much you're looking forward to the weather."

"That's wonderful that I can go to Florida," Mom said. Then she added, "I'm glad to know that the mouth sores won't be bad. I didn't like them at all." She said this as though mouth sores were a matter of taste, something some people actually enjoyed.

"No, I expect not," Dr. O'Reilly said with a smile. "They're miserable, aren't they?"

"But the rinse you gave me helped a lot," Mom added.

"And do you have any other questions?" Dr. O'Reilly asked.

Mom shook her head no.

"Well, I have one more for you," Dr. O'Reilly said. "Will your grandchildren from Geneva be coming to visit in Florida?"

Mom beamed. "Oh yes, and the Paris one and New York ones as well."

On the way back to the waiting room, Mom said she'd expected the news about the tumors. She could feel them growing. So what she was focusing on was going to Florida, having us all come and visit, seeing her friends there, and being warm.

That day at chemo, we talked once more about the ending of *The Reluctant Fundamentalist*. "I just really want to know which character dies. I've read the ending again and again," I said. "I hate not knowing."

"I do too. That's why I always read endings first. But sometimes you just can't know what's going to happen, even when you know everything there is to know. So you prepare for the worst but hope for the best."

The weather was not great when we finally left Sloan-Kettering. It was a bitterly cold January day. But Mom still insisted on waiting for the bus, so I waited with her.

The Year of Magical Thinking

A few months after Mom was diagnosed with pancreatic cancer, so was the actor Patrick Swayze, star of *Ghost* and *Dirty Dancing*. He was much younger than Mom, and she'd liked his films, but she'd never thought all that much about him—until he had the same cancer. There was to be a Barbara Walters interview with him right before Mom was to leave for her month in Florida. I forgot about it until I was channel surfing and stumbled upon it. It was very powerful because, just like Mom, Swayze was completely comfortable stressing his hope and his resolve and his dedication to fighting the cancer—all the while acknowledging that he knew the cancer would most likely kill him.

As soon as the show was over, the phone rang.

"Wasn't he wonderful?" Of course, I knew Mom was talking about Swayze. "That's exactly what I'm going through." She was particularly impressed by how he spoke frankly and without embarrassment about the severe gastrointestinal symptoms caused by the treatments. Mom, too, spoke frankly of these—the cramps and diarrhea and constipation—but noted that it often made people uncomfortable. Still, she persisted—her time in the refugee camps had taught her not to be squeamish about such things, and she didn't think other people should be either.

Throughout everything, Mom hadn't talked to or met other people with pancreatic cancer. It was tough to do so because most don't last more than a few weeks or months. Now she felt she had met someone else, even if only on television. She would take the tape to Florida, she said, and show the Swayze interview to all her friends there.

The day Mom arrived in Vero Beach, she was so ill that she thought she'd made a terrible error coming at all. She had fever, chills, diarrhea; her feet and hands were numb; she was nauseated. But a day later, after recovering from the indignities of air travel—all the standing around and taking shoes on and off and waiting in hot corridors or amid too much air-conditioning—she felt a lot better. And in a rare moment of ill humor, she briefly railed against people who used wheelchairs at airports as a way of cutting to the front of screening queues when they really didn't need them, leaving people like her standing in long, slow-moving lines.

"Mom, you know you could use a wheelchair at the airport?" I reminded her on the phone.

"But there are people who really need them," she answered. (Mom was still giving up her seat on buses for older people, pregnant women, and even children—because she knew they didn't have the strength to hold on when the bus swerved. She glared at healthy young adults who would never think of giving up a seat for anyone.)

As always, Mom had an elaborate schedule for Florida—

and a new set of medical and nonmedical routines that gave structure to her days. As soon as I arrived at the Vero Beach condominium she'd rented, she filled me in. My being with her allowed Dad to go back to New York for a week, as he'd done the year before, to look after his business. David would be coming to join me in a few days. My siblings and their partners and all the grandchildren had already visited.

"First thing in the morning, we see the manatees. Adrian, Milo, Lucy, and Cy all loved the manatees."

So every day began with this ritual. After a cup of coffee that Mom had already made—no matter how early I was up, she had awoken before—we walked past the fountain and through the gate and across the street to the harbor. Then out on the pier, to the edge of the pier, to wait and see if any of those glorious, misshapen gray lumps of sea creature would show up.

"I really hope the manatees come today," Mom said.

It had been, I realized then, a year and a half filled with many odd superstitions that would come over me suddenly—what Joan Didion would call "magical thinking." All I could focus on was the following nonsensical equation: If the manatees came, it would be a good day. Mom would feel "better." If they didn't show, if they had been there before us or came after, then it would be a "not great" day. I stared deep into the water, hoping to see one. I looked over at Mom, who was pursing and unpursing her lips, the way women do who are trying to even out their lipstick. But she wasn't wearing lipstick—her lips were dry and cracked and must have been painful in the wind.

Then I saw one manatee and then another, and then one more. The harbor was filled with a jumble of powerboats, the hulls of which were linen-crisp against the murky water and the bright blue of the sky. The boats were still, unmanned. The manatees moved slowly around and between them. But in the distance were boats at full power, churning the water. And when you stared at the backs of the manatees, you could see great gashes that had scabbed over.

"They get cut up by the boats," Mom said. "It's terrible."

After going to see the manatees, we had breakfast back at the condo. Mom would sit with me while I ate. She would try to eat some cereal, or an English muffin, but was having trouble with her appetite. We would later get *The New York Times*. Over breakfast we read the local paper, with Mom paying special attention to houses and apartments for sale.

"We could buy a small condo down here and everyone could use it. The kids would love it."

After breakfast came the trip to the computer center, where Mom would check her email; then the liquor store (where I bought myself wine for the evening or a small bottle of whiskey); then the gourmet store, for the evening's dinner; and then the market. There might be dry cleaning to pick up.

And so it was, with afternoons for napping and reading, until four P.M. That was Mom's favorite time. When the clock turned four, on the dot, not before, we headed out to walk to the beach. The book club had gone mobile. Mom loved the physical beauty of the beach, but it wasn't complete for her until it had a smattering of people walking or jogging alongside their dogs. Mom had a nodding acquaintance with many of the people and more than nodding with some.

"Wait until you see, there's the most beautiful cocker spaniel. And the woman who owns it is from San Diego and works with children who have learning disabilities. Her daughter is in the army."

I didn't want to see the cocker spaniel. Or meet the woman from San Diego. Or hear about her daughter. I didn't want to talk to anyone other than Mom. I wanted to talk about books with her, or just stare at the ocean, drugging myself on the sound of the gentle waves. Sure, I like dogs. But all those strangers with their lives and stories made the landscape less beautiful for me, not more. They marred it. And as the clock ticked, I resented other people for interrupting the limited number of conversations we had left.

How, I wondered, could anyone always want to talk to everyone? Waiting for chemo, in cabs, in lines at airports, at the market, in refugee camps and black-tie dinners. "Aren't there some times, Mom, when you just want to be by yourself, or be alone or talk to people you already know?" I asked. "It seems like you always want to meet people everywhere."

"I don't always want to meet people."

"That's just not true, Mom. You're always wanting to meet people."

"No, sometimes I don't. But it's not very hard to make yourself. You can't know if you want to meet someone until you've met them, until you've started to talk and, most important, asked them questions. I've met the most wonderful people that way. And I don't see other people as interruptions—they give us more to talk about. Just the way books do." She paused. "But I don't always want to meet people."

Suddenly, padding up to us, ears flopping in the afternoon breeze, came a cocker spaniel. And behind it a woman.

"Hi, Susan. This is my son Will."

"Nice to meet you. I'm just in from New York," I began. And then: "Mom tells me you work in San Diego with special needs children. How is your daughter? She's in the army, right?"

ONCE WE WERE back at the house, I tried to remember how old I was when I'd come home from school and asked my mother how her day was, or inquired of my dad whether, say, that slight rasp in his voice meant that perhaps a cold was coming on. I do remember asking them such things once I went away to boarding school, but I would do so in a perfunctory way, at the end of the conversation.

It's incredibly hard for me to ask and to listen, really listen, and not try to prompt an answer that feeds my innate sense of optimism, my hope that it's always possible for things to be a little better, as opposed to a steady slide from worse to still worse. And what mother wants to disappoint her son, to be feeling worse when he so desperately wants her to be feeling better?

I'd brought a copy of Joan Didion's *The Year of Magical Thinking* to Florida. Mom and I had both read it when it came out a few years before. I wanted to read it again. Didion writes about her life after the sudden death of her husband, which she describes in the first few pages—and about their daughter, who becomes deathly ill and then, seemingly, recovers. (Tragically, Quintana Roo Dunne would later die, of pancreatitis, but it would be after her mother's book was written and just as it was about to be published.) *The Year of Magical Thinking* is a book about death and grief and illness.

Didion contrasts her grief after the death of her husband with how she felt after the death of her parents:

> Grief, when it comes, is nothing we expect it to be. It was not what I felt when my parents died: my father died a few days short of his eighty-fifth birthday and my mother a month short of her ninety-first, both after some years of increasing debility. What I felt in each instance was sadness, loneliness (the loneliness of the abandoned child of whatever age), regret for time gone by, for things unsaid, for my inability to share or even in any real way to acknowledge, at the end, the pain and helplessness and physical humiliation they each endured.

I found myself immersed in the book and turning frequently to that passage. Mom was not dead; she was very alive. I was sad but not yet lonely. And I had an opportunity to do and say things so that I wouldn't feel regret; I had the chance to acknowledge and assuage Mom's pain and helplessness and physical humiliation.

That's easier said than done. Mom was both dying and living. She wanted to talk about her friends and her work and the grandchildren and real estate and the books we were reading (especially the Didion, which she reread as soon as I was finished) and about music and movies and the traffic and funny stories and old times and about my business and . . . the list was huge. She wanted to spend time with me and all her family but meet new people too.

I came to see great wisdom in Didion's choice of words: *share* and *acknowledge*. And I realized I could share by talking about anything Mom wanted to discuss, or by sitting quietly with her, reading. And I could acknowledge without probing or dwelling or fixating.

It had been a good day. Soon it was dark, and I made myself a drink. We heated the turkey tetrazzini from the gourmet store. After dinner, we watched a documentary about the political operative Lee Atwater. We both loved it—but it ended with his death from cancer and some gruesome footage of how transformed he was by the disease.

During the film, I looked over several times to see if I could tell how Mom was doing. When it was over, I asked her how she was feeling. I continued to try really hard to form the question just as *The Etiquette of Illness* had taught me: Do you want me to ask how you're feeling? And I still think that's great advice. But after a while it seemed artificial and too formal—like raising your hand for permission to speak when it's just you and the teacher in the room. It was one thing on the phone, but odd when I was there with her in the house in Florida.

"Better," she said. I hoped that was true. After all, we had seen the manatees.

Olive Kitteridge

In March 2009, Mom came back to New York just in time for another helping of slush and snow and freezing rain.

My image of her at this point is of an increasingly frail person determined not to appear so. Daily she would head out—if not to the office she shared at the International Rescue Committee, then to the nearby Asia Society to meet someone for lunch, or to listen to a concert rehearsal or see a ballet. She was managing to keep her weight over one hundred pounds. I can still see her walking on the sidewalk toward her building, wrapped in a quilted down coat, wisps of her white hair showing underneath a silk scarf, the hair so fine, like corn silk; proceeding gingerly so as not to slip on a patch of ice, but unaided; planting each foot firmly and deliberately as other New Yorkers barrel past her. I try not to call out to her—I don't want to startle her, as I know this walking on ice takes great concentration. Instead I walk up softly beside her and then greet her, a second before gently taking her arm to guide her the rest of the way home.

Just as parents don't really notice gradual changes in their children—how is it that the toddler is, suddenly, a foot taller?—so I didn't immediately notice how much frailer Mom had become. It was only by looking at pictures—even of her at Christmas—that I could see she was, to use her words, fading away. More and more came the not-good days, and each one seemed to leave its mark, with Mom ever so slightly frailer afterward. On the not-good days, her stomach failed her—and she'd have to go to the toilet ten, eleven, twelve times a day. Sometimes her feet swelled up so much she could barely walk. But she continued to go to the rehearsals and the lunches, to see her grandchildren, to museums, and to her office.

We did not, however, need to navigate these changes by ourselves. Nina had a friend named Dr. Kathleen Foley, a leader in palliative care, who referred Mom to an extraordinary nurse practitioner named Nessa Coyle. Dr. Foley and Nessa work in tandem with Dr. O'Reilly at Memorial Sloan-Kettering and specialize in helping cancer patients and their families with both quality-of-life concerns during treatment and also end-of-life care. Nessa is tall, English, and thin, with somewhat wild gray hair, a soft voice, and a wide smile. The first time I met her, I was reminded of a nanny right out of an English children's novel. As I would later learn, I wasn't far off the mark; she'd started her training as a midwife.

Whenever we saw Nessa, she would greet me warmly but direct almost all her conversation to Mom, often taking Mom's hands in hers. And I mention both these things because so often over the course of Mom's dying, I noted how people would avoid touching Mom or talking to her, addressing comments and queries to us, even when she was right there. ("Does your mother want something to drink?")

Nessa was always available with sound advice and kept us all from having to bother Dr. O'Reilly with every small question; she helped us figure out what needed to be brought to Dr. O'Reilly's attention and what we could handle on our own. It took me a while to understand Nessa's role. But then it struck me: athletes and executives have coaches; Nessa was a coach too, with wisdom that none of us had, even though we'd all lost people we loved. I came to see her not just as a death coach but as a life coach as well.

It was Nessa who suggested to Mom that she do the things that were important to her while she still felt well enough to do them. If Mom wanted to write a letter to each grandchild, to be opened sometime in the future, she should do that right now. If Mom wanted to go somewhere and see something, she should. But if Mom simply wanted to stay home and have quiet times, reading and listening to music—that was fine too. Nessa encouraged Mom to see her friends for morning or afternoon tea, as opposed to meals, so Mom wouldn't have to worry about moving food around on the plate to make it look like she was eating if she wasn't hungry. Mom was pleased when Nessa acknowledged how tough it was not to be self-conscious about such things. Whenever we had a question (Who could install guardrails in the bathroom? How could we find a Reiki practitioner? What should we say to a friend who stopped by a bit too often?), we called Nessa.

At the end of the month we would celebrate Mom's seventy-fifth birthday—which created its own set of problems and questions. I don't think that when Mom was diagnosed, eighteen months earlier, she thought she would live to see it. I don't think we did either. So Mom was determined to have a party, but she was worried about her stamina. At first, her idea was to invite as many as 150 people to Dad's club around the corner. But she suspected that that would prove far too ambitious, and Nessa agreed. She and Nessa reasoned that if she had a smaller group, then she could have the party at home and spend as much time as she needed to in the bathroom or in her room. And there would just be fewer people to greet. So we set about making a list—family, of course; just a few co-workers, as she didn't want to offend people by inviting many and not all; and only people who had been in touch in the last year or so, but no one from outside New York, as she didn't want anyone to travel. "It's not *This Is Your Life*," she told me, referring to the famous 1950s television show. "It's more for the people I've seen, for whatever reason, in the last year, and to thank some of the friends who have been so wonderful." She knew she would forget to include people. "They'll just have to understand," she said.

The plan was this: A friend of Mom's would do simple buffet food. It would last two hours, six to eight. There would be champagne, and Mom would have a few sips, her first since months before she was diagnosed.

And there would be two absolute and inviolable rules that I was to put on every invitation: no presents and no toasts. Mom looked over my shoulder at the electronic invitation (my idea) on my computer screen as I composed it and shook her head. I hadn't done it quite right. She typed in what she wanted: NO PRESENTS AND NO TOASTS. All caps. Better.

But the party wouldn't be until her actual birthday, March 31, the end of the month. And there was a lot to do in the meantime, including several doctor appointments, which would give us much time to read and talk. She also needed to find a present for grandson Adrian. After some searching, she found a handsome early edition of *The Hobbit* for his ninth birthday. "No more plastic toys," she said. "Just books."

We settled on two books that we would read next and swap. One, a book called *In Other Rooms, Other Wonders* by Daniyal Mueenuddin, had just been published. The other was a Pulitzer Prize–winner, *Olive Kitteridge* by Elizabeth Strout, which had come out the year before. Both are books of collected but related stories. She would start with the Strout; I with the Mueenuddin.

The chemo continued with a new combination of drugs and no longer with the Baxter infusion, the bottle strapped to her chest, but the old-fashioned way, the drip—although connected to the port rather than a vein. The routine is otherwise the same familiar one.

We first sit in the waiting room chairs, maybe reading, maybe still talking about this and that, and periodically one of the nurses announces a name. After a while, it's Mom's. "Mary? Mary Schwalbe?" We then pick up our coats, our books, and our half-drunk mochas and follow her through the swinging doors into the room with the treatment cubicles.

Mom sits in the recliner; I sit alongside; coats get shoved under my chair. They rarely keep you waiting long once you are in your cubicle—someone usually comes in right away. Today I hope it's Curt, Mom's favorite nurse. Curt is a few inches taller than me, and handsome—not movie-star handsome, but the kind of person you would cast in a film to play a very attractive minor member of an army platoon, or a male nurse in a hospital drama, for that matter. Mom beams when it's Curt and asks him about his apartment, whether he's taking any vacation, how he's feeling.

There's a slight clenched-jaw quality to Curt's face, and while he's never distracted, you feel that he is aware that he has a limited amount of time for each encounter. He will chat while he's doing what he's doing, but not for too much longer. A friend's father introduces himself to the waiter at the start of every New York restaurant meal by saying: "Hi, I'm Eric, and this is Susie, and we're from Vermont." My friend cringes ever so slightly whenever his dad does this. I cringe a little when Mom is talking to Curt, thinking that he doesn't want to chat; he's trying to concentrate; she's just another old person dying of cancer. But this isn't true—it's just the childish embarrassment we all develop about our parents: they are too effusive, try too hard; they just aren't being cool.

Mom likes a blanket (she's always cold) and a pillow under her arm. Some apple juice—warm, not cold. She doesn't ask for them but accepts them gratefully when they are offered, almost surprised. If these items don't materialize, she still doesn't ask but sometimes offers a tentative question: "Usually when I come here, they give me a glass of apple juice. Am I supposed to be drinking something?" But often she doesn't.

"Mom, do you want to ask about the apple juice?"

"No," she says, a little annoyed at me. "I don't have to have it every time."

"I'll ask."

"Okay."

There's always their list of questions—How is Mom feeling? Is she tired? How are her bowel movements? Then another nurse is brought in for the chemo check, Mom confirms her name and date of birth, and the nurses confirm with each other that she's the right person getting the right dose of the right stuff. With that, the bag is attached to its hook and slung upside down like Mussolini on that meat hook. The saline is set to flow, and with one eye we will watch it drip.

"Anything else I can get you?" asks Curt.

"No, and thank you for everything, Curt. You've been just wonderful," says Mom, as though Curt were her host for a country weekend and she was just settling in for a nap in a duvet-covered bed after a long journey.

It's quiet. People doze or talk in hushed voices. Machines beep. The nurses walk briskly in and out on sneakered feet. Depending on the treatment, we now have anywhere from one to four or five hours. This Tuesday in March, treatment stretches to more like six or seven hours. It's a busy day, and there are delays all around. It's the last treatment before Mom's next scan and next doctor appointment. She's convinced the new treatment isn't working. Not in a pessimistic or fatalistic way. She's just matter-of-fact. She feels she's getting sicker, and she's looking sicker too.

"I'm loving *Olive Kitteridge*, the Elizabeth Strout. Maybe partly because Olive is a schoolteacher, but not like most teachers in books; she's got strong opinions and very sharp edges—like so many of the best teachers I worked with. She's a real New Englander, too. And I love that she has many more fears than she's willing to admit—for herself and her family. There's an extraordinary passage about loneliness. Just like we talked about with *Kokoro* and *The Price of Salt*. Here—read this." She points her finger at a page in the book.

In the passage Mom is showing me, Olives notes that "loneliness can kill people—in different ways can actually make you die. Olive's private view is that life depends on what she thinks of as 'big bursts' and 'little bursts.' Big bursts are things like marriage or children, intimacies that keep you afloat, but these big bursts hold dangerous, unseen currents. Which is why you need the little bursts as well: a friendly clerk at Bradlee's, let's say, or the waitress at Dunkin' Donuts who knows how you like your coffee. Tricky business, really."

And as I finish reading, in comes Curt.

"Almost done. Would you like some apple juice?" Curt asks.

"Oh, thank you, Curt. I'd love that."

I wish I'd told Curt then and there how grateful I was to him for looking after my mother so well, for the little bursts, which make all the difference in the world to someone dying of cancer, and to the people who love her. I hope he could see that.

AFTER OUR LONG day at Memorial Sloan-Kettering, I had to put in long hours at work, and the next few days were busy ones, with business dinners every night. Then it was time for me to go to a tech conference in Austin. I couldn't wait for the plane ride—five hours each way alone with a book. Mom had finished *Olive Kitteridge* and given me her copy. I devoured it on the way there and the Mueenuddin on the way back.

AT THE NEXT doctor's visit, on Tuesday, March 24, 2009, Mom was told something she had suspected—the scan revealed that the present treatment wasn't working at all. The tumors had not only continued to grow, but they were growing even more rapidly. And the present treatment was the very last standard treatment. So now it was time to talk about experimental treatments.

The experimental treatments being considered were in various stages. Which one Dr. O'Reilly would recommend depended on a lot of different factors: whether there were spaces available; the type of cancer Mom had; whether she was willing to be poked and prodded and tested the way one needed to be for some of the trials; whether she was willing to put up with the side effects already experienced by other people trying them. We would discuss it all in two weeks, when Mom returned for another checkup.

Dr. O'Reilly was her usual kind self. She was a little more soft-spoken this time, her Irish accent a bit more pronounced. She spent some extra time with us.

"The experimental treatments we're looking at have shown some promise in slowing the growth of tumors," she said. Afterward Mom said, "She's not giving up yet." And Mom also said, "Do you realize that this means for the first time in eighteen months I'll have had a whole month without a treatment?" So for Mom, that was the silver lining. A month without treatments—a month without side effects—feeling good for her birthday party. As for her tumors growing—well, we'd face that two weeks from now.

We had to wait around for some paperwork after the visit with Dr. O'Reilly, so I had the chance to spend a little more time talking with Mom.

"Are you discouraged?" I asked her.

"No," she said. "I expected it. And it's not over yet. I'm going to plan some wonderful things for the summer and for the fall, and I'll do what I can."

We sat in silence for a while.

"Do you have the Mueenuddin stories?" she said.

"You're going to love them," I said. "They're quite dark—but totally absorbing."

"Where are they set?" Mom asked.

"Lots of places. In Pakistan, in the countryside and in Lahore and Islamabad. But also Paris—there's a wonderful story that takes place in Paris."

Oddly, and maybe partly because I read both books on planes to and from Austin, *In Other Rooms, Other Wonders* reminded me of *Olive Kitteridge,* not just because both were books of connected stories, but because they share a tone: poignant, but also a bit acerbic. Many of the characters in the Mueenuddin are blunt and opinionated, just like Olive.

"Of all the places I've been, the place I most want to go back to is Pakistan," Mom said. "But I don't think that's in the cards. Nancy and my other friends there say it's even more dangerous now than Afghanistan. But obviously I'm not worried about getting killed." Mom smiled. "No, I just think that I've probably made my last trip. Though we'll see—maybe I'll get one more trip to London or Geneva." She looked sad, a bit defeated. She bit her lower lip, the way she did when lost in thought or in pain. She closed her eyes briefly. I sat quietly next to her.

MOM WAS TERRIBLY sick in the days leading up to her party. She would give me the report on the number of Imodiums she'd needed to take and how many times she'd been to the bathroom. I asked her if Nessa had any advice for her; she said she'd checked and picked up some tips on what to eat to settle her stomach. Mom didn't feel like reading much that week, but she did love *In Other Rooms, Other Wonders,* the Mueenuddin book, as I'd predicted. There's a story near the end called "Lily" about a couple named Lily and Murad—it's a tale of a marriage that's gone seriously off the rails. We talked about that story the most—about how much the collapse of the relationship was Lily and Murad's fault as individuals, but also about how, even though they came from the same social class, they were trapped between different worlds—Lily's fast life in Islamabad and the isolation of Murad's farm, which Lily thought she wanted.

"I think this is one of the saddest things we've read all year," I told her.

"I agree," Mom said. "Everything is too much against them—they really don't have a chance. What makes it so sad is how much hope they have at the start—all the plans they make."

Our conversations then turned from the stories and Pakistan to neighboring Afghanistan and the progress on the library, for which detailed architectural drawings were well under way. Very much in our minds was what had happened to David Rohde. He was still held hostage in Afghanistan, and we'd still had no word about his health, or condition, or even if he was still alive. Mom told me she continued to pray for him every night without fail and also checked her email constantly for any news.

The day before the party a colossal array of flowers arrived—from Mom's last class of students at Nightingale, the high school where she taught and was an administrator before she became director of the Women's Commission. Girls from the class of 1990 had found each other through Facebook for the sole purpose of joining together to send Mom a stunning bouquet with a note of thanks for all she'd done for them.

When Mom showed me the flowers and note, she burst into tears. It was the first time since she had gotten sick that I saw her do so. And then, just as suddenly, she brightened, and it was clear that she was going to be well enough for her seventy-fifth birthday. Soon the guests started to arrive. She stood the whole two hours and then some. She greeted everyone at the door and kissed everyone good night. She even went ahead with her plan to have a few sips of champagne. It was actually Dad who looked frailer that night—I suddenly noticed the physical toll all the stress and worry were taking on him.

Maybe it was adrenaline or Ritalin or the antibiotics or the flowers or the energy in the room or sheer force of will, but Mom looked better that night than she had in months, and if you hadn't known her, you never would have guessed that this was a woman a year and a half into treatment for pancreatic cancer, to whom the doctor had just said that all the usual treatments were now of no use. On the way out, a friend whose wife had died of cancer years before said to her, "This must be exhausting for you."

And Mom didn't answer yes or no. She just smiled and said, "It's my last party."

THERE WAS ONE moment of concern after the party was over—there were too many finger sandwiches left. In recent months, Mom had become almost hysterically concerned about any kind of waste, and looking at the trays of little sand-wiches was making her miserable.

I saw David and Nancy, my sister-in-law, whispering. Then they both approached Mom and asked her if she'd mind if we all took some of the sandwiches home.

Crisis averted.

THE NEXT DAY, when I called Mom, she said she'd had the most wonderful time. And her fever was gone.

"What fever?" I asked.

"I didn't want you all to worry—but I had a fever of 102."

Girls Like Us

When I was growing up, there was a television show called *All in the Family* that became famous for pushing social boundaries. One episode featured a riddle that stumped every character in the show—and just about everyone watching it. It went something like this:

"A father and his son are in a terrible car crash. The father is killed instantly—but the son survives, barely, his life hanging in the balance. He's rushed to the hospital and into surgery, but there's only one doctor there, and as soon as the doctor sees the boy, the doctor says, 'I can't operate on my own son!' How could this be, if the boy's father was killed in the crash?"

In 1971, when the show aired, people walked around for days trying to figure it out and created elaborate scenarios to explain it: "Maybe the father had an identical twin brother who thought he was the boy's father . . ."

Often as we walked into the office of Dr. Eileen O'Reilly, I thought back to that riddle. The doctor who said, "I can't operate on my own son" was the boy's mother, of course. Even today people still get stumped by this riddle.

PERHAPS BECAUSE THE clock did seem to be ticking much faster and louder than it had over the past two years, we began to read many books at once. So even before we'd both finished *The Bolter* (a wonderfully quirky book that had just been published and told the true story of a woman who scandalously, frequently, and impulsively shook up her life in the early decades of the twentieth century in England and Kenya), we were on to a few others, one of which was George Bernard Shaw's 1923 play *Saint Joan,* in an edition that has the more-than-sixty-page preface Shaw wrote the year after the play opened.

Shaw celebrates Joan as someone who "refused to accept the specific woman's lot, and dressed and fought and lived as men did." Mom pointed out to me a wonderful Shavian sentence in which he says that any biographer of Joan "must be capable of throwing off sex partialities and their romance, and regarding woman as the female of the human species, and not as a different kind of animal with specific charms and specific imbecilities."

My mother considered herself a feminist. As one of the first generation of women in America who worked by choice and not necessity (not counting the women a few years older, the Rosie the Riveters who kept the factories humming, and worked due to a combination of choice and necessity), she was aware of the trailblazers of her generation who had made these advances possible and was proud to have been, in her own way, one of them, racking up a collection of "firsts"—the first woman president of the Harvard Faculty Club, the first woman director of admissions at Harvard and Radcliffe. My father is a feminist too, though he would most likely describe himself as a social anarchist, someone who believes that all people should be free to do as they like. Mom and Dad agreed on both the ends and the means—but he was less interested in discussing the specific rationale.

Idina Sackville, the Bolter, was, according to Frances Osborne, her biographer and great-granddaughter, passionately, though not violently, devoted to the campaign for Votes for Women. Osborne writes "Idina was not a militant suffragette. Instead her East Grinstead, England, organization was a signed-up branch of the NUWSS (National Union of Women's Suffrage Societies), which believed that women's suffrage should be achieved by peaceful means." But this didn't stop the members of this organization from being menaced by

> a mob of fifteen hundred anti-suffragists marching against them, hurling "pieces of turf, a few ripe tomatoes and highly seasoned eggs," reported the *East Grinstead Observer*.
>
> The first house the suffragists sheltered in was charged by the mob and its front door slowly and steadily bent until it cracked. The police dragged the women out the back to the branch's headquarters at the top of the Dorset Arms pub, where they were trapped for several hours, listening to the crowd outside continuing to bay for their blood.
>
> It was the only violent outburst in the entire six-week campaign, but Idina and her mother's involvement in the group was enough to confirm society's unfavorable opinion of Idina.

Both my parents loved *The Bolter*—my father mostly because he's always been obsessed with that period. For Mom, it was the era and the fact that it was the story of such a strong woman: the kind that she could relate to on an almost personal level. Mom read books by and about women whenever possible.

I'm not sure how she found her way to *Eleanor Rathbone and the Politics of Conscience* by Susan Pedersen, but that's what we read next. Rathbone was a British feminist and parliamentarian, and Mom was fascinated by this new biography—the political journey and also the parts that spoke of Rathbone's four-decade relationship with another woman. When I asked her what in the biography impressed her most, she answered:

"She had to figure out a life for herself. Nothing was handed to her—personally or professionally. There was no path. And it's just fascinating to see how much work—how much organizing and planning—went into the suffrage movement. I think too many young women take that for granted, and it just makes me so cross when I see young women who've had every opportunity and then I find out they can't be bothered to go and vote. People need to read the stories of these women—to learn how much effort went into getting the right to vote, so they won't take it for granted."

Oddly, we both simultaneously discovered our next book, which continued the theme of reading about women's lives: *Girls Like Us* by the journalist Sheila Weller, a book about the singer-songwriters Carole King, Joni Mitchell, and Carly Simon. I'd never known Mom to be a particularly big fan of the music of any of these women—though I think she liked them all, and I can recall her humming along with "You've

Got a Friend" and "Both Sides Now" if they came up on the radio—and I believe my sister listened several thousand times to Carly Simon and James Taylor singing "Mockingbird," and that was also a favorite of Mom's. These women weren't of her generation; they were an important decade younger, born at or near the end of World War II as opposed to growing up during it. But Mom was interested in their lives with the same big-sisterly affection she lavished on the younger women with whom she had worked.

Mom felt that a special burden had been placed on the women of the generation that followed hers; because they were the first to have certain opportunities and choices, theirs hadn't been an easy road. Weller writes about the "hurt, anger, and heightened self-regard shared by female age mates whose elevated expectations had left them unwilling to be pushed aside in the same 'due course' of life that had bound earlier generations of women." Because Mom was in the first generation to make a new kind of life—one with marriage and children and a career—she said she'd really been too busy to stop and think about what kind of expectations she'd had, if any.

"I do think back," Mom told me, "on my wonderful headmistress at Brearley, the one who told us we could have everything we wanted. She always said, 'Girls, you can have a husband and a family and a career—you can do it all.' And when you three children were little and I was trying to go to all your school events—and make things for your bake sales—and do my full-time job—and look after you when you were sick—and look after your father—and cook dinner—and make sure the house was tidy—and everything else, I would think about what we'd been told as girls and just keep on going, even though I was exhausted so much of the time.

And then, years later, I went back for a reunion, and I told the headmistress that I had, indeed, managed to have it all—a husband, a career, three children—but that I was tired all the time, exhausted in fact. And she said, 'Oh, dear—did I forget to mention that you can, indeed, have it all, but you need a lot of help!' "

Mom made a point of telling this story to the young women who came to her for advice, but she also made sure they knew that help could come in many forms—an extended family, a stay-at-home spouse, or friends who were willing to pitch in, for example, in addition, of course, to any hired helpers a family might be able to afford.

Also, Mom told these young women that she didn't have regrets about her work or her family life—that her friends with regrets were more likely to be the ones who hadn't tried to do it all, who had devoted themselves solely to marriages that fell apart or to jobs that jettisoned them when they got to be a certain age.

ON TUESDAY, APRIL 7, 2009, Mom and I found ourselves again in the waiting room at Memorial Sloan-Kettering, so the book club was in session. Mom's feet were swollen, her ankles bulging out above her flats. I asked her if she was in pain.

"No," she said. "Not pain. Just uncomfortable."

This day was important for two reasons—it was the fourth birthday of Mom's youngest grandchild, Cy, and at the appointment Mom would find out if she qualified for any experimental treatments.

Before we were called into Dr. O'Reilly's office, I asked Mom if she remembered the *All in the Family* riddle. "Of course," said Mom. "I think that did a lot to change people's attitudes. Even people who thought they were very progressive were alarmed when they realized they'd spent hours puzzling it out, assuming without question that a doctor must be a man."

I had been thinking about the women in *Girls Like Us,* and about the women who were my contemporaries, and their daughters. "Did you ever think things would come as far for women as they have in your lifetime?"

"Sure I did," she said. "All you had to do was see the extraordinary young women at college in the sixties and seventies—nothing was going to hold them back. And it was an exciting time—there were so many discussions and meetings and books. But I do worry now that people don't understand how much is at stake. I think women should have choices and should be able to do what they like, and I think it's a great choice to stay at home and raise kids, just as it's a great choice to have a career. But I don't entirely approve of people who get advanced degrees and then decide to stay at home. I think if society gives you the gift of one of those educations and you take a spot in a very competitive institution, then you should do something with that education to help others. I know lots of people don't agree with me on that."

I was about to say something when Mom began again, on a slightly different topic.

"But I also don't approve of working parents who look down on stay-at-home mothers and think they smother their children. Working parents are every bit as capable of spoiling children as ones who don't work—maybe even more so when they indulge their kids out of guilt. The best thing anyone can teach their children is the obligation we all have toward each other—and no one has a monopoly on teaching that." I had a feeling that Mom had said this many times and to many young women. But while she was telling me, color came back into her face, and I got a strong sense that she was not yet ready to call it quits. She had more she wanted to do.

And so did Dr. O'Reilly.

When we were called into the office, Dr. O'Reilly was already there. She leaned against the examining table across from Mom and told us the good news first. Mom's tests had revealed that the most recent bacterial infection was gone—so the antibiotic had worked. There would be ultrasound for Mom's feet, to make sure there was no blood clot, but a simple diuretic should reduce the swelling. The abdominal discomfort was gastrointestinal and not directly related to the cancer. Nor was Dr. O'Reilly overconcerned about the fever.

"As for treatment . . ." Dr. O'Reilly began. Then she paused, though her eyes didn't leave Mom's. "Well, I think some of the experimental treatments may need to be ruled out, because you would need a new biopsy just to see if you qualified. We made the original diagnosis off a sample that's too small to stain. A new biopsy might be rough on you. So I don't suggest that."

"No," said Mom right away, "I don't want a new biopsy. I definitely don't want that."

"But there are some promising trials, and you might fit the criteria for those, so I'll put you on the list, and if you meet the criteria and space opens up, well then, you can decide later. In the meantime, I think we should try mitomycin—it helps slow the growth of tumors in some people who've been through many different courses of treatment, as you have. It's just going to be one treatment a month, and we'll try it for two or three months while waiting to see if a spot opens up in one of the trials." Dr. O'Reilly then described all the usual chemo side effects: nausea, mouth sores, hair loss, fatigue. But Mom shrugged them off—she was used to them by now.

The next scan would be in two months.

"How are you feeling?" Dr. O'Reilly asked. "Is your appetite coming back? Are you very tired?"

"I'm trying to eat as much as I can," Mom said. "But nothing tastes good. So I eat a lot of Jell-O. I still have enough energy to see friends and go to afternoon concerts and read. No matter how tired I am, I can always read. But maybe that's because of raising three children while working full-time. I think I got used to being tired all the time. If I'd waited until I was well rested to read, I never would have read anything."

Suite Française

When we talked about anything other than Irène
Némirovsky's *Suite Française* that next week, we found
our conversation constantly moving back to it.

Mom had another doctor's appointment, so I met her in
the waiting room as always. On this particular day, we had to
sit on the long sofa in front of the windows, as every chair was
taken. Before a holiday weekend, people are keen to squeeze
in another course of chemo.

"So, any news from The Angels?" asked Mom. "The Angels" was my shorthand for a group of angel investors who had
expressed some interest in the cooking site. They had been on
the verge of funding it for months. I was getting down to my
last dollars.

"Nothing." We both looked down at our copies of *Suite
Française*. "Did you find space for the Afghan project?"

"No. You would think with the way the economy is, someone would be able to rent us a desk."

"You would think."

"I'm going to close my eyes for second," Mom said after a pause, but she didn't.

"Okay, I'll read a bit."

"Where are you in the book?" Mom asked.

"I'm just at the part where the son has run off to join the French army."

"He shouldn't have done that," Mom said. And then she closed her eyes.

Long prior to her cancer and its brutal treatment, when we were growing up, whenever Mom "closed her eyes," it was never completely clear to us if she was sleeping, meditating, or simply and quite literally closing her eyes. So we exercised caution, as it always seemed that she would open her eyes just in time to catch us in the middle of doing or saying something we shouldn't.

Mom kept her eyes closed, and I read on, eager to see what was going to happen to our boy soldier and suspecting the worst. After a little while, I noticed Mom's eyes were again open.

"I agree," I said. "He shouldn't have run off to join the soldiers. It was clearly futile—France was lost! And he had no training, so he could only get in the way."

"That's not what I meant," Mom said. "The reason he shouldn't have gone is that he was a child and children shouldn't fight in wars. When I read that part, I kept thinking about Ishmael Beah's memoir of his life as a boy soldier in Sierra Leone, *A Long Way Gone*. And about the child soldiers in Burma."

Mom closed her eyes a few minutes more, then continued: "And our lack of empathy is astonishing, When parents look at photographs of their children, can they imagine them with real guns in their hands, killing? They see them with toy light sabers and water pistols, but what about with machetes and Kalashnikovs?"

Still, even the dramatic incongruity of a child with a real weapon doesn't tell the full story, because Mom had also seen how thin the veneer of civilization is and can be, that it doesn't take the most extreme situations for order to break down. We talked not just about Beah and Eggers but also again about *Lord of the Flies,* the ultimate work about how quickly people can become savage and cruel. And how deep the scars are then for everyone and how long they last.

Mom did believe that there was a life and future for the child soldiers. That was the lesson of Beah—who had gradu-ated from college in 2004, published his book in 2007, and become a champion of human rights—and also of other chil-dren Mom had met and seen around the world. In 1993, in Liberia, Mom had visited the War Affected Children's Home. She wasn't allowed to take any pictures there, not even of the gardens the children were tending. "War Affected" was the term they used for child soldiers—it was first called a "deten-tion center," but the children liked it better when they were told they were going to a home. The children were kept there for six months. The place consisted of three dorms for the boys, who ranged in age from nine to sixteen. Originally, they were going to have fourteen be the upper age limit, but they soon learned that the sixteen-year-olds were really children too. Mom wrote in a report, "They sleep in bunk beds—they have little of their own. But for children who have come from terror, torment, and trauma, I saw boys who were smiling, quiet, friendly—and nice to each other."

They were kept to a firm schedule—up at six A.M. to do

chores and take baths, if there was water. Breakfast at seven thirty. Literacy class until noon. Then an hour of group therapy with different social workers. Lunch followed, which they helped prepare. Then rest, vocational training, recreation, supper—and bed at eight P.M.

"It's amazing," Mom said, "just to see the effect of a schedule. They're children, and they want to be told what to do. That's both the problem and the way back."

So the responsibility on all of us, as Mom saw it, was not just to attend to those who were conscripted and forced to do terrible things or who found in themselves the same terrible impulses that the *Lord of the Flies* kids found in themselves, but also to look to those parts of the world where children were likely to be impressed into service and try to stop it before it happened.

Mom and I had both intended to read *Suite Française* from the moment it was finally published in America a few years before, but neither of us had gotten around to it until now. The fact that the book exists at all is miraculous. When the Nazis occupied Paris, Némirovsky, a Jewish writer who with her husband had converted to Catholicism, sent their daughters to Burgundy and eventually joined them there. But in 1942 Némirovsky and her husband were betrayed and shipped to Auschwitz, where she died of typhus. Before being sent to her death, Némirovsky gave her daughter Denise a suitcase containing a notebook.

Denise and her sister survived the war in a convent. Only in the 1990s did Denise realize that the notebook, which she'd managed to save, with its tiny, cramped script, contained not random scribbles but two completed parts of an extraordinary novel, written during the occupation, called *Suite Fran-çaise*. "I'm working on burning lava," Némirovsky had said while writing the book. This was it.

My copy of the book was the U.S. version; someone had given Mom a copy from England, or she'd bought it on one of her trips. I was with Mom when she was reading the epilogue to the English edition, which had been the preface to the French. It said, "On 13 July 1942, the French police knocked at the Némirovskys' door. They had come to arrest Irène."

July 13 is my birthday—though 1962, not 1942. Némirovsky was arrested exactly twenty years to the day before my birth. Obviously, this is a totally insignificant numerical coincidence. But it did force me to remember anew how recently it had all taken place. I remember first learning as a child about World War II and thinking it was a million years ago, as a quarter century is to a five-year-old. But the older I get, the more recent it becomes: events in my life from twenty or so years ago often seem like yesterday. And as Mom constantly reminded me, you don't need to look far back in history, or even at history at all, to find atrocities. The genocides in Rwanda and Darfur, to name just two, took place under our watch.

Suite Française is a book about refugees, and life under occupation, by a refugee. (The IRC, the organization for which Mom worked, had actually been started at roughly the same time as the novel—at the suggestion of Albert Einstein—to rescue Jews from Nazi Europe.) It's a subtle book, with scenes of comedy and violence, that is devastating to read both because of the power of the writing and also in light of the murder of its author and so many millions more by the Nazis and their collaborators.

IT WAS NOW May 2009, there had still been no news about David Rohde, and Mom was increasingly worried. She was also determined that they break ground on the library, something that had been postponed for all sorts of reasons, mostly involving the difficulty of building anything in Afghanistan. They still had no office for the lone staff member, a woman who was working night and day raising money and awareness for the project. They were also busy editing a video of one of the mobile libraries, and of Nancy Hatch Dupree in action, which they would use for fund-raising; they needed more money to finish the library once they started and to pay for the traveling collections. A friend of mine had shot the footage; that he had returned safely from Kabul was a huge relief. In all, there was so much to do that Mom didn't know how she would get it done. But she said she would.

We were back at chemo for Mom's dose of mitomycin and found our conversation moving back, once again, to *Suite Française*. I also mentioned, again, my insomnia—I'd finished the book on a night when I couldn't sleep at all.

"I just feel guilty that I'm not doing more in the world," I said. "I mean, it's so easy to read *Suite Française* and think, 'Why didn't people in America know more and do more?' But here I am, and there are things going on all over—child soldiers and genocide and human trafficking—and I'm hardly doing anything."

Mom tilted her chin to the left and pursed her lips, giving me the same quick, mystified look she used when I'd forgotten to call someone she wanted me to contact, or when I'd asked again for directions to somewhere when she was sure she'd already given them to me. "I loved the people I met on all my trips, Will," she said. "I loved hearing their stories and getting to know them and finding out what if anything we could all do to help. That's enriched my life more than I can say. Of course you could do more—you can always do more, and you should do more—but still, the important thing is to do what you can, whenever you can. You just do your best, and that's all you can do. Too many people use the excuse that they don't think they can do enough, so they decide they don't have to do anything. There's never a good excuse for not doing anything—even if it's just to sign something, or send a small contribution, or invite a newly settled refugee family over for Thanksgiving."

"And what about going to expensive restaurants and things like that?" I asked, risking The Look again.

"It's fine to give yourself treats, if you can afford it, but no one needs to eat like that every night. It should be special. If you are fortunate enough to have these questions, it means that you have an extra responsibility to make sure you're doing something. Oh, and I don't mean just something that helps you. I'm always so disappointed when I hear of wealthy people who only give money to the schools where their children go while their children are still going there—that's charity, of course, but it's quite selfish. There are also so many wonderful schools that help children who have very little. If they gave a fraction of what they give to their children's school to one of those schools, too, just think of what they could do."

"Lots of my friends say they want to do something but just don't know how to start. What do you tell people who ask you that?"

"Well," Mom said, "people should use their talents. If

you're in public relations, you can offer public relations help to a charity. And charities are always looking for people to raise money, and everyone can help do that. I always have people come to me who have professions—bankers, lawyers—and they want to go right away and get a paid job working in the field with refugees. And I say to them, 'Would you hire someone who had no other qualification than working with refugees to be a banker in your bank, or to argue a case in court? It's a profession.' So I tell these people to start by volunteering or giving money and then decide if they want to train to do this kind of work. But if they really want to help, then money is the quickest and fastest way, even if you can only afford a little."

Then Mom added, with a smile, "And there's something you can always tell people who want to learn more about the world and who don't know how to find a cause to support. You can always tell them to read." She paused. "But all this isn't what's keeping you up at night, is it?"

"No, Mom, it isn't." I took a moment before continuing. "I'm up at night thinking about what we're going to do . . ." I wanted to say "without you" but stopped myself. I just couldn't say it. I couldn't even let myself think it.

Mom reached out and touched my cheek, as if to wipe away a smudge of dirt or a tear.

"Aren't you angry?" I blurted out. "I am."

"Sometimes, sure," she said.

It turned out that she had one more thing to tell me that day—or rather, to show me. When she got up to go to the toilet, she left *Daily Strength for Daily Needs* open on her chair. The day's passage was by Ralph Waldo Emerson. It read:

That which befits us, embosomed in beauty and wonder as we are, is cheerfulness, and courage, and the endeavor to realize our aspirations. Shall not the heart which has received so much, trust the Power by which it lives? May it not quit other leadings, and listen to the Soul that has guided it so gently, and taught it so much, secure that the future will be worthy of the past?

The Bite of the Mango

Across the street and up a block from the main entrance to Macy's, in the middle of Manhattan, is a banquet building called Gotham Hall that was once a bank: a large structure with a cavernous main room. It's incredibly grand, built at a time when banks were temples to money and no expense was spared in creating spaces that would awe visitors and give them confidence in the abilities of the owners to take their money and make vast sums for their customers.

Gotham Hall is where more than a thousand people, mostly women, have come together to celebrate, on this day in 2009, the twentieth anniversary of the Women's Commission for Refugee Women and Children, recently renamed the Women's Refugee Commission.

It's a bit cold in the hall. I look over at Mom, but she seems warm enough; she's wearing her pearls, a brightly colored scarf, and a pistachio-green mandarin-collar silk blouse, but she has left her coat on. She's surrounded by people she's

worked with in the organization's New York office and people
with whom she's traveled all over the world: to Khartoum and
Rangoon and Khost and Monrovia and Gaza. It's been eighteen months of chemo: of mouth sores, swollen feet, nausea,
headaches, weight loss, lack of energy, diarrhea, constipation,
cramps, and fevers, and hours in doctors' offices, emergency
rooms, and hospitals. And it's been thousands of dollars of her
own money and tens of thousands of dollars of Medicare. But
how can you put a price, in suffering or in dollars, on seeing
her here, among her friends and colleagues, celebrating twenty
years of helping women and children all over the world, and
recommitting to continuing to help in whatever time she, or
any of us, has left?

Or what price could you put on Mom's lunches with her
oldest friends—some of whom she'd kept in touch with since
grade school—or her time with her grandchildren, or a trip
she was making to visit the extraordinary women she loved
who had been directors of admission at Radcliffe's six "sister" colleges? These women, who ranged in age from late sixties to mid-nineties, had been getting together every year for
more than thirty years. What price could you put on the daily
calls and movies and meals she shared with two of her and
Dad's best friends, a renowned Harvard scholar, now retired
nearby, and a college president Mom had met while serving
on a board, who was one of the few people with whom Mom
enjoyed shopping for clothes, because her friend's enthusiasm
for this activity was so intense and infectious? How could you
even put a number on something as simple as the hours Mom
spent listening to music, or reading, or looking at the wonderful shapes and shadows of the pottery she loved?

And yet Mom was calculating that price. And she'd made it very clear to all of us. There would come a time when she would say enough.

THE ROOM WAS so packed, there was barely space for the waiters to get between tables to clear the dishes. Mom thinks this kind of lunch should be one plate, no clearing, with cookies already on the table for dessert—something she will later remind her friends at the Women's Refugee Commission.

Liv Ullmann, a co-founder of the organization, gave a speech and included a tribute to Mom, in which she said that Mary Anne Schwalbe made her proud not just to work with the commission but proud to be a woman. Carolyn Makinson, the director of the commission, had spoken before, describing, with humor and love, how Mom first approached her for funding, then became a friend, and eventually roped her into running the organization. How great, I thought, to honor people while they are still alive.

After the tributes, and a film on the history of the commission and Mom's role in the early years, and the lunch, and the conversation about this and that, came the recipients of the Voices of Courage awards. Dr. Shamail Azimi was the first woman doctor to return to Afghanistan after the fall of the Taliban—bringing a team of women doctors from Pakistan to deliver maternal and child-related medical services that no male doctor would ever have been allowed to perform. I thought of my talks with Mom about courage and about what needs to be done in the world.

And then came Mariatu Kamara, the other recipient of a Voices of Courage award, a young woman who had written a

book called *The Bite of the Mango,* which Mom had chosen for
our club and which we'd both read the night before.

One of the first things everyone noticed about Mariatu
Kamara was that she has no hands. You couldn't help but see
this as she accepted her award, holding it proudly with her
stumps before gently placing it on a table behind her. A gorgeous presence, with long braids wrapped like a crown around
her head, she spoke in a loud, clear voice, with a distinct African accent, dotted with some Canadian vowel sounds. She
wore a golden African-print gown and a tangerine-colored
shawl.

Mariatu was born in Sierra Leone and was only twelve years
old when she was captured by rebels, adult and boy soldiers. At
first she was forced to witness unimaginable horrors—the torture and murder of people she knew from her village as well as
others. In her book, she describes how the rebel boys boarded
up a house where twenty people had taken shelter—and then
set it on fire.

After being held captive for a while, Mariatu thought she
might be allowed to leave physically unscathed. But just as
she was walking off, she was stopped and told she must first
choose a punishment. It wasn't much of a choice: Which hand,
they asked, did she want to lose first?

"Three boys hauled me up by the arms. I was kicking now,
screaming, and trying to hit. But though they were little boys,
I was tired and weak. They overpowered me. They led me behind the outhouse and stopped in front of a big rock."

She begged them not to do it, reminding the boys that
she was the same age as they were. That they spoke the same
language. That they could perhaps even be friends. She asked
them why they would want to hurt someone who liked them.

The boys replied that they needed to chop off her arms so she couldn't vote. They told her that they wouldn't kill her—they wanted her to go to the president and show him what they had done to her. They said, "You won't be able to vote for him now. Ask the president to give you new hands."

It took two attempts for the boys to cut off her right hand. "The first swipe didn't get through the bone, which was sticking out in all different shapes and sizes," she writes. It took three tries to cut off her left hand.

The book continues: "As my eyelids closed, I saw the rebel boys giving each other high-fives. I could hear them laughing. As my mind went dark, I remember asking myself: 'What's a president?'"

If anyone at the lunch had any doubt about why they were there, or if their money was well spent, Dr. Azimi and Mariatu dispelled it. The title of Mariatu's book, written with the Canadian journalist Susan McClelland, refers to the moment when Mariatu, after regaining consciousness, and after using her feet to wrap cloth around her arms, and after walking all through the night on snake-infested paths, finally comes across a man who is willing to help her. He has a mango and starts to bring it to her lips, but she shakes her head. "I couldn't eat from his hands. It felt wrong to be fed like a baby." She manages to take a few bites of the fruit by cradling it in her injured arms. She had to do that one thing—feed herself. That meant everything, that she might live.

The Bite of the Mango is written elegantly but simply. It's also the story of how the author survived rape; how she reconnected with friends from her childhood whose arms had also been cut off; how she created a family for herself among other victims of violence in Sierra Leone; how salvation came in the form of a theater troupe she joined, to educate others on the war and on HIV/AIDS, where she found her voice; and how she managed to emigrate to Canada and make a new life for herself while keeping her ties to Sierra Leone and her commitment to build homes for abused women and children there.

Perhaps the most moving thing about Mariatu's book is how she learned forgiveness. She describes a play she performed with the theatrical troupe she discovered in the camp for displaced people where she was living. In one part of the drama, they enacted scenes of the rebel commanders giving the boys drugs to "make them strong men" and beating a boy rebel who refused to take them.

> In the second-to-last scene, the boy rebels huddled together, crying. They admitted their crimes to one another and wished they could return to their own villages and their old lives—much like all of us . . . were wishing we could do.
>
> As I sat on the ground and watched, I realized that the boy rebels who had hurt me must have families somewhere. I thought back to the rebel who'd said he wanted me to join them in the bush. "Would he have asked me to kill?" I wondered.

At the book's end, the author describes how she was offered the opportunity to meet Ishmael Beah, the former child soldier from Sierra Leone who had written *A Long Way Gone*. At first she was unsure she wanted to or could, but then impulsively decided she would. And Beah wound up writing the foreword to her book. He, too, was present at the Women's Refugee Commission lunch.

When the speeches were over, I waved goodbye to Mom, who was not yet ready to go home. She was absolutely mobbed by friends and colleagues who wanted to tell her how much they loved her and how happy they were to have her there. There's no price I wouldn't have paid for Mom to be at that lunch, or to have witnessed it myself and to be able to hold that image in mind: a small, gray-haired lady surrounded by people she adored and admired, people who felt exactly the same way about her.

IN THE DAYS after the lunch, Mom got steadily sicker. It's as though she'd tapped into some hidden reserve of energy to get herself through it, and now there was little left. When I went to see her at home the following week, I found her biting her lower lip. She looked particularly uncomfortable. Still, she had several things she wanted to talk to me about.

"When I had my first MRI, soon after I got sick, they warned me that the sound would be terrible, the clanging of the machine, and that many people found it frightening and unnerving. But really, I told them afterward, it's nothing like the sound of the Russian helicopters that used to take us around to the refugee camps in West Africa. Still, it got me thinking that I might want to write something. Something about how lucky those of us with health care are, and how much we take for granted—and about that remarkable young woman who wrote *The Bite of the Mango* and who spoke at lunch. I'm not sure what—but help me think."

Mom had *The Bite of the Mango* open on the table in front of her. She'd flagged a section in which a friend of the author who works for the Canadian government tells her, "In North America, a lot of kids take getting an education for granted. But when you're from a poor country, you know what an education can do. It can open doors. You may not have hands, but you still have your mind. And I think you have a very sharp mind. Make the most of what you have and you will make your way in the world."

"I also want to write about refugees and courage," Mom said, "and get people to imagine what it would be like if they had to flee right now and leave everything they know and love behind. And I want to write about young people all over the world and how amazing they are—and how little they are trusted or often trust themselves. And about refugee boys—how we need to find things for them to do. And about education in wartime—how it's the most important thing—it's what gives children stability and hope. Even when bombs are falling, you need to find a way to keep kids learning. But I don't know if I feel well enough to write anything right now."

"I could help you write it."

"You don't have time for that."

"But I do. And I'd like to."

"I've been thinking too," Mom continued, "about all the books we've been reading. There must have been other books you wanted to read more than the ones I kept giving you."

"Really, no. Well, maybe at first. But I've loved all of it. Even *Joseph and His Brothers*."

"Me too," Mom said. "But you didn't read all of *Joseph*, did you?"

"No, but I still might."

"You really don't have to," Mom said. It seemed like an odd thing to say. I knew she'd loved that book, even though she at first found it daunting. Then she added: "You've done enough. You've all done enough."

We sat without talking for a while. I was aware that I could hear Mom breathing a little more heavily than usual. She closed her eyes—this time clearly not sleeping but concentrating, as if trying to remember something. Or maybe she was in pain.

"Are you okay, Mom?" I said. I wanted to say so much more—about the book club, about all she'd done for me, about how grateful I was for everything—but it didn't seem the time, it just never seemed the time. And I knew I would start to cry and didn't want to. Not then. Maybe I didn't want Mom to have to comfort me. Or maybe I was scared that once I started, I wouldn't be able to stop.

"I'm fine. I just need a second," Mom said, and abruptly got up and left the room. Ten minutes passed and I wondered if I should check on her, but when she came back, it was with a tea tray. Not mugs with bags, but a teapot, strainer, two cups, milk, sugar—even a tea cozy. I immediately got up and took it from her to place on the table, but Mom poured. "I think some tea will help."

The tea did help. After a few sips, she seemed a little better. "Sometimes," she said, "it makes me feel better just to do something, even to make tea."

"And you said there were other things you wanted to talk to me about?" I asked.

"My obituary. I've put together my résumé, and a list of the places I've been, and some other things. I know it will be time-consuming, but I'm afraid that you're going to have to write it. And I also have letters I've written, one for each of the grandchildren, for when they get older. I want them to know how much their grandmother loved them and how special they all are. I'm trusting you to keep the letters safe and make sure they get them."

At that moment, my brother arrived.

"Good. Now that your brother is here, I want you both to have another look at the wig. I think it's better. Now it's not as dark. And it's not as big, Also, Doug, I want to talk to you more about the service for me: what hymns and what readings." Mom and Doug had already had several conversations about this after their initial ones.

"And one other thing. I'm really trying to make it clear to people that if they're going to cry all the time, then they can't come over. I'm getting ready, but I'm still here."

ON A SATURDAY in May 2009, David and I went for the first time that season to visit our friends Tom and Andy, who'd hosted the first Thanksgiving after Mom's diagnosis, at their house on Fire Island, a gorgeous sunbaked spit of land. David and I call ourselves perma-guests: We are there constantly, but Tom and Andy don't seem to mind. An hour after we arrived, the phone rang. It was Larry Kramer, a great friend of Mom's from the theater world in the 1950s, and of mine from when I was in college and the two of us, along with another friend, wrote a television show together. I'd become very happily entangled in Larry's complicated life as an author and a gay activist, helping him place the rights to his books and edit his massive new novel. David and I had also become very close to his partner, another David. It was one of those calls where you can hear, instantly, in the voice, that all is not well.

"Will, it's Larry," he began.

"Hi, Larry. What's up?"

"Rodger killed himself. He drove from Denver to a town in New Mexico called Truth or Consequences, and he shot himself in the head." Larry was devastated; he and his David and Rodger had been best friends.

As soon as Larry and I finished talking, I called Mom. It had been eighteen months since that first call when Rodger's predictions had so frightened her. In our most recent conversations with Rodger, he'd said that his back continued to bother him terribly and that no surgery had ever done enough to help. He'd also talked to Mom about the loneliness of working on gay rights, how no one in the movement was very nice to anyone else. Mom had suggested he do refugee work—no matter how bad things were in the field, the staff of all the various organizations really looked after one another. More than anything, though, both Mom and I thought he was depressed.

According to Larry, Rodger had always said he would kill himself one day—and that he wanted people to know that if he ever did it, it was because he wanted to. "Yes," Mom said. "People may want to kill themselves. But no one wants to be depressed, or in pain, or lonely, or hurt. When this is all too much, I'm going to choose not to have anything more done for me. But, of course, I'd rather it didn't all get to be too much. Rodger was such a wonderful man and did so much for so many people. I'm going to church tomorrow, Will. And I'm going to pray for him."

I couldn't think of anything to say, so I asked Mom to remind me when the next appointment was with Dr. O'Reilly.

"Friday. After a new scan on Wednesday. I have to decide between now and then if I'm going to do an experimental treatment—that is, if a space is open. I've sent all the paperwork on to your sister. I'm thinking probably not. The one they have in mind is a stage one trial—so they don't really know what dose to give or if it does anything yet. And it involves being in the hospital, and lots and lots of tests. I want to do it if it can help other people—someone has to do these trials. But I also don't want to spend whatever time I have left in hospitals if I can help it. We'll see what the doctor and your sister say, and then I'll make up my mind.

"But between now and then, I'm going to see the Mark Morris production of *Romeo and Juliet*. It's three hours, and I know I probably won't feel up for it, but if I'm going to feel rotten, I'd rather feel rotten watching something wonderful than just sitting in the living room, looking at the wall. Plus, it's that funny Prokofiev version. You know what happens in his version, don't you?"

"I don't," I said. "What happens?"

"It ends happily! The friar alerts Romeo to the fact that Juliet isn't really dead, just drugged, and both Romeo and Juliet live. I think I could use a cheerful *Romeo and Juliet* right now. I think we all could."

The Elegance of the Hedgehog

The Elegance of the Hedgehog by Muriel Barbery came into our lives just when we needed it. Mom, for the first time since I can remember, hadn't been able to find anything she wanted to read. She picked at books—reading a chapter or two and then leaving them by her bedside or in the lobby of her building for her neighbors. I think this was because she was feeling rotten but wouldn't own up to it. We read some poetry. We both loved Mary Oliver's poems—their thoughtfulness and introspection, the way they make you look at the natural world differently. We especially liked the poems that show some irritation with how impatient we all can be, and with our lack of appreciation for the world around us. We read some Nikki Giovanni poems, and some Wallace Stevens. And then someone told Mom about Barbery's *The Elegance of the Hedgehog*. The author, a philosophy teacher, was born in 1969 in Casablanca and now lived in Japan; the book had been published in France a few years before.

First Mom fell in love with the setting of the novel, the

building at number 7, rue de Grenelle, which Barbery so simply describes: the eight luxury apartments, "the old wood-paneled elevator with a black grille and double doors"; and then Mom fell for the "very grand and very beautiful" apartment of one of the characters, Monsieur Ozu. Our co-narrator, the concierge, expects a Japanese interior, "but although there are sliding doors and bonsai and a thick black carpet edged with gray and objects that are clearly Asian—a coffee table in dark lacquer or, all along an impressive row of windows, bamboo blinds drawn at various levels, giving the room its Eastern atmosphere—there are also armchairs and a sofa, consoles, lamps, and bookshelves, all clearly European." In the novel, the apartment is an oasis—of civility, kindness, and elegance.

It may sound strange to fall for an apartment in a novel, but that's exactly what Madame Michel, the concierge, does—not out of avarice but out of awe and respect for the values that created and would be needed to curate such a place. When she enters the apartment, she's able to imagine a different kind of life for herself.

Mom loved talking about real estate, and I think it was in the same way that Madame Michel loved Monsieur Ozu's home—the fantasy of imagining a different life for yourself, or your same life lived differently. Whether the real estate was real or fictional was almost beside the point, because Mom created her own fictional narratives around real places as well as imagined ones. She was constantly looking through circulars and brochures at pictures of houses and apartments. When her eye settled on something she liked, she would start planning.

"We could use this every summer—just for a few weeks—and rent it out the rest of the time. Nico and Adrian will love the loft. There's a hotel nearby for you and David"—somehow David and I usually wound up in the imaginary plans in a hotel nearby, which was fine with us, as I love hotels and I could then join in the planning, adding details about how we would walk over in the morning for a cup of coffee, but still be able to go back in the afternoon for a nap and a trip to the spa—"and a bedroom for Milo and Cy. And Lucy will love the pullout sofa because it's in the dayroom and the sun streams in . . ."

In her last years, as we sat waiting for doctors or chemo, the houses in the real estate section that we looked at were mostly near New York City. But sometimes, depending on what book we were reading, Mom looked farther afield: the Dalmatian Coast or Botswana or the Black Forest or Surrey or Provence or Hua Hin.

The Elegance of the Hedgehog placed Mom and me squarely in Monsieur Ozu's Paris apartment—or perhaps another, similar one. We started to plot our family's life there. We worried about Dad and the tiny elevator, so thought a second-floor apartment (or rather, first, in the European fashion) would make sense. Proximity to museums was key, of course, and the grandchildren would need to be near a park—the Luxembourg Gardens, perhaps. And if the novel teaches you anything (and of course it teaches you much more than this), it's that traffic can be a problem. The children weren't to cross the Boulevard Montparnasse by themselves under any circumstances—at least not until they were ten or so.

We redecorated all sorts of literary apartments and fit our lives into and around them. Never movie apartments or TV apartments—those spaces were too literal, too fleshed out, with no room for the imagination. We went back again and again to a room with a view of the Arno (it would be heaven to stay there two weeks before heading up to Fiesole) or palazzos in the Venice of Donna Leon. And there were always the details—that's what kept it interesting. Just how many nights would we stay? Would we eat in or out?

But as we were falling in love with Barbery's building, we were also falling in love with her characters: Madame Michel, Monsieur Ozu, and Paloma, a jaded little girl bent on both committing suicide and also setting her apartment on fire before she turns thirteen. *The Elegance of the Hedgehog* is, in many ways, a book about books (and films): what they can teach us, and how they can open up worlds. But it's really, like most great books, about people—and the connections they make, how they save one another and themselves. When Madame Michel tries sushi for the first time, she experiences a form of ecstasy. And in the conversation that follows, she gets more than ecstasy—she gets absolution, and she is able to bestow it on Paloma, too.

It's not giving away too much, I hope, to say that the novel ends in death—but also in a kind of reverie about life. And just as Barbery ends with a paradox—the "always" that lives in "never"—so Mom and I found ourselves discussing a related one: even though *The Elegance of the Hedgehog* leads to a death, the experience of reading the book is even more joyful than seeing a *Romeo and Juliet* where they both live. I asked Mom why she thought that was, and she pointed out that joy is a product not of whether characters live or die but of what they've realized and achieved, or how they are remembered.

"I'm not scared to die," she said suddenly. "But I would like this one more summer."

ON JUNE 5, we went to the doctor. We so wanted news that wasn't entirely bad that we at first not only presented an optimistic spin to others but also believed it ourselves. Mom, as always, wrote the blog entry in my voice for me to post. She composed the entry right after we left Dr. O'Reilly's office:

> Very briefly, there was both bad and good news when Mom saw the doctor today after her scan on Wednesday. The bad news is that the tumors are growing; the good news is that there is a spot open in a clinical trial for a drug that may help slow the growth of tumors. Mom can start at the end of June (she will decide about that after reading the material and talking to the doctor next week). This also means that there is no more chemotherapy.
>
> More after she and the hospital have made a decision.
>
> As always, thanks for all your care and support.

Mom then consulted with my sister and read through the materials and quickly came to a realization: the trial made no sense for her. It would start early in July, just as Nina and Sally and Milo and Cy were arriving for the summer. Mom had always said she would choose quality of life over quantity; the procedures would be invasive and time-consuming, and even if there was reason to hope that this trial might slow the growth of the tumors, it was not remotely any kind of a cure.

"I feel very selfish," Mom told me. "I know they need people for this trial. But it's not for me."

"Mom, I don't think that's selfish. And maybe your not participating frees up a spot for someone else—so maybe it's the opposite."

All through Mom's illness, it was hard enough to persuade

her to do something with the logic that it would help her—we often had to make a case for the greater public good. She liked the idea that someone else would be able to take part because she'd declined.

June 2009 would be a month of turning points. Mom's decision not to go ahead with the trial meant that she would no longer be taking any treatment whatsoever to slow the growth of the tumors, as she'd exhausted all the traditional chemotherapies, and the others, like the monthly mitomycin she'd tried, had too many bad effects and not enough good ones. From now on, emphasis would simply be on making Mom as comfortable as possible as the tumors grew.

There would be more visits to the hospital—the C. *diff.* would return with a vengeance. There would be a tumble in front of two of the grandchildren—Mom would be okay but shaken and worried at having scared them. Another time she would fall, late at night, in the apartment—my father would need to summon first a neighbor and then the building's porter to help lift her off the floor. There would be a fund-raiser for the Afghan project, hosted by an IRC friend of Mom's whom she'd drafted to the library cause, that would bring in more than $25,000, an evening for which Mom had helped sweat every detail. There would be the hunt for a first edition of Mann's *The Magic Mountain* to give Nico for his summer birthday. There would be more concerts and movies, and more meetings of our two-person book club.

And there would be a miracle.

The Girl with the Dragon Tattoo

Mom was on a bus on June 21, 2009, when she got a cell phone call about the miracle from our friend Andy, who was now also serving on the Afghan library board. "Have you heard the news?" he asked. Their fellow board member David Rohde, the *New York Times* reporter who had been taken captive by the Taliban and for whom Mom had been praying, had managed to escape along with an Afghan journalist who had been captured with him. After seven months in captivity, they were safe. No one yet knew the details—just that they'd somehow managed to break free of their captors and find their way to safety. Mom told me she couldn't stop smiling even as she sobbed all the way home on the bus. The only other time during her last two years when a piece of news had made her so happy, she said, was when Obama was elected. As soon as she was home, Mom's first response was to call her minister.

"The prayers helped!" she said. "You can take 'David' off the list."

Several weeks later, Mom and Dad made a long day trip to be at the wedding of the child of two of their oldest friends. They didn't know that one of the bridesmaids would be Kristen Mulvihill, David's wife, to whom he'd been married for only a few short months when he was seized. So Kristen and David were at the wedding. David was gaunt and pale, Mom said, as one would expect—but full of energy and remarkably well, all things considered. "We just sat there and held hands," she told me. "I still can't believe he's okay."

I thought back to my conversations with Mom about the Didion—and about magical thinking. There was that morning in Florida when I was convinced that if we saw the manatees, Mom would have a good day. And I also realized that there was a different type of magical thinking—that certain things had to happen if Mom was to have the exit from life that she wanted. One of them was that Obama had to win the election. Another was that David Rohde had to come back safe. In addition to her personal affection for him, I think she regarded him as a talisman of sorts for the fate of the earth. If the David Rohdes were destined to perish, then what hope was there for the world? Whenever anyone doing humanitarian or refugee work or the hard task of journalism in troubled areas was killed or injured, Mom felt it pushed the balance toward chaos. But if a David Rohde could come back from near death, then maybe there was a future for the region and for us all. And if there was, then Mom could leave us all a more peaceful world than the one in which she'd lived. It would be easier for her to let go of life if she believed that everything would be okay. For Mom and David to meet again at a wedding was not just a miracle; it was a sign.

AT THE NEXT doctor visit, the news was worse, as we now expected. The disease was progressing. Mom's fevers and lack of energy were now clearly a result of the cancer—as there was no chemo, and she'd finally gotten rid of the C. *diff.* and other infections. To help with her flagging energy, they tried to give her a transfusion but had to stop because she developed a high fever. There wasn't much to say. The main thing was to concentrate on the next few weeks, when she'd be in the country, in Pawling, New York, with Nina and Sally and their kids. Doug and Nancy and Nico and Adrian and Lucy would also be spending time there. Dad would divide his time between the country and the city; David and I would come to visit. The house, which belonged to one of my father's two sisters, was an old clapboard, with grand trees, fields, and a pool. My aunt had told Mom she could be there as much as she wanted and have all the grandchildren come stay with her there. My father's other sister had also been thoughtful at every turn—visiting, dropping off food, and performing dozens of other kindnesses.

It was time to choose another book—and neither Mom nor I had yet read Stieg Larsson's *The Girl with the Dragon Tattoo*. Everyone had been raving to us about how addictive this book was: a mystery set in Sweden that teamed a journalist who was recovering from a libel verdict with a young Goth woman computer hacker. Larsson himself was a crusading anti-extremist Swedish journalist who had died of a heart attack in 2004 at age fifty, leaving behind three (or possibly four) unpublished novels, of which this was the first. Apparently he'd written them largely as a way to relax after work.

When Mom finally tucked into the Larsson, she was hooked. Lisbeth Salander reminded her, she said, of some of her quirkiest and most interesting students—the high school girls she had taught and admitted to college who'd had lonely and painful childhoods but who'd nevertheless managed to make lives for themselves using their brains and resolve. Lisbeth shared with many of the refugee women Mom knew a special kind of courage and determination, along with a distrust of authorities bred by experience of corruption, capriciousness, and cruelty. It's a book with a strong feminist current—and one that inspires revulsion at the sickening way women around the world are battered and tortured and abused. Mom said it also made her think of all the extraordinary women she'd met in refugee camps who spoke to aid workers and one another about the rapes and other acts of sexual violence committed against them, regardless of the stigma or the risks that came from making their voices heard.

Our next book club meeting (preceding Mom's monthly doctor visit, for which she'd come back into the city) was all about this book. The bizarrely prompt Dr. O'Reilly was running late—so even though Mom had stopped chemo, there was plenty of time to read and chat. To help her conserve her strength, we often now spent as much time reading together as discussing the books.

"You know, Will—I think Stieg Larsson has probably done as much for the things I care most about with this book as any other writer I can think of. It would be very hard to read this and not understand what the Women's Commission has been working for all these years. It's a book I never would have read if so many friends hadn't told me that I must. But now I can't imagine not having read it."

(I had an odd thought about what would have happened if Lisbeth had been one of my mother's students. I was fairly certain Mom would have put her computer skills to work helping reunite "unaccompanied minors" with their families, or redoing the content management system for the library in Kabul.)

We both noted that reading plays a big role in the novel. Bloomkvist needs to comb through thousands of pages of documents to try to solve the mystery and still, when he wants to relax, reaches for a book. Over the course of the novel, he reads Sue Grafton, Val McDermid, and Sara Paretsky, among other mystery writers. While Lisbeth Salander finds what she needs on the computer, Bloomkvist looks to books and genealogies and photographs (and to old-fashioned interviews) for his discoveries. The two characters complement each other, as do their approaches to knowledge.

I thought of the contrast between the physical and digital worlds as we sat together that day. Mom was finishing up the Larsson, holding the book in her lap. I was reading it on an electronic reader. She was turning the pages; I was clicking through them. I showed her the device—she, as always, had no interest.

"I can't see giving up real books," she said. "And I love that I can give away my books after I've read them. Think of the first edition of *The Magic Mountain* I'm giving Nico. It was printed along with the first copy that went to Mann himself. It's got a history."

"But electronic books are good for trips," I said.

"Yes, I can see that. And maybe for books you don't want to keep."

And then something occurred to me. "You know: the thing about our book club is that we've really been in it all our lives."

Mom agreed but pointed out that she'd been doing the same with others too—talking about books with my sister and brother and some of her friends. "I guess we're all in it together," she said. And I couldn't help but smile at the other meaning of the phrase. We're all in the end-of-our-life book club, whether we acknowledge it or not; each book we read may well be the last, each conversation the final one.

I was still waiting to have the big talk, the one where I would tell Mom how much I loved her, and how proud I was of all she had accomplished, and how she had always been there for me—what a great mother she was. And she would tell me, then, how proud she was of me—but she would undoubtedly be carrying some guilt about something or other, and she would tell me that, and I would absolve her completely by genuinely not even knowing what she was talking about.

There had been many days when we'd almost had the big talk but didn't.

On this particular afternoon, I accompanied her home after the doctor's appointment, and we sat for a moment in the living room. Suddenly I heard myself say something that had just popped into my head. "I think I might want to write something—about the books we've read, and the conversations we've had—about our book club."

"Oh, sweetie, you don't want to spend your time doing that. You have so many other things to do and to write."

"I have an idea. And I want to do it." And then my voice broke. "Because I'm proud of you."

I think I initially meant to say "because I love you," but then I heard myself saying "proud" and thought, *I know that Mom knows I love her, but I don't know if she knows I'm proud of her.* So maybe I'd said it that way for a reason.

Mom looked at the floor. I was due to leave soon, so I hurriedly kissed her on the cheek—gently, for fear of bruising her skin—and before I knew it, I was outside the door of the apartment. For the longest time, I stood there, unwilling or unable to push the elevator button and go home. I stared at her door and for the first time let myself realize fully that soon would come a day when she wouldn't be behind it, when she'd be gone, when I'd be unable to talk to her about books, about anything. I felt a sharp pain and for a moment thought I was having a heart attack, but it was just panic. And finally, grief. I rang for the elevator and took the subway home.

The next day I got an email from Mom. She'd put together a list of all the books we'd read, with notes—for my book. Mom kept sending me additions to the list and emails with thoughts she'd had. That op-ed she'd wanted to write, about Mariatu Kamara, the young woman from Sierra Leone—that should be in my book. Also something about the need for health care reform. And a piece of advice that she thought was one of the most important things she wanted to pass on: You should tell your family every day that you love them. And make sure they know that you're proud of them too.

Brooklyn

An eight-hour day at the hospital for a transfusion preceded a trip back out to the country house my aunt had loaned us. The transfusion had to be interrupted twice as Mom's fever spiked. A friend of hers sat through the whole thing with her. When I asked Mom that night how she felt, she said, "A little guilty to be taking that much blood—but for fifty years I've donated blood to the Red Cross every time there was a blood drive, so I guess it's okay if I take a little bit of it back."

The first days after she returned to the country went smoothly, though it was taking a titanic effort for her to make it through each day. Still, just sitting in the July sun, watching her grandchildren and reading when she had the energy, was enough. It had been twenty months, almost two years, since she'd been diagnosed—and she was well aware that she had survived far longer than anyone had expected. Then one day she woke up with a fever that got worse and worse. My sister and Sally and the boys were in the pool. Mom didn't tell Nina and Sally there was a problem; she just called a car service to bring her back to the city. All they had available was a limo, and Mom didn't want to bother anyone, so she said she'd take it. By the time the limo got there, a half hour later, she was able to convince my sister to let her go to New York by herself. Everyone waved to "Gram" as she went off in the limo.

We had reached a point when it was hard to tell if any visit to the hospital would be the one from which Mom would never return. She was so frail—well under a hundred pounds. Later, my sister said she wasn't sure it would be the worst thing if the boys' last memory of their grandmother was of her getting into a limousine. My father and I met Mom at the hospital. They soon had her on a gurney. The port, implanted in her chest for her chemo treatments, was now protruding from her skin, a foreign object that no longer served any purpose, like a gas pipe that jutted into an apartment now heated by steam and electricity.

Mom's stent, the device that kept the path open between her bile duct and her liver, had become blocked and infected—she would spend three days in the hospital having it replaced. My sister was desperate to come back into the city with her kids—but no, that was out of the question. They were to enjoy the country and the pool. Mom would be back, and Dad would stay by her side in the meantime.

When I went to see Mom the second day in the hospital, I asked her if she had enough to read—she did. While she dozed, I picked up *Daily Strength for Daily Needs* from beside her bed. That day's entry read, "This is of great importance, to watch carefully,—now I am so weak—not to over fatigue myself, because then I cannot contribute to the pleasure of others; and a placid face and a gentle tone will make my family more happy than anything else I can do for them. Our own will gets sadly into the performance of our duties sometimes" (Elizabeth T. King).

Four days later, Mom returned to the country house. There was no way she was going to miss spending time with her grandchildren. She was back just in time for a birthday party she'd organized—Milo's sixth and Nico's seventeenth and my forty-sixth. As all our birthdays were in July, Mom wanted one big party for us all together, as well as separate parties for each of us.

Mom and Dad had bought lots of presents for everyone that day, including two for me. The first box I opened had a cream-colored sweater in it. It was nice, but it just didn't seem like the kind of thing I would wear. I thanked her but stuck it aside. She'd also bought me a wonderful assortment of books. She hadn't read any of them, but she did have her own copy of one, *Brooklyn* by the Irish novelist Colm Tóibín, which had just been published. We decided that it would be the next book for our club.

We'd both already read several novels by Tóibín: *The Master* and *The Story of Night* and *The Blackwater Lightship*. Tóibín's portrayal of the relationship between gay men and their mothers, a theme that features in several of his works, was a topic Mom and I never discussed—perhaps because it seemed a little too close. I had come out to my parents when I was twenty and was taking a term off from college during my junior year to work in television in Los Angeles. I'd told everyone at college I was gay the day I arrived—yet I waited more than two years to tell Mom and Dad because I was worried that it would change our close relationship. Eventually, I felt I couldn't wait any longer. While I was in Los Angeles, I'd submitted a very gay short story I'd written to a national gay literary magazine, which had accepted it—so I felt it only fair to warn them before it appeared on newsstands. I did so with a letter.

Because I'd written them a letter, Mom replied by mail. Her letter admitted that her first reaction had been to be upset—and then she'd been upset at herself for being upset. She wrote that being married and having children had been her greatest joy, and she'd always wanted the same for all of us. Also, she wrote, she knew that, with the prejudice of society, being gay meant I would have a harder life, and no one wanted a harder life for a child. She added that if I wanted to be a writer, she hoped I'd be a writer, not a gay writer.

Dad was fine with it all, she wrote—his only worry was that I was going to want to talk about it all the time. The letter ended with her telling me that they loved me and we could all talk more about it later. We never did—but after a short period of some awkwardness, from then on I was able to count on their love and support. They took to David as soon as they were introduced. My sister came out to them a few years after she'd graduated from college. I don't think Mom saw that coming either.

Then as now, I looked to books to help me make sense of my life. Most important to me had been Christopher Isherwood's *Christopher and His Kind,* a memoir in which he wrote about his life from 1929, when he moved as a young man to Berlin (mostly, as he wrote, to meet boys), to 1939, when he moved to America. During that time, he'd palled around with his school friend the poet W. H. Auden; amply sampled Berlin's louche nightlife; fallen in love with a German man, and wandered all over Europe trying to avoid the Gestapo, which was pursuing them; and written *The Berlin Stories,* his classic work, which was later made into the play *I Am a Camera,* the Broadway musical *Cabaret,* and the film of the same name.

I don't know whether Tóibín prefers to be called a gay writer or just a writer. Though you could argue *Brooklyn* is written from a gay sensibility, there's nothing gay in the plot.

COME AUGUST 2009, my sister and Sally and their kids had returned to Geneva; Mom and I and the rest of the family were back in New York, sweating our way through the month. Our book club met again as we waited for our appointment with Dr. O'Reilly. Mom and I had arrived almost an hour early for no reason we could figure out.

We both sat reading *Brooklyn,* side by side in chairs at the Memorial Sloan-Kettering waiting room. The novel tells the story of a young woman named Eilis who, after bravely establishing a new life for herself in 1950s Brooklyn, finds a part of her that wants to stay in Ireland after her return there.

I kept pausing to point out to Mom some of my favorite passages. Before Eilis leaves for Brooklyn, she watches her sister going about daily tasks. Tóibín writes of Eilis, "And then it occurred to her that she was already feeling that she would need to remember this room, her sister, this scene, as though from a distance." As I showed it to Mom, I was struck by the thought that I was attempting to be fully present while also, like Eilis, trying to fix images in my head—just as I'd tried to freeze time with a camera nearly two years before in Maine, when I'd taken that picture of Mom with all her grandchildren.

Tóibín also writes of Eilis: "What she would need to do in the days before she left and on the morning of her departure was smile, so that they would remember her smiling."

Eerily, just then, from across the room, a woman rose and caught my eye, as if to ask permission to interrupt, which she then did.

"Excuse me," she said to Mom, "but I've seen you here before, and I just have to say that you have the most beautiful smile."

Mom looked a little surprised, and then beamed.

"Is this your son?" continued the woman.

"Yes, this is Will, my second son. I also have a daughter."

"Your mother," she said to me, "has the most beautiful smile."

Then she went back to the sofa.

Reading further, I came to "Some people are nice . . . and if you talk to them properly, they can be even nicer."

"Wasn't she nice," said my mother. "That woman. So nice." And Mom went over to her and sat next to her, and they held hands and talked. Or rather, Mom listened.

I kept reading as they talked. Soon I was at a vivid part of the book, the transatlantic crossing, a rough one, in which Eilis is desperately seasick and vomits everywhere.

Of course, the irony of reading about nausea while surrounded by people undergoing chemotherapy wasn't lost on me, or on Mom, when I mentioned where I was in the book.

DAD MET US there, right before it was time to see Dr. O'Reilly. Mom was now officially on home hospice, meaning that the only goal was to make her as comfortable as possible while she died, preferably at home. She could have home visits from hospice nurses and attendants whenever she wanted and as often as she needed. She was also told that she could resume treatment at any time, if she wanted. Nessa had come back and had met with us all, explaining how it worked and all the services available, including massage and guided meditation; the use of a hospital bed; round-the-clock care at home when the time drew close; and medicines we would store in the refrigerator and could give Mom to help with the pain as she neared death. Mom had no doubt whatsoever that home hospice was the right course for her. She'd always said she would let us know when it was time. It was time.

So it would be a very different kind of doctor's visit. As if to mark that, we met in an examination room where we'd never been. It was identical to the others, but different, a little smaller. It had been raining all day, so I had with me an umbrella, which kept falling over. Dad and I had to cram together a bit for Dr. O'Reilly to draw the curtain and do her examination.

Why wouldn't the damn umbrella stop falling over?

Mom had her usual list of questions—the swelling, the Ritalin, the steroids, Megace for the appetite. Dr. O'Reilly answered them all and then told us what we knew: the tumors were growing very rapidly.

I looked at the sheet of questions Mom had prepared. The last item on the list wasn't a word or words but punctuation: a single lone question mark.

"Mom," I prompted, "was there something more you wanted to ask the doctor?"

There was silence.

"Well, first, now that I'm on hospice, they said I could still come see you. And I wanted to see if that was okay."

"Of course," said Dr. O'Reilly. "We'll make an appointment for a scan and another visit in September." Mom had been breathing quite shallowly. I could now hear her breathe more easily. We were planning things for September.

"And I have some questions about the hospice. Nessa was wonderful. But I just want to ask again what my family should do when I die."

"Well, they'll call the funeral director. We can give you one, or you can find one through the church."

"And," said Mom, "I need to have a copy of my 'Do Not Resuscitate' for home."

Dr. O'Reilly suggested we just do a fresh one—Mom could fill it out, and she would sign it. She had someone bring one in—one of the other nurses Mom loved who had been helping. Mom asked me to fill it out for her, and I began:

M-A-R-Y A-N-N-E

Mom looked over—her face a bit panicked. "Sweetie, you've done it wrong. There's no *e* on the end. It's Mary Ann."

"But you've always spelled it with an *e* on the end," I said.

Then I realized that even though Mom had indeed spelled her name with an *e* at the end of *Anne* ever since she was a little girl—maybe because she liked the more English *Anne,* as in Queen Anne—her name was actually Mary. And her middle name was Ann. Without an *e*. I'd never known Mom's real name.

I thought of Wouk's Marjorie Morgenstern, who had changed her name to Morningstar. I hastily scribbled over the *e* with the pen. And that's how the DNR order remained—with one scribbled-out letter. I worried from that point on that they would ignore Mom's wishes and hook her up to all sorts of dreadful machines, all because of an irregularity in the paperwork—all because her son didn't even know her name.

At the end of the appointment, Mom had her usual questions for Dr. O'Reilly just as she had for her other favorites there. Mom wanted to know about their families, their vacations, what they were reading. But this time Dr. O'Reilly asked Mom something she'd never asked before.

"Do you mind if I give you a hug?" she asked Mom.

The two of them embraced, gingerly, but for what seemed like an entire minute. They were both the same height. Dr. O'Reilly was in her white doctor's coat. Her short blond bob grazed her collar. Mom's hair had grown back a bit now that she'd been off chemo. She was wearing a coral-colored mandarin-collar shirt, made of silk. Dad and I sat awkwardly, not sure whether to look at them or away. It's not a very hopeful sign when your oncologist gives you a goodbye hug—but that only went through my mind later. It was a hug of genuine sweetness and affection: two people comforting each other, like sisters parting before one left on a long trip to a distant land.

My Father's Tears

※ ※

The part of *Girls Like Us,* the book about Joni Mitchell, Carly Simon, and Carole King, that didn't have anything to do with Mom was the creative struggle of the three of them—their need and desire to express themselves by making music. Mom was not a creative person—she didn't compose songs or lyrics or even play an instrument, didn't write poetry or fiction, rarely kept a diary, didn't paint or draw or make sculptures, cooked decently but not creatively, liked to have some nice clothing but didn't spend too much time thinking about it. (To complement her pearls, she had some artisan and family brooches she liked, and quirky jewelry, made from watch innards and such, bought abroad and at craft fairs; but she wasn't otherwise interested in jewelry.) I asked Mom if she missed acting (she didn't) and if she wished she'd written (she said definitely not, though she did enjoy the time she tried to write a proposal, with a friend of mine, for a book on volunteering).

So there was no competitiveness whatsoever in Mom's love for music, art, pottery, and literature.

It's almost taken for granted now that people—children especially—should be encouraged to create, and one of the obvious benefits to mankind brought about by the Internet is that it has opened up worlds of creativity. Mom certainly appreciated that. But she also was content not to make things but just to enjoy them.

"Everyone doesn't have to do everything," she told me. "People forget you can also express yourself by what you choose to admire and support. I've had so much pleasure from beautiful and challenging things created by other people, things I could never make or do. I wouldn't trade that for anything."

This had been a theme throughout her life. She had always gone to museums and galleries and had a rule for herself about buying art, which was to try whenever possible to buy works at galleries by young artists at a point in their career when a sale really made a difference. She still went to see as much art as she could, although walking around galleries was now proving too tiring.

What captured her attention most as she became increasingly frail was pottery. Just as one book leads to another, so one potter had led to others; with the help of her friends in England, her love of the jolly geometric art deco work of the British potter Clarice Cliff had led her to the work of the master potters Lucy Rie and Hans Coper, and then to a new generation of young British potters, who worked with monochrome glazes and simple forms and celebrated the human touch: the slightly off-kilter shape, the uneven lip of a vase, the subtle imperfections and slight asymmetries that give character and life to inanimate objects. This was a passion she and Dad shared. Among their favorites were Edmund de Waal, Julian Stair, Rupert Spira, Carina Ciscato, and Chris Keenan.

Looking at the pots, now from one angle, now from another, arranging them in various ways, eggshell delicate next to sturdy, watching the light come across them and cast shadows, feeling their weight and texture—all of this was a form of meditation for Mom. I would come over and see her admiring the pots with a kind of middle focus—not staring at them but quietly taking them in. Living with these beautiful objects gave her great pleasure and peace.

Part of curating, collecting, and appreciating was editing—Mom never had much patience for junk or for crassness, and less so now that she knew her time was limited. I, on the other hand, continue to waste a significant portion of my life watching reality television, learning about the lives of dubious celebrities, and consuming cultural garbage with the feigned irony and faux populism that's a hallmark of my generation and the ones that immediately follow. It was inconceivable to Mom why I would want to go see *Return to the Blue Lagoon* or sit glued to the television watching a Sunday reality-show marathon. When I'd tell her what I'd been up to, she never said anything critical, but she would make a face and quickly try to get me to change the subject. In the middle of that August, while visiting Mom at home, I started talking about a reality television show that just about everyone was discussing. When I paused, Mom asked me if I wanted to read the new Updike collection, a volume published posthumously a few months before called *My Father's Tears: And Other Stories*.

"How are they?" I asked

"They're wonderful. They're so well written. And you know, there was a very smart kid in a freshman seminar I took when I was at Radcliffe. I never really caught his name, and years later I realized it was John Updike. He was clearly brilliant even back then. And the stories bring back so many memories—like our trip to Morocco that we took as a family. And there are ones set in Cambridge, of course. Just start with one, and see what you think."

"Which story is your favorite?"

"The title story. It's a lot about death. Here . . ." And Mom showed me a section. It was a passage about a fifty-fifth high school reunion. It began:

The list of our deceased classmates on the back of the program grows longer; the class beauties have gone to fat or bony-cronehood; the sports stars and non-athletes alike move about with the aid of pacemakers and plastic knees, retired and taking up space at an age when most of our fathers were considerately dead.

It continued:

But we don't see ourselves that way, as lame and old. We see kindergarten children—the same round fresh faces, the same cup ears and long-lashed eyes. We hear the gleeful shrieking during elementary-school recess and the seductive saxophones and muted trumpets of the locally bred swing bands that serenaded the blue-lit gymnasium during high-school dances.

MOM'S SCHEDULE FOR the next two weeks was mostly filled with short meetings with friends and family, and with sending emails to the ones she wasn't able to see: her child-hood friends; college classmates; the women she'd worked with day after day and who had traveled to so many places with her; her fellow admissions officers; other teachers from the schools where she'd taught; her friends on boards with whom she'd served for years and decades; students and cousins and nieces and nephews. It gave her not only hap-piness but strength—in the eyes of her oldest friends and colleagues and extended family, she wasn't a painfully thin seventy-five-year-old gray-haired woman dying of cancer—she was a grade school class president, the friend you gossiped with, a date or double date, someone to share a tent with in Darfur, a fellow election monitor in Bosnia, a mentor, a teacher you'd laughed with in a classroom or faculty lounge, or the board member you'd groaned with after a contentious meeting.

Updike was dead. But when she read him, she read a book by that smart-as-a-whip classmate who was in her freshman seminar, and the truths that he had to impart about aging and relationships spoke to her.

I read *My Father's Tears* cover to cover that night and re-turned it to her so she could give it to someone else. We didn't talk about it. I had nothing to add. But every time we men-tioned the title, it felt odd, as though we were talking about Dad after Mom's death—something she rarely touched upon, and then only lightly: planning trips for us all to take without her, or dinners we would have at his club. Ever since we'd read *Crossing to Safety,* the Stegner, and Mom had let me know that she was sure Sid would be okay after the death of his wife, Charity, well, we had left it at that—and never returned. So we stopped mentioning the title of the new Updike. We just called it The New Updike.

THE THIRD BOOK we read together in August was the wildest: *Big Machine* by Victor LaValle, a thirty-seven-year-old novelist and short-story writer. Mom had read an article about it in *The Wall Street Journal* while she was at my aunt's house in the country. I mentioned this to a friend who'd published the book, and to whom Mom had given some school advice for her daughter, and before we knew it, a copy was waiting for Mom. Mine I bought.

It's a fantastical story—a porter/janitor, on the prompting of a note, and with the gift of a train ticket, whisks himself off to a strange Vermont colony of African Americans dubbed The Unlikely Scholars, a group tasked with investigating odd phenomena. What follows is a saga of odd beginnings, male pregnancy, Native American lore, demonology, serial killers, and feral cats. Mom was thrilled with it. Sure, she'd read the end first, but it provided barely any clues at all as to what would take place in the rest of it.

I was excited to talk with Mom about *Big Machine*. One of the things that had been bothering me about so many of the books I'd read over the last decade was their sheer ordinariness and predictability. It's not that I liked lunacy for the sake of lunacy, but if a writer can truly surprise me without throwing logic completely out the window, then that writer has me for good. Most book surprises aren't surprising at all but follow a formula, like the dead body that's certain to lurch out of a wreck being explored by deep-sea divers in just about every book that involves wrecks and divers.

"What did you think?" I asked Mom.

"It's fascinating—I think I read it in one sitting. I can see why they compare him to Pynchon."

"I've never read Pynchon," I admitted. Mom gave me a look. "But I will!"

"Everybody's scared of Pynchon; I always thought he was great fun to read. But I think my favorite thing about the La-Valle is what it has to say about second chances."

At the end of the book, a character named Ravi (aka Ronny) asks the narrator if people can really change, even people like him. Ronny is an odd fellow who can "wiggle his long nose in a way that looked both funny and sexual." He'd been a gambler and a lout—his brother had thrown him out, and everyone now shunned him. What he's seeking isn't redemption but an invitation back into the world of people, "just the possibility of relief."

The narrator in the book says that people can indeed change. LaValle writes, in the narrator's voice, "To be an American is to be a believer. I don't have much faith in institutions, but I still believe in people."

"That's really so much of what I think about," Mom said. "And that's one of the things I loved about my work with the refugees. They're just people like us who've lost everything and need another chance. The world is every bit as surprising as what happens in this novel—crazy things do happen when people least expect it. But it takes so little to help people, and people really do help each other, even people with very little themselves. And it's not just about *second* chances. Most people deserve an endless number of chances."

"Not everyone?"

"Of course, not everyone," Mom said. "When I think back

to Liberia and the horrific way Charles Taylor terrorized his country, and what he did to Sierra Leone, and the millions of lives he destroyed, and the cruelty and savagery—well, he's pure evil. He will never deserve another chance. If you believe in good, you also believe in evil, pure evil."

We found ourselves talking quite a bit about *Big Machine*. It's a fun book to discuss, but also the perfect book to read and dissect when you are all hopped up on Ritalin, as Mom was then. One of Mom's greatest fears was that she wouldn't be able to read in the weeks leading up to her death, that she'd be too sick or too tired or unable to concentrate. And she had many days when she was too sick to read—days that found her watching videos or old episodes of *Law & Order* or endless amounts of CNN and other political commentary. When she would say of a book like *Big Machine* that she'd read it in one sitting, it was both praise for the book and a way of letting all of us know that she was still herself, able to concentrate, stay awake, and be enthralled. As long as she could read books in one sitting, the end wasn't quite in sight.

LATER IN AUGUST, I went over one afternoon to Mom and Dad's apartment to help Mom with some errands. She'd been finding it harder and harder to eat. She'd rediscovered aspic, that classic of the 1950s, and one of my partners at the cooking website had made her some she loved, as had a family friend who was a caterer. Another friend, who'd been married to my father's best pal, found a shop that sold jellied consommé. It was a return to the 1950s and 1960s, to the fancy dinner party food of Mom's youth—all those strange, savory gelatinous dishes. Mom could eat corn, too—and friends brought her that. And blueberry muffins, which several people provided. But little else.

Mom was starting to waste away. She was dramatically thinner and frailer than even a week before, when we'd strolled off to a café a few blocks uptown for muffins, and when Mom had been able to talk for hours on camera to a friend in the building who was making a documentary about women who inspired her. Now, just seven days later, we had one errand: to cross the street and go to the bank's cash machine. Mom shakily took my hand as we headed out. Every step was deliberate and tentative.

New York is a place that inspires hypocrisy. When I'm walking, I curse the cabs that race through yellow lights, but I tip generously when I'm late and my driver does just that. And I barrel down busy sidewalks—but now, when I was with my mother, so unsure of each step, so fragile, I couldn't believe the rudeness of the people who raced by us, swinging their arms or recklessly toting ungainly bags or backpacks. It was terrifying just making it to the corner and crossing the street. No one even paused for the lady with the thin gray hair, so determined still to take part in the life of the city, not yet ready to lie in bed and die.

My sister was soon back in town, as she'd been so many times over the last two years. Dad took Mom on other trips around the city, as did my brother and sister-in-law and many friends. Mom wouldn't use a wheelchair or a walker—but she did take a cane. Most errands she did with one of us. Others she insisted on doing on her own—despite everyone's pleas—like going to a dress shop to get a black dress for my sister. Only later did Nina realize that Mom thought Nina should have something new and smart to wear at Mom's funeral. My nine-year-old nephew Adrian was studying the Harlem Renaissance—so Mom kept making forays to various galleries to see if she could find him an affordable print by James Van Der Zee, one of the great photographers of the 1920s and beyond. She couldn't, but kept trying.

Mom and I found ourselves talking more and more about the conversations she had every day with her grandchildren. It's not an exaggeration to say that she lived for them, especially in her final weeks.

Friends came over, and she continued with alternative treatments—the biofeedback and also Reiki massage. A former student sent her lots of information about New Age philosophy and psychics. "Your father would have a fit," she said to me. But Mom was open to it and touched by how much this young woman cared, though she never did go to a psychic.

MY FATHER ACTUALLY had very few fits anymore. He's a big man with a big personality, but he tiptoed through the house so as not to disturb Mom when she was resting. His office is a few blocks away, and Mom had to beg him not to come home during the day—he was approaching his eighty-second birthday, and she was worried about him charging around in the August heat.

Some of Mom and Dad's friends and family expressed surprise at the depth of his care and devotion. Theirs had been one of those relationships where he was known as the difficult one. Dad was irascible; Mom made peace. Dad had limited patience for noisy children and people asking for favors; Mom was endlessly welcoming. Dad talked to select people; Mom to everyone.

Yet throughout their lives together, Dad's anger was frequently on behalf of Mom—he was always ferociously protective of her. They enjoyed each other's company; they made each other laugh; they loved most of the same things—sharing remarkably similar tastes in music and art—and many of the same people.

All you had to do was to talk with one when the other was away to see how much they worried about each other and missed each other. In private, Dad has always been generous and even sentimental: his opposition to Mom's endless stream of good works usually took the form of proud teasing, which almost always made her smile. And when he got too obstreperous or opinionated, she could usually control him with an "Oh, Douglas!" and a look that was more loving than stern.

Actually, a large percentage of Dad's volatility has always been purely for show. In fiercely liberal Cambridge, he delighted in telling everyone he'd voted for Richard Nixon; only a few years ago did he admit that he hadn't. It was just too much fun for him to see the reactions. He also jokingly referred to himself as the meanest dad in Cambridge, based on the occasional philosophical positions he would take, such as asking kids who were trick-or-treating for UNICEF to choose between candy and a donation. "The idea is to see if *you* are willing to give up candy in favor of a donation to starving children," he would instruct some candy-crazed child in a witch costume, "not to see if I'll give you candy *and* a donation. So which is it?" It was always the candy, proving a point to Dad but making Mom shake her head in aggravation in the background.

But as her illness progressed, he no longer insisted on this type of social experiment; he answered the phone (which he still hated) and was even polite to the dozens of callers. From time to time, my mother insisted my father go out to dinner with my brother and me. But other than that, he was home every night, with as much dinner as Mom would eat.

ON MONDAY, AUGUST 24, Mom sent me a new post for the blog. She'd written it, as she'd written all the others, but she was anxious about this one. Did I think it was okay? "Please edit or tell me if it's a bad idea." I told her I thought it was a terrific idea. It was titled "Hospice and Health Care."

Mom wants everyone to know that she has an excellent Hospice team—nurse, social worker, nutritionist—who are taking good care of her. And, with Dad's help and a dose of Ritalin, she has been able to get to some morning Mostly Mozart rehearsals and two afternoon performances. She is not going out in the evening anymore.

We see the doctor next week and will have another medical report after that.

But she also wanted anyone reading this to put full support behind some kind of health care reform. She feels she is so blessed with the care she has received and that it is terribly unfair that people who have worked as hard as she has have no access to care—either because they have lost their jobs or had jobs that didn't provide insurance or have pre-existing conditions that do not allow them to get (or afford) insurance. There is no perfect solution, but some kind of bill has to be passed this fall.

We all send our best to all friends and family.

As word got out, through the blog and otherwise, that Mom was in hospice care, most people correctly understood that meant Mom's death would be very soon—so more and more messages came in. I learned anew a valuable lesson: send those messages. Mom loved reading emails and hearing directly, or through us, from people whose lives she touched. Because she knew I would be writing about her, she started to share them with me.

The following email had come from David Rohde in early August:

Mary Anne:

Thanks so much for your notes. My apologies for not responding to your first message. We went up to Maine to visit family after Madeline and Judson's wedding. Unfortunately, I fell way behind on my email. It was wonderful to see you at the wedding. You looked well. At times, I thought of my imprisonment as a long battle with cancer. I didn't know the outcome, but knew I had to continue to do my best to survive. I was treated well by the Taliban. As I told you, I was never beaten. I was given bottled water and they even allowed me to walk in a small yard each day. In short, I never experienced the physical pain you are suffering.

In some ways, captivity is easier than cancer. I could try to talk to them, at least, and appeal to their humanity. You can't have a conversation with a disease. Your courage through all of this inspires me. Please let me know if there is anything I can do to help you. I'd be happy to get together at any time—if you're eager to hear stories about the Taliban that will take your mind to other places. If not, I completely understand. Rest. Relax. Do not reply to this email. Your body needs time to recover. As a prisoner, I realized that the basics—sleeping and eating— were the most important things in keeping me going.

I'm sending prayers your way, just as you sent prayers my way. In the end, we decided our fate was in God's hands. We fought, of course, but we knew God would decide what happened to us. That gave us comfort in what seemed an impossible situation. Then—suddenly and against all expectations—we escaped and survived. From the bottom of my heart, I wish you the same.

Best,

David

Too Much Happiness

There were no doctor appointments in the last weeks of August, so our book club met at Mom and Dad's home while Dad was at his office.

On this late August day, I had come over to help with errands, and then, when I finished, I sat next to Mom on the sofa, and we both prepared to read. First we had to find her reading glasses. She'd misplaced them. She always used cheap ones, from the drugstore. After her death, Doug and Nina and I would go through the apartment to gather them. We found twenty-seven pairs, tucked away everywhere: in cushions, in cabinets, in drawers and pockets, behind vases and frames. Every time she misplaced a pair, she'd buy another.

Today, we find a pair—and she's excited to be reading *The Miracle at Speedy Motors,* a new mystery by Alexander McCall Smith from his The No. 1 Ladies' Detective Agency series. Mom soon comes across a passage she wants to show me, and hands the book over to me, finger-marking a place:

Mma Makutsi was right about villages, even the bigger ones, like Mochudi, where Mma Romtswe had been born. Those places were still intimate enough for a rough description to suffice. If somebody had written a letter addressed to "That man who wears the hat, the one who was a miner and knows a lot about cattle, Mochudi, Botswana," it would undoubtedly have been correctly delivered to her father.

This passage makes me smile. I know Mom is watching my face as I read it, waiting for me to show that I enjoy it. But that's not enough, of course. We need to discuss it.

"That's wonderful," I say. "You really feel you know the place. It's a great description."

"I went to so many villages like that when I was in Africa," says Mom. "He's got it absolutely right."

When I looked at Mom in that moment, I saw not a sick person, but not quite the same Mom I'd known all my life. After reading so much together, and after so many hours together in doctor's offices, I felt I'd met a slightly different person, a new person, someone quirkier and funnier. I was going to miss my mother dreadfully but also miss this new person, too—miss getting to know her better.

Mom had one more thing she wanted to show me that day, before I left, and one more thing she wanted to tell me. First: There was a new edit of the video my friend had shot in Kabul. The video now began with two large bags of books being stowed in the back of a car; it showed a pine bookshelf being lashed to the top of the car; then it followed the car as it made its way to a school an hour from central Kabul. It showed dozens of Afghan girls reading books and laughing and pointing out passages to one another, and beaming with pride as Nancy Hatch Dupree looked on. They were reading, really reading, real books. Sure, there were only five hundred books for eight thousand students. But they'd never had any books at all before.

As for the one other thing Mom wanted to tell me that day:

"You mustn't let my frequent flyer miles go to waste after I'm gone. I'll give you my passwords. Delta is for you; BA for your brother; American Airlines for your sister."

DAD'S EIGHTY-SECOND BIRTHDAY was at the end of the month, and we had a small dinner party for him. On my way out the door, Mom stopped me. She wanted to know if I'd remembered to call one of her former students who was moving to New York and wanted some job advice. I told her I had. Then she whispered something to me, with a conspiratorial smile: "A friend left me a plant—to help me have an appetite. I made it into a tea just like she said. But I didn't like it, so I'm not doing that again."

It took me a minute to figure out that Mom was talking about marijuana. We'd occasionally teased her and Dad for being the only two people we knew in Cambridge in the 1960s who were progressive Democrats and who'd never tried pot. Once when I asked her why they hadn't, she said it was because no one ever offered it to them. I have a hard time believing that.

<hr />

NOW THAT WE'D finished the Updike, and *Big Machine,* and the McCall Smith (well, she had—I was behind), it was time to decide on a new book.

We had two lined up: *Feasting the Heart* by Reynolds Price, a collection of short pieces that this great American novelist had been delivering aloud on National Public Radio since 1995; and *Too Much Happiness,* a new collection of Alice Munro stories. It had just been published in England but not yet in America; a friend of Mom's had brought her a copy.

Our last visit to Dr. O'Reilly was on September 1. I have no recollection whatsoever of what we talked about. There just can't have been that much to say. The next day, I went over to have lunch with Mom, or to have lunch while Mom sat and watched me. She was down to ninety-four pounds and trying to eat but not able to do much more than have a few bites of something, or a little soup.

I was due to fly to San Francisco for a quick trip the next week and wasn't at all sure I should go. My trip was to meet with venture capitalists on Sand Hill Road in Silicon Valley to see if I could convince someone to add funding to the business. The website was going fairly well, but we were desperately in need of cash. Mom was adamant that I should go on the trip and not worry about her—she was feeling a little better, she said.

We talked, that day, about family, plans, and an upcoming show of one of my sister-in-law's paintings. The second-richest family in India had commissioned Nancy to do a giant mural for the ballroom of the house they were building in Mumbai, which would be the tallest private house in the world; Nancy was going to display the mural in her studio, for family and a few friends, before shipping it off. Mom didn't want to miss that—and neither did I, so I would fly back in time to see it. Nina was coming in for a few days to see Mom—so she'd be able to see it too. As Mom and I talked about Nancy's show and everything else, it seemed like a normal family day, devoted not to literature or to melancholy, just to logistics, with Mom in her role as air traffic control, directing all the various comings and goings of the family. She was still looking ahead, and so I took my cues from her. Did she want to talk about how she was feeling? Not today. Today she wanted to plan.

Even the books were scheduled. I would take the Price on my trip, as Mom had already read most of it; she would read the Munro while I was gone and then loan it to me.

THAT MONDAY, LABOR Day, I flew to San Francisco to stay with an old college friend and go to my meetings. I had no idea how tired I was—most of the first evening, Labor Day, I spent in his living room, reading, dozing off, and listening to his monster stereo. When I called Mom the next day, she could talk only for a few minutes. She really wasn't feeling great.

I finished the Reynolds Price—fifty-two brief personal essays. Price describes an unusual childhood and looks back on himself in a cowboy uniform but with a Shirley Temple doll. He writes about the England that Mom loved in the 1950s, when "professional theater was incomparably brilliant, and ticket prices were laughably small," and includes a very moving tribute to teachers. He recounts his obsession with being on time and his frantic worry for (and growing irritation with) people who aren't. And he reflects, amid chapters on more mundane topics, on sickness—on the devastation and sadness of AIDS, on being in a wheelchair, and on death. "We've reached a point in American history when death has become almost the last obscenity. Have you noticed how many of us refuse to say 'he or she died'? We're far more likely to say 'she passed away,' as though death were a sterile process of modest preparation, followed by shrink-wrapping, then rapid transit—where? Well, elsewhere. In short, it's the single thing we're loath to discuss in public." That page was dog-eared by Mom.

My first day of meetings with the venture capitalists was not fun. I'd come from the world of books, which was a big strike against me. It was like walking into Boeing and seeking a job with a résumé full of experience with horses and carriages. That afternoon I called Mom again, and we had a quick chat. She didn't sound like she was any better, but she told me she was.

I slept uneasily and woke up early for my second day of meetings. When I called Mom, she was clearly in pain and could talk only a minute. But she wanted to know how the meetings were going—and wanted to tell me that under no circumstance was I to cut my trip short. I still had two more days of meetings scheduled. When I called again later in the day, she mentioned that she'd stopped eating. I canceled everything and drove straight to the airport to catch the red-eye home.

There is no place more perfectly lonely than an airport at night when you fear someone you love is dying and you're rushing to see that person. I drank two Scotches, took an Ambien, woke up in New York, and took a cab straight to Mom and Dad's apartment.

I'D CALLED DAD to tell him I was rushing home. The fact that he didn't advise me not to told me all I needed to know about how much things had deteriorated over the last forty-eight hours. My sister arrived at our parents' apartment a few hours before me. She was sitting next to Mom, who was upright in bed in her bedroom when I walked in. I saw a look of real anger flash across Mom's face.

"What are you doing here?" she said. She was more than angry—she was furious.

"The trip wasn't going well, so I decided to cut it short," I said. "I have a lot to do here this week, and it was crazy to be out there having meetings that weren't going to amount to anything."

We left it at that, but Mom continued to glower at me. I'd deviated from the plan—that was part of the anger. But the bulk of it, I'm convinced, was her anger at death. She wasn't quite ready to go. She still had so many things to do. And my rushing back made it that much harder to believe that there was world enough and time. I spent the rest of the day at the apartment with Nina and Dad. Eventually Mom's face softened, and she either stopped being mad at me or forgot that she was. We had dinner at the dining table, and Mom came in and sat with us. She'd put on one of her favorite blouses and a turquoise scarf and her pearls. She was still making plans—including for Nancy's opening. But she recognized she might finally need to use a wheelchair. I volunteered to find a taxi or car service that could take one. Now she weighed less than ninety pounds, but to me she looked like herself, just a paler, smaller version. Frail but strong.

I'd brought back the Reynolds Price book and put it on her

shelf. That afternoon, when Nina had gone for a run, I'd sat next to Mom in her bedroom.

"We haven't heard anything about Patrick Swayze recently, have we?" she asked, referring to the actor who had been diagnosed with pancreatic cancer soon after she had and who'd done the television special she so admired.

"No, we haven't," I said.

"I guess he's doing as badly as I am."

We then talked about the books. She'd finished the Alice Munro stories and loved them. "They kept me happy all weekend," she said. There was one that she wanted me to read. Set in Munro's native Canada, it was called "Free Radicals," and it was about a woman named Nita, a big reader, who is dying of cancer. Munro describes the way Nita reads:

> She hadn't been just a once-through reader either. *Brothers Karamazov, Mill on the Floss, Wings of the Dove, Magic Mountain,* over and over again. She would pick one up, thinking that she would just read that special bit—and find herself unable to stop until the whole thing was redigested. She read modern fiction too. Always fiction. She hated to hear the word *escape* used about fiction. She might have argued, not just playfully, that it was real life that was the escape. But this was too important to argue about.

In the story, Nita finds herself in mortal danger, from something other than the cancer, and manages to save herself from the immediate threat with a story she makes up about a murder. It's a darkly funny tale with a Somerset Maugham ending—the kind Mom and I loved. Books save Nita's soul, and a story saves her life, or at least it does so temporarily.

When I got home that night after dinner, I went right to sleep—but woke up in the middle of the night and read *Too Much Happiness* until dawn, skipping just the title story, or rather, saving it for later. Nita was nothing like Mom, other than the fact that they were both readers. But I could see why Mom loved that story the most. All readers have reading in common.

The next day was Friday, September 11. I came back to spend more time with Mom. She was in bed most of the day. We all—Dad, Doug, Nina, and I—spent time with her. She had *Daily Strength for Daily Needs* on her bedside, with the same colorful handmade bookmark holding her place, the one she'd brought back from a refugee camp she'd visited years before.

After some more hours of my trying to find a car service that could take a wheelchair, it became clear that a visit to Nancy's studio to see the mural before it shipped to India was too ambitious. That night we again had a family dinner at the table, and Mom again joined us. She hadn't eaten for days now and had trouble focusing on the conversation. But she was determined to sit with us and did. We told funny stories from our childhood. Mom occasionally grimaced in pain, even though she said she was just uncomfortable. But she also smiled at some of the stories, particularly those that involved Bob Chapman, the theater director she'd fallen in love with as a student at Harvard who'd become the sixth member of our family.

That morning I'd posted the very first blog post I'd written myself. I'd shown it to Mom for her approval. It was she who suggested I add the sentences about Obama. It read:

Starting last Monday, Mom has been feeling much worse. Phone calls are difficult—so it's far better to send her emails than to call. She reads all her emails, but may not be able to answer promptly as she has been spending more time in bed, and has had, for the last few days, a much more limited amount of energy. Her spirits remain strong.

Also, Nina is here from Geneva—and that's great for all of us.

Mom watched Obama's speech and was encouraged by it. She thinks he did an excellent job on the speech, and that it will help get us some kind of health reform this fall, which the country desperately needs.

We all hope everyone had a good Labor Day—and will keep you posted on any news.

Saturday arrived, and Mom was much worse. She spent the whole day in bed, drifting in and out of consciousness. We'd been in touch with Dr. Kathy Foley (Nina's palliative care guru friend) and the hospice people a great deal over the last few days, and they now sent a nurse called Gabriel to walk us again through what we would need to know about delivering pain relief to Mom as she needed it. A vigil had begun, with all of us taking turns sitting an hour at a time with Mom, talking when she was awake, holding her hand when she wasn't. As we'd been told to expect, her breathing was becoming more and more labored.

That afternoon I updated the blog. I did not read it to Mom:

Mom's illness is progressing quickly. She is resting quietly and her pain is being controlled. She is not taking any phone calls or visitors and is not checking her email. We will update the blog every day and thank everyone for your kind thoughts.

It's difficult for us, too, to answer the phone or reply to emails, so please do continue to check the blog for updates.

Again, our thanks to everyone for all your support.

By evening, Mom's pain seemed to increase, so we gave her some morphine. She drifted in and out of consciousness. One of the phrases she kept uttering was "It is what it is." But everyone, including David and Nancy, had one more good conversation with her. With Doug, she talked about the service she wanted. He also asked her if she had any regrets. She said she did have one: She'd always wanted a castle in Scotland. I don't think this was delirium. I think she really did. Mom's minister came by. Doug sat with him and Mom, and they all recited the Lord's Prayer. She'd been very agitated when her minister arrived—she knew what that meant. But after his visit, she did seem, somehow, changed. Lighter, perhaps—as though partially here and already somewhere else.

Then things rapidly deteriorated.

I'd seen so many movies where characters sit by beds as their loved ones die. They give speeches, hold hands, and say, "It's okay—you can let go." What none of those books and movies conveys is how tedious it is. My sister and brother both felt the same. We would hold Mom's hand, give her sips of water from a cup, tell her how much we loved her, listen to her labored breathing to try to hear if it was getting more so, and five minutes would have gone by, with fifty-five more to go before another sibling would come in to take over.

Soon there was a hospice nurse to sit with us as much as we needed, and to help us keep Mom clean and comfortable. I would glance over, and the nurse would be adjusting Mom's pillow or dabbing the corners of her eyes or giving her gentle sips of water. It was an extraordinary sight—a stranger tending to our mother with infinite care. David and I ran out to get a little toothbrush with toothpaste preloaded on it, so we could keep her teeth clean. It was something to do when it wasn't our turn to sit with Mom. The alternative was to pace back and forth in the living room.

One unintentionally cruel thing was the phone. There was a local election coming up, and Mom and Dad's number was on every autodial of every politician. All our friends and family were respecting our need for quiet—but the phone kept ringing and ringing, and we would pick it up, on the chance that it was a call from her minister or the nursing service, only to have a recording blared at us trying to convince us to vote for one candidate or another.

AT ONE POINT we all found ourselves out on the terrace—it was one of the brief moments when just the nurse was with her. It was chilly—a true New York autumn evening. We were all exhausted and bracing ourselves for what was to come. And my brother said something that made an immense difference to me. It was an echo of what Mom had said all along—how lucky she was.

"You know," Doug said, "think of it as a deal. If someone said to Mom, 'You can die now, with three healthy children, your husband of almost fifty years alive and well, and five grandchildren whom you love and who love you, all well, all happy'—well, I think Mom would have thought that wasn't a bad deal."

ON SUNDAY, MOM did not have many moments of what seemed like consciousness. She did sit up and smile when David walked into the room. And she did seem to respond to our questions and expressions of love. We were with her constantly. I was wearing for the first time the cream-colored cotton sweater she'd given me for my birthday that year. I think she recognized it. When her hand brushed against it as I was sitting beside her, she smiled. Of course, she was right—it's far and away the nicest and best-fitting sweater I have. It's more than that. It's beautiful.

I was supposed to be at the bat mitzvah of my youngest god-child that weekend and was going to read a Mary Oliver poem as part of the service. But a friend would be reading it in my stead. Since Mom loved Mary Oliver's poetry, I decided to read it to her. It's from a 2004 collection called *Why I Wake Early.*

WHERE DOES THE TEMPLE BEGIN,
WHERE DOES IT END?

There are things you can't reach. But
you can reach out to them, and all day long.

The wind, the bird flying away. The idea of God.

And it can keep you as busy as anything else, and happier.

The snake slides away; the fish jumps, like a little lily,
out of the water and back in; the goldfinches sing
    from the unreachable top of the tree.

I look; morning to night I am never done with looking.

Looking I mean not just standing around, but standing around
   as though with your arms open.

And thinking: maybe something will come, some
   shining coil of wind,
     or a few leaves from any old tree—
       they are all in this too.

And now I will tell you the truth.
Everything in the world
comes.

At least, closer.

And, cordially.

Like the nibbling, tinsel-eyed fish; the unlooping snake.
Like goldfinches, little dolls of gold
fluttering around the corner of the sky

of God, the blue air.

    I felt a bit self-conscious reading it—like someone with
headphones on who suddenly realizes he's singing in the subway. But I like to think that Mom's eyes fluttered when she
heard me say the word *God*.
    When I was finished, I looked around at Mom and Dad's
bedroom—and at Mom, resting relatively peacefully, but with
that rasping breath that means there isn't much time left.
She was surrounded by books—a wall of bookshelves, books
on her night table, a book beside her. Here were Stegner and

320 THE END OF YOUR LIFE BOOK CLUB

Highsmith, Mann and Larsson, Banks and Barbery, Strout and Némirovsky, the Book of Common Prayer and the Bible. The spines were of all colors, and there were paperbacks and hardcovers, and books that had lost their dust jackets and ones that never had them.

They were Mom's companions and teachers. They had shown her the way. And she was able to look at them as she readied herself for the life everlasting that she knew awaited her. What comfort could be gained from staring at my lifeless e-reader?

I also noted a special pile of books. They were to be the next ones for our book club. They were in their own small stack, separate from the others.

MY SISTER TOOK charge, which was a huge relief. She and Mom had always had a bond beyond mother-daughter, something forged when they worked together in the camp in Thailand. My brother read the Bible to Mom, and both he and my sister updated Mom on all the goings-on with her grandchildren. My father spent a lot of time alone with Mom, recounting, as he said, what a grand adventure they'd had together, and how he never could have dreamed of the life that he'd had with her. By this time, she was sleeping all the time, mostly peacefully.

In the hours I spent beside Mom, I talked with her about the books we'd read together, about the authors and characters, about favorite passages. I promised to share them with others. I told her that I loved her.

Mom died at three fifteen in the morning on September 14. The minister had told us that she would likely die in the middle of the night. I'd left at two A.M. to go home and shower. Nina, who was with her when she breathed her last, called me, and I raced back, as did my brother, who was a bit worse for wear, having taken an Ambien. But he was there, as he always has been.

We each spent some time with Mom's body. And in the morning, my sister and I waited for them to remove it. Doug and Dad didn't want to be around for that, so they went out to a diner to get something to eat. Nina and I opened the window to let out Mom's spirit. And just then I noticed a shaft of light touch a tiny picture of the Buddha that my sister-in-law Nancy had painted and that Mom had hung in a place where she could see the light hit it as she lay in bed. It's a beautiful turquoise Buddha—and it glowed.

Next to Mom's bed was *Daily Strength for Daily Needs,* still with the bookmark in it marking the entry for Friday, September 11. I looked in the book first at the Bible passage for that day. It was the shortest entry in the whole book, just three simple words:

Thy Kingdom Come.

Then I read the rest of the page. At the bottom was a quote from John Ruskin:

If you do not wish for His kingdom, don't pray for it. But if you do, you must do more than pray for it; you must work for it.

I believe those were the last words Mom ever read.

Epilogue

For the longest time after Mom's death, I would suddenly be seized with paralyzing guilt over something I'd neglected to tell her during one of our book club meetings: Why didn't I say this thing or that thing? I'd had the perfect opportunity when discussing this book or that. Eventually I came to realize that the greatest gift of our book club was that it gave me time and opportunity to ask her things, not tell her things.

Of course the book club also gave us a welter of great books to read—books to savor and ponder, to enjoy, and to help Mom on her journey toward death and me on mine to life without her.

Since Mom's death, I've heard from all sorts of people who also talked about books with Mom. There are dozens of people whose lives were touched by and touched Mom's—like Brother Brian, who runs the amazing De La Salle Academy in Manhattan, one of Mom's favorite schools; or my "siblings" Ly Kham and John Kermue and Momoh and Dice and Winnie, all friends Mom made when they were refugees—who have mentioned to me conversations they had with her about books or an important book that she insisted they read.

I've also talked with many people who have shared with me stories about times they spent reading or talking about books with someone they loved who was dying: a father, a sibling, a child, a spouse.

The memorial service for Mom was held in her church, Madison Avenue Presbyterian, during a blizzard in February. One of the artists Dad represents, Emma Kirkby, sang Mozart's *Laudate Dominum*. My siblings and I spoke, and so did Nico, representing the next generation. Mom's brother recounted childhood stories about his big sister, including how she'd told him he should really read more books so that he'd have something to talk about with adults—and with girls.

The former head of the IRC spoke of Mom's work with refugees. Harvard's dean of admissions talked of their early days working together, combining Harvard's and Radcliffe's offices. A friend from those days spoke of Mom as role model, friend, and mentor. The president of Kingsborough Community College, the friend who was one of the few who could get Mom to shop, told of their time on boards together, of their travels, and all she'd learned from Mom about life and death.

Walter Kaiser, the Harvard scholar and lifelong friend who'd called Mom every morning, recounted a story about a college trip to Rome with Mom, and how she would smile at absolutely everyone, including young men, and how this frequently led to misunderstanding. Back then he'd said to her, remonstrating: "Mary Anne, you've just *got* to stop smiling at strangers!" Now, at her memorial service, he said, "Who could have foreseen that she would spend the rest of her life doing exactly that—smiling at strangers?"

I OFTEN THINK about the things Mom taught me. Make your bed, every morning—it doesn't matter if you feel like it, just do it. Write thank-you notes immediately. Unpack your suitcase, even if you're only somewhere for the night. If you aren't ten minutes early, you're late. Be cheerful and listen to people, even if you don't feel like it. Tell your spouse (children, grandchildren, parents) that you love them every day. Use shelf liner in bureaus. Keep a collection of presents on hand (Mom kept them in a "present drawer"), so that you'll always have something to give people. Celebrate occasions. Be kind.

Even though nearly two years have passed since her death, I'm occasionally struck by the desire to call Mom and tell her something—usually about a book I'm reading that I know she'd love. Even though she's not here, I tell her about it anyway. Just as I told her about the three million dollars the U.S. government has committed to building the library in Afghanistan. By the time this book is published, the Kabul library will be finished. I like to believe that she knows that.

My mother's friend Marina Vaizey wrote an obituary that ran in London's *The Guardian*. It began: "Mary Anne Schwalbe, who has died aged 75, was one of my closest friends for more than 50 years. We met when she was the head girl at school—and a subtly effective leader at that early age. Mary Anne was an outstanding listener and teacher, which even encompassed passing on grandparenting practice."

It then described some of Mom's passions and jobs and accomplishments. It ended: "This dynamo of energy was contained in a small, quiet, smiling, elegantly dressed woman, who could appear as conventional as a lady who lunched, but travelled the world often in desperately trying circumstances: she was an electoral observer in the Balkans, and was shot at in Afghanistan. Mary Anne saw the worst and believed the best."

I think Marina got it exactly right. Mom taught me not to look away from the worst but to believe that we can all do better. She never wavered in her conviction that books are the most powerful tool in the human arsenal, that reading all kinds of books, in whatever format you choose—electronic (even though that wasn't for her) or printed, or audio—is the grandest entertainment, and also is how you take part in the human conversation. Mom taught me that you can make a difference in the world and that books really do matter: they're how we know what we need to do in life, and how we tell others. Mom also showed me, over the course of two years and dozens of books and hundreds of hours in hospitals, that books can be how we get closer to each other, and stay close, even in the case of a mother and son who were very close to each other to begin with, and even after one of them has died.

ACKNOWLEDGMENTS

I mentioned people in this book according to whether they happened to be involved in a particular story or incident, and not according to their importance in Mom's life or mine. I want to thank our wonderful friends and extraordinay extended family, who answered questions, provided letters and stories, and encouraged me in the writing of this book. I decided not to try to list you below only because I was too worried about accidentally leaving someone out; but I am grateful beyond words to all of you.

I received invaluable help on the manuscript from James Goldsmith III (my uncle Skip), Stephanie Green, Jean Halberstam, Lisa Holton, Beena Kamlani, Larry Kramer, Pablo Larios, Georganne Nixon, Mary Ellen O'Neill, Bill Reichblum, David Shipley, Peternelle van Arsdale, the Tutorial, Leslie Wells, and Naomi Wolf. Alice Truax provided, once again, probing questions and an eagle eye.

I'm grateful to Mary Oliver and also Regula Noetzli.

Doug Stumpf and Lisa Queen were among my first readers. Lisa gave me daily encouragement, wisdom, and laughs.

I couldn't have written this without her. Doug was, as ever, ridiculously generous with his time and genius.

Some of this book was written at the Fire Island home of Andy Brimmer and Tom Molner. I owe them (literally) for this and for so much more.

For their help with information about the Women's Refugee Commission and the IRC, immense thanks to Susan Stark Alberti, George Biddle, Carolyn Makinson, Diana Quick, and Carrie Welch.

I'm endlessly grateful to John Brockman and Katinka Matson, and also to Max Brockman, Russell Weinberger, and Michael Healey. There are no better people to have in your corner.

Lisa Highton, publisher of Two Roads UK, helped me more than I can say with her humor, empathy, brilliant counsel, and steadfast faith in this book and me.

I owe huge thanks to Sonny Mehta, for his immediate and unwavering support, and to the amazing team at Knopf: Paul Bogaards, Gabrielle Brooks, Andrew Michael Carlson, Carol Devine Carson, Chris Gillespie, Erinn Hartman, Lynn Kovach, Nicholas Latimer, Victoria Pearson, Anne-Lise Spitzer, and Jeff Yamaguchi, along with their colleagues.

Marty Asher is simply the editor of my dreams. Marty encouraged me to do this book. He coaxed and pushed and edited and guided me through draft after draft. Finally, he told me I could stop. The myriad flaws and failings are all due to my not listening sufficiently to Marty. But even in the face of my intransigence, he remains as extraordinary a champion and friend as any book or writer could ever have.

This book is in memory of my mother, of course, but also of Mary Diaz and Al Marchioni, who both died of pancreatic cancer, and of Beverlee Bruce. Mary and Beverlee were two of Mom's most beloved colleagues and were an inspiration to her and all of us. Al Marchioni was one of the best people I will ever know. I was blessed to have him as my boss, friend, and mentor.

Again, my father and Doug and Nina provided constant and selfless help and loving support, while encouraging me to write the book I wanted to write.

As for David Cheng: I don't deserve someone as wonderful as David, and he sure doesn't deserve someone as trying as me. But I'm insanely lucky and he's incredibly patient. He's the light of my life.

And finally, I want to thank my mother.

APPENDIX

An alphabetical listing of the authors, books, plays, poems, and stories discussed or mentioned in *The End of Your Life Book Club:*

Louisa May Alcott, *Little Women*
Dante Alighieri, *Purgatorio*
W. H. Auden, "Musée des Beaux Arts," from *Collected Poems*
Jane Austen
Russell Banks, *Continental Drift*
Muriel Barbery, *The Elegance of the Hedgehog,* translated
    by Alison Anderson
Ishmael Beah, *A Long Way Gone*
Alan Bennett, *The Uncommon Reader*
The Holy Bible
Elizabeth Bishop
Roberto Bolaño, *The Savage Detectives,* translated
    by Natasha Wimmer
The Book of Common Prayer
Geraldine Brooks, *March; People of the Book*

The Buddha, *The Diamond Cutter Sutra,* translated by
    Gelong Thubten Tsultrim
Lewis Carroll, *Alice's Adventures in Wonderland*
Robert Chapman, *Billy Budd,* play and screenplay, with
    Louis O. Coxe
Sindy Cheung, "I Am Sorrow"
Julia Child, *Mastering the Art of French Cooking*
Agatha Christie
Karen Connelly, *The Lizard Cage*
Pat Conroy, *The Great Santini*
Colin Cotterill
Roald Dahl, *Charlie and the Chocolate Factory*
Patrick Dennis, *Auntie Mame*
Charles Dickens
Joan Didion, *A Book of Common Prayer; The Year of*
    Magical Thinking
Siobhan Dowd
Nancy Hatch Dupree
Dave Eggers
T. S. Eliot, *Murder in the Cathedral*
Ralph Waldo Emerson
F. Scott Fitzgerald
Zelda Fitzgerald
Ian Fleming, *Chitty Chitty Bang Bang*
Ken Follett, *The Pillars of the Earth*
Esther Forbes, *Paul Revere and the World*
    He Lived In; Johnny Tremain
E. M. Forster, *Howards End*
Anne Frank, *Anne Frank: The Diary of a Young Girl*
Erle Stanley Gardner
Nikki Giovanni

William Golding, *Lord of the Flies*

Sue Grafton

Günter Grass, *The Tin Drum*

The Haggadah

David Halberstam, *The Coldest Winter*

Susan Halpern, *The Etiquette of Illness*

Mohsin Hamid, *The Reluctant Fundamentalist*

Patricia Highsmith, *Strangers on a Train; The Price of Salt;
     The Talented Mr. Ripley*

Andrew Holleran

Khaled Hosseini, *The Kite Runner; A Thousand Splendid Suns*

Henrik Ibsen, *Hedda Gabler*

John Irving, *A Prayer for Owen Meany*

Christopher Isherwood, *The Berlin Stories; Christopher
     and His Kind*

Jerome K. Jerome, *Three Men in a Boat*

Ben Johnson, *Volpone*

Crockett Johnson, *Harold and the Purple Crayon*

Erica Jong, *Fear of Flying*

Jon Kabat-Zinn, *Full Catastrophe Living; Wherever You Go,
     There You Are; Coming to Our Senses*

Walter Kaiser

Mariatu Kamara, *The Bite of the Mango,* with Susan
     McClelland

Carolyn Keene, Nancy Drew series

John F. Kennedy, *Profiles in Courage*

Elizabeth T. King

Larry Kramer

Jhumpa Lahiri, *Interpreter of Maladies; The Namesake;
     Unaccustomed Earth*

Anne Lamott, *Traveling Mercies*

Stieg Larsson, *The Girl with the Dragon Tattoo,* translated
    by Reg Keeland
Victor LaValle, *Big Machine*
Munro Leaf, *The Story of Ferdinand,* illustrated by
    Robert Lawson
Dennis Lehane
Donna Leon
C. S. Lewis, *The Chronicles of Narnia*
Alistair MacLean, *The Guns of Navarone; Where Eagles Dare;*
    Force 10 from Navarone; Puppet on a Chain
Malcolm X, *The Autobiography of Malcolm X: As Told to Alex Haley*
Thomas Mann, *Tonio Kröger; Death in Venice; The Magic Mountain;*
    Mario and the Magician; Joseph and His Brothers, translated by
    John E. Woods
Ngaio Marsh
W. Somerset Maugham, *Of Human Bondage; The Painted Veil;*
    Collected Short Stories, including "The Verger"
James McBride, *The Color of Water*
Val McDermid
Ian McEwan, *On Chesil Beach*
Herman Melville, *Billy Budd*
James Michener
Arthur Miller, *Death of a Salesman*
Rohinton Mistry, *A Fine Balance*
Margaret Mitchell, *Gone With the Wind*
J. R. Moehringer, *The Tender Bar*
Toni Morrison
Daniyal Mueenuddin, *In Other Rooms, Other Wonders*
Alice Munro, *Too Much Happiness*
Iris Murdoch

Nagarjuna, *Seventy Verses on Emptiness,* translated
   by Gareth Sparham
Irène Némirovsky, *Suite Française,* translated by Sandra Smith
Edith Nesbit, *The Railway Children*
Barack Obama, *Dreams from My Father*
John O'Hara, *Appointment in Samarra*
Mary Oliver, *Why I Wake Early,* including "Where Does
   the Temple Begin, Where Does It End?"
Frances Osborne, *The Bolter*
Sara Paretsky
Randy Pausch, *The Last Lecture,* with Jeffrey Zaslow
Susan Pedersen, *Eleanor Rathbone and the Politics of Conscience*
Harold Pinter, *The Caretaker*
Reynolds Price, *Feasting the Heart*
Thomas Pynchon
Arthur Ransome, *Swallows and Amazons*
David Reuben, M.D., *Everything You Always Wanted to Know
   About Sex: But Were Afraid to Ask*
David K. Reynolds, *A Handbook for Constructive Living*
F. W. Robertson
Marilynne Robinson, *Housekeeping; Gilead; Home*
David Rohde
John Ruskin
Tim Russert, *Big Russ and Me*
David Sedaris
Maurice Sendak, *Where the Wild Things Are; In the Night Kitchen*
Peter Shaffer; *Equus; Five Finger Exercise*
William Shakespeare, *King Lear; Othello*
George Bernard Shaw, *Saint Joan*
Bernie Siegel, M.D., *Love, Medicine and Miracles*

Alexander McCall Smith, *The No. 1 Ladies' Detective Agency: The Miracle at Speedy Motors*

Aleksandr Solzhenitsyn, *The Gulag Archipelago*

Natsume Soseki, *Kokoro,* translated by Edwin McCellan

Wallace Stegner, *Crossing to Safety*

Edward Steichen, *The Family of Man,* prologue by Carl Sandburg

Wallace Stevens

Lydia Stone, *Pink Donkey Brown,* illustrated by Mary E. Dwyer

Elizabeth Strout, *Olive Kitteridge*

Josephine Tey, *Brat Farrar*

William Makepeace Thackeray

Michael Thomas, *Man Gone Down*

Mary Tileston, *Daily Strength for Daily Needs*

Colm Tóibín, *The Story of the Night; The Blackwater Lightship; The Master; Brooklyn*

J. R. R. Tolkien, *The Hobbit; The Lord of the Rings*

William Trevor, *Felicia's Journey*

Liv Ullmann

John Updike, *Couples; My Father's Tears*

Leon Uris

Marina Vaizey

Sheila Weller, *Girls Like Us*

Elie Wiesel, *Night*

Tennessee Williams, *A Streetcar Named Desire*

P. G. Wodehouse

Geoffrey Wolff, *The Duke of Deception*

Herman Wouk, *The Caine Mutiny; Marjorie Morningstar; The Winds of War*

Brief excerpts were originally published in different form in *The New York Times* (May 13, 2012).

Grateful acknowledgment is made to the following for permission to reprint previously published material:

The Charlotte Sheedy Literary Agency Inc.: "Where Does the Temple Begin, Where Does It End?" from *Why I Wake Early* by Mary Oliver, copyright © 2004 by Mary Oliver (Boston: Beacon Press, 2004). Reprinted by permission of The Charlotte Sheedy Literary Agency Inc.

Random House, Inc., and Curtis Brown, Ltd.: Excerpt from "Musée des Beaux Arts" from *Collected Poems of W. H. Auden* by W. H. Auden, copyright © 1940 and renewed 1968 by W. H. Auden. Reprinted by permission of Random House, Inc., on behalf of print rights and Curtis Brown, Ltd., on behalf of electronic rights.

A Note About the Author

WILL SCHWALBE has worked in digital media, as the founder of Cookstr.com; in book publishing, as senior vice president and editor in chief, first of William Morrow and Company and then of Hyperion Books; and as a journalist, writing for publications including *The New York Times* and the *South China Morning Post*. At Hyperion, he created Hyperion East, an imprint devoted to Asian fiction in translation. He is on the boards of Yale University Press and the Kingsborough Community College Foundation. He is the coauthor with David Shipley of *Send: Why People Email So Badly and How to Do It Better*.

A Note on the Type

The text of this book was set in Requiem, created in the 1990s by the Hoefler Type Foundry. It was derived from a set of inscriptional capitals appearing in Ludovico Vicentino degli Arrighi's 1523 writing manual, *Il Modo de Temperare le Penne*. A master scribe, Arrighi is remembered as an exemplar of the chancery italic, a style revived in Requiem Italic.

Typeset by Scribe,
Philadelphia, Pennsylvania

Printed and bound by Berryville Graphics,
Berryville, Virginia

Designed by Cassandra J. Pappas